Queer (Un)Friendly
Film and Television

ALSO BY JAMES R. KELLER

Anne Rice and Sexual Politics:
The Early Novels
(McFarland, 2000)

Queer (Un)Friendly Film and Television

by JAMES R. KELLER

McFarland & Company, Inc., Publishers
Jefferson, North Carolina, and London

Library of Congress Cataloguing-in-Publication Data

Keller, James R., 1960–
    Queer (un)friendly film and television / by James R. Keller
      p.   cm.
    Includes bibliographical references and index.
    ISBN 0-7864-1246-1 (softcover : 50# alkaline paper) ∞
    1. Homosexuality in motion pictures.   2. Homosexuality on
television.   I. Title: Queer unfriendly film and television.
II. Title.
PN1995.9.H55K45   2002
791.43'653 — dc21   2001008124

British Library cataloguing data are available

Cover photograph ©2002 PhotoDisc

Manufactured in the United States of America

*McFarland & Company, Inc., Publishers
  Box 611, Jefferson, North Carolina 28640
  www.mcfarlandpub.com*

Contents

Preface   vii

Introduction   1

1. Queer and Self-Loathing: The Gay Male Conversion Fantasy   7

2. Courage Teacher: The Portrait of an Aging Artist with an
   Angry Young Man   46

3. "Naught's Had, All's Spent": Shakespeare, Queer Rage, and
   The Talented Mr. Ripley   68

4. *Gladiator:* Family Values and Promise Keepers in the
   Colosseum   82

5. *Twilight of the Golds:* Jews, Gays, and Eugenics   97

6. Forbidding Desire: Profanity, Protest Masculinity, and
   The Usual Suspects   108

7. *Will & Grace:* The Politics of Inversion   121

8. Rehabilitating the Camera: Loquacious Queens and Male
   Autism in *Flawless*   137

9. Queering the American Family   153

10. Scared Straight: Rehabilitating Homophobia and the Dread
    of Proximity   175

Conclusion   199

Film and Television Listing   203

Bibliography   205

Index   209

Preface

In January of 2000, I was one of the final candidates for a position as Assistant Professor of Eighteenth Century Literature at a university in Florida. One of the stipulations that the search committee articulated for my being hired was that I produce a book during my tenure earning years, an interval which would be accelerated by my substantial previous experience. I was eager for the position because it meant returning to Florida where my family resides and escaping from the intransigently conservative environment of rural Mississippi. However, the stipulation that I produce a book within three years was troubling because I had only recently completed my work on Anne Rice, one which had not yet been released, and I was already faced with the necessity of writing another.

While I waited for resolution of the interviews, I began to consider subjects that would lend themselves to a two or three year study. I felt the necessity of getting started quickly because for the first year I would be occupied with preparing new courses. Over the previous several years, I had published multiple essays on the 'New Queer Cinema,' and my original proposal was to collect these published articles and perhaps add a few new ones to the group. I was subsequently informed that a collection of previously published articles would not be desirable because library budgetary limitations deterred many universities from purchasing previously released materials. I then decided to produce a manuscript with all new essays.

In the interim, I received the demoralizing news that the position which motivated me had been offered to an internal candidate whose qualifications in publication, teaching, and service were inferior to my own. I decided nevertheless to complete the new book, motivated mostly by lasting interest in the aesthetic and social value of the subject, but also by outrage over being subjected to a fake search and interview. The reader might wonder how I can be certain that the process was not legitimate. One important clue was the failure of one of the two search committees to show up to interview me, but most convincing was the chair's rejection letter which admitted that I would have stood a better chance if the successful candidate were not already in the position doing a good job.

The professional disappointment that partially motivated the writing of this book retains more than a causal relationship to the content. The experience dramatizes the material in several aspects. I am not speaking of anything as simplistic as discrimination, although I do not consider the group above such a practice. (I recall the look of panic and confusion on committee chair's face when he thought he was going to have to comment on sexuality when responding to my query about campus diversity.) Instead, the parallel I address includes the idea of invisibility, of the absent presence. Within the ruse of the fake interview, the candidates who are invited to campus only to keep up appearances that satisfy the legal obligation to conduct a national search are in effect invisible. Their qualifications and contributions to academia are irrelevant, and their performance in the interview is immaterial. The search has a foregone conclusion. They are engaged in a public performance for the benefit of those who may or may not be monitoring such events. The same invisibility defines the experience of gays and lesbians where our personal lives and specifically our relationships are considered unspeakable or at least unimportant for most of America. Paradoxically, the absent presence of gays and lesbians is easily recognizable in the effort to represent alternative sexual identities in the media, film and television, where it is acceptable to acknowledge the existence of gays and lesbians but where there is a real reticence to examine the subject in detail. This is true of the portrayal of same sex intimacy, and the public is particularly squeamish about intimacy between men. The media announces its commitment to a diversity with which it is clearly uncomfortable and for which it is unwilling to risk ratings or profits defending.

The expression "New Queer Cinema" applies broadly to films of the past decade that reveal a new openness toward the portrayal of gays and lesbians in film. These works are the product of a generation of filmmakers who are less willing to compromise with the dominant culture and who object to the conventionality of previous gay politics. The purpose of this study is to demonstrate that even these works fall short of an ideal and uncompromising promotion of gay rights. The American audience is experiencing an unprecedented, yet cautious and reticent effort to reconstitute the public image of gays and lesbians through the production of positive imagery in the popular media. These images are qualified by their negotiation with the homophobia of heterosexist culture. While Holly-wood is laboring to improve the public image of gays and lesbians, it is also mindful of mainstream values; too often its project is to represent the conformity of gay men and women to the values of middle class America in order to remove the stigma that portrays gays as a threat to social stability. The new queer film and television, therefore, avoids the revolutionary, opting instead for accommodation and reconciliation.

This collection of essays includes some studies that are singular in focus, concentrating on individual films, and some that are plural, applying a single social theory to a group of cinematic narratives. All the chapters observe the dynamic interplay between the social and the aesthetic, addressing issues such gay marriage and families, cross-dressing, verbal and physical abuse, coming out, rage, aging, and romantic fantasies. The chapters have a distinctly masculinist bias, concentrating on the particular experience of gay males and observing the subtle binary construction of manhood within the popular representations of gender. Contemporary men's studies is a branch of feminism that discusses the diversity within multiple constructions of manhood. It is interested in the social forces that legitimize and prioritize particular performances of masculinity over others.

The collection of essays makes no pretense to objectivity in its examination of gender politics since the treatment of gays and lesbians over the past century has been anything but fair and impartial and the effort at objectivity would suggest that the homophobes might be correct in their criticism and condemnation. Indeed, people with alternative sexual identities have been and still are subjected to public sentiments and policies that at their best moments are irrational and frequently absurd. Consider for example that the group most committed to portraying gay men as a menace to the social order is the same that is responsible for virtually all rape, assault, murder, theft, child abuse, spouse abuse, and war, yet no one suggests that heterosexual males are a threat to peace and should subsequently be deprived of their constitutional rights, and they constitute a social category that is determined by the same criteria that constructs and defines gay men — sexual object choice. This study is committed to exposing cultural paradoxes of heterosexism and heterocentrism even within media programming that is ostensibly gay friendly.

Several years ago a student asked me to help her fulfill a class project by describing the sentiments that motivate me professionally. When I responded with the following list — outrage, jealousy, revenge, and fear of failure — she invited me to be serious. I asked if she would like me to invent an inspirational answer or to tell her the truth. My film criticism seeks to expose the mechanisms of homophobia while celebrating and encouraging the social progress that has been made. My project is satirical, but not in the comedic sense. It is a response to the absurd and often intolerable conditions to which gays and lesbians are subjected within American culture, and it is committed to the ideal that invisibility, silence, and homophobia are unacceptable.

Introduction

The Showtime series *Queer as Folk* has been marketed as an innovative program that introduces to American television a formerly taboo subject matter in an uncensored fashion. Dramatizing the lives of a group of gay men living in Pittsburgh who divide their time between work, workout, and play — mostly play — the program offers an unconflicted glimpse of the gay life and gay sex, images formerly censored in the mainstream media, either because of the culturally imposed silence on the issue or because of the effort to confront the physical and political necessities of the pandemic with socially responsible imagery. The characters in *Queer as Folk* exhibit little of the shame and self-loathing that is a staple in the mainstream depictions of gays and lesbians, nor do they make an effort to apologize for their behavior to the uninitiated and the unsympathetic. The show is a strident affirmation of the personal choices of a collection of young adults.

Even the title of the series reveals a previously unprecedented and uncompromising socio-political bravado. "Folk" is a cognate for the profane expression "fuck." The Canadian/American series is based upon a British program set in Manchester, and in the vernacular of central England the pronunciation of "fuck" often sounds like "folk" to an American. Moreover, in British vernacular some words that include the syllable "folk," such as "Norfolk" and "Suffolk," are pronounced "Norfuck" and "Suffuck." The title of the program recuperates the homophobic epithet "queer" and blatantly offers it as a description rather than a denigration, while adding the profane to intensify the impact of the former slur. The result is an expression that suggests a brazen refusal of the victim pose that has defined gay representations of the past, a repudiation of stigma, shame, and social oppression; the characters are "queer as fuck."

The content of the program dallies with subjects that are controversial even within the gay community. Each episode concludes with a disclaimer maintaining that the characters are not representative of the entire gay populace. The warning is clearly not directed at the potential heterosexual audience, but at gay apologists and capitulationists who might object to the politically reckless content of the series. The program reinforces some highly negative assumptions about gay men, some that the community has struggled to refute for decades, particularly characterizations of gay men as promiscuous and non-committal. The characters spend their evenings at a dance club appropriately named "Babylon" (an allusion to pagan decadence), engaging in anonymous sex in the backroom when they cannot manage a traditional "one night stand." They abuse drugs and solicit male prostitutes. Perhaps the most controversial aspect of the show is the inclusion of an under aged character, Justin (Randy Harrison), whose sexual experimentation involves adult men. The depiction feeds the homophobic hysteria over child molestation. The producers appropriately anticipated the objection to this facet of the series and included in the disclaimer an assertion that all the actors are over the age of consent. Justin's character addresses the problems facing gay teens who are isolated within the high school community, often cut off from information that is requisite to their personal development. Finally, *Queer as Folk* offers an unblushing look at the sexual practices of gay men, frequently depicting the actors in various stages of undress and in sexually suggestive poses, stopping short only of the full frontal nudity of the principal characters or images of penetration.

On the surface, *Queer as Folk* refuses to coddle hysterics and homophobes, yet the show nevertheless retains the didactic quality that characterizes most gay friendly art, striving to reach a crossover audience. While the series seems preoccupied with the depictions of the Dionysian sexual abandon of its protagonists, it nevertheless pauses in the very first episode to offer a lesson on safe sex. Before Justin and Brian (Gale Harold) become dangerously intimate, Brian instructs his partner on the necessity of safety, a lecture that seems addressed more to the television audience than to his uninitiated partner: "We always practice safe sex." The cautionary example is almost sarcastic in its simplicity, but it reveals a recurring strategy for the instructional mission of the program. In the education of Justin, *Queer as Folk* simultaneously edifies the uninitiated of its audience, offering an enlightening glimpse into gay culture. Beyond his instruction in safe sex, Justin also learns about the universality of discrimination and intolerance, and the existence of a gay support network. Justin's evolution is parallel to that of his mother, who is striving to understand her son and who is subsequently offered instruction in the subtle balance between loving support and non-interference. The mother's experience is instructive, offering a paradigm of behavior for gay friendly parents who want to be supportive in spite of their reticence.

Even the most brazen aspect of *Queer as Folk*, the explicit sexual depictions, frequently have a voyeuristic quality that stands in for the camera's and the audience's prurient interests. The lovers have the look of lovers being looked at. There is an element of flaunting in front of the camera that forces the audience to gaze directly at the taboo practices that have been so over-determined in the public imagination. This aspect of the program is even depicted as the lurid imaginings of Justin's parents, who are not content to accept their son's orientation in the abstract but must visualize him in the sodomitical act. The voyeurism of the camera and the audience has a broader social project: to demythologize the queer sex act, to desensitize the audience.

This glimpse into the private lives of gay men reveals a paradox at the heart of the series. At the same time that the characters of the drama unblushingly parade their sexual practices in front of the audience, refusing to trade in their object choices for more conventional pursuits, they are nevertheless appealing to and expecting the audience's understanding, and offering the requisite arguments and explanations calculated to elicit that understanding. While Brian indulges in a veritable orgy of anonymous sexual encounters, he nevertheless takes the time to explain that he practices safe sex. While even the most responsible and likable characters engage in illicit drug use, the narrative includes a cautionary tale concerning the dangers of substance abuse: Ted (Scott Lowell) ends up in a drug induced coma. The most scandalous element of the plot is, of course, the sexual experimentation of seventeen-year-old Justin. The program is careful to expose the complexities and the delicacies of the subject. Justin initiates the sexual encounters while impersonating a consenting adult, and he is particularly intelligent and mature for his age. The inclusion of his parents in the narrative serves to mitigate the scandal somewhat. The mother is convinced that there is nothing she can do to dissuade her son from an alternative lifestyle, remembering her initial sexual encounter at the age of sixteen. She is persuaded that experimentation at seventeen is normal, although she admits that she expected Justin to experiment with someone his own age. Justin's father is extremely hostile toward his son's sexual orientation, leaving the boy no alternative but to seek the affection and support of an adult male elsewhere. Most importantly, Brian is thoroughly punished for his reckless involvement with an underaged boy. His car is smashed, and he is physically assaulted on the street by Justin's irate father. However, the most bitter consequence for Brian is having to accept temporary responsibility for Justin's homelessness, housing and supervising the unwanted teenager, a circumstance that undermines Brian's hedonistic lifestyle.

The example of *Queer as Folk* reveals that even a presumably uncompromising glance at gay lifestyles, one that enjoys the added license of pay television, must nevertheless engage in cultural diplomacy to gain and maintain its audience. Queer art employs the narrative practices that Jonathan Dollimore has identified as "strategies of inclusion" (51), demands, capitulations, and reconciliations between dominant and emergent cultural practices, a contest in which the latter attempts to negotiate and occupy a space within mainstream visibility and permissibility. While maintaining a defining semblance of its former self, the culturally abject constructs and fashions itself as safe and productive, friendly to the values of the white, heterocentric, middle class populace. The purpose of this study is to expose and analyze the mechanisms of these cultural negotiations through analysis of a sample of recent films and television programs. The title of the book is intended to capture the duality of the project. *Queer (Un)Friendly Film and Television* does not refer exclusively to the increased visibility of gay subject matter, nor to the greater availability of Hollywood's coveted financial resources for gay projects, nor to the increased representation, influence, and visibility of gay men and women in the industry, nor to the improved portraits of gay lives, images that defy negative stereotype. The title invokes the efforts of queer art to portray itself as amicable to the interests and values of mainstream America, to portray gays as innocuous and inoffensive. While ostensibly such efforts constitute a capitulationist strategy because they jettison materials that are retrograde to the interests of the homophobic mainstream and subsequently seem to validate compulsory conformity, they nevertheless engender opportunities for experimentation, winning the necessary visibility and accessibility requisite to social change.

The study adopts usage of the rehabilitated homophobic epithet "queer" not because it is a convenient synonym for "gay," but because it is a specifically social constructionist appellation that captures the way in which sexual identity is spatially determined through its marginal relationship to mainstream normativity. Accordingly, most of the film and television analysis within this study adopts a relational approach to the formation of sexual orientation and gender performance, exposing the semiotics of literary and filmic representations, the praxis in which characterization is developed through opposition. The specific preoccupation of the subsequent chapters is with comparative productions of diverse and even antithetical masculinities. The study has a masculinist preoccupation that is not intended to slight lesbians or to suggest that dramatic art by or about women is inferior, unimportant, or unworthy of inclusion. A legion of important scholarly studies about lesbian film have been published, and I leave such ruminations to those most qualified to produce convincing commentary on the subject — lesbians. I will focus on what I know best, which is men — straight and gay. This study is a perpetuation of the project of men's studies, which is to reveal masculinity as a gender performance that is socially constructed and diverse, and to reveal the mechanisms of coercion that a culture deploys to force compliance with the stipulations of hegemonic masculinity — those qualities of male gender performance that are socially and temporally constituted as permissible. For the purposes of this study, I will reveal the ways in which heterosexual/homosexual binary is repeatedly erected and deconstructed to the occasional adulation, but more frequent denigration, of gay men.

The characterization of film as an ongoing conversation between oppositional voices and vying cultural factions is a bow to the cultural theory of Mikhail Bakhtin and specifically his ideas on "heteroglossia" and "polyphony." "Heteroglossia" refers to the multiplicity of discourse types and their attendant ideologies present within a single text, a "diversity of social speech types ... and a diversity of individual voices, artistically organized." These may include "social dialects, characteristic group behavior, professional jargons, generic languages, languages of generations and age groups," etc. (Bakhtin 262–263). Similarly, "polyphony" alludes to the "collective quality of the individual utterance," the capacity of the utterance to "embody someone else's utterance," creating a "dialogic relationship between two voices" (Park-Fuller 2). The individual utterance occurs within a language that has a long socio-political history, one laden with "shared thoughts, points of view, and value judgements" (Bakhtin 276). Thus the seemingly unitary voice "cannot fail to become an active participant in social dialogue," speaking the collective, even speaking its own opposition (Bakhtin 276).

The polyphonic quality of queer film is inherent even in the term "queer" itself, which invokes a long history of abusive discourse directed at gays and lesbians, but has been recuperated within the past decade not to erase the historically vituperative significations of the term, but to embrace them and fling them back into the tormentors face: "turning our tortures into horrid arms." While the term "gay" became increasingly conventional and capitulationist, "queer" revels in difference, dissension, and protest. However, at the same time that "queer" voices its dissident opposition to the quiet desperation of gay and lesbians, it, nevertheless, resurrects the homophobe's vitriol with every iteration. The potential plurality of the individual utterance is nowhere more evident than in the social discourses where gay and lesbian issues are endlessly debated without any evident progress in gaining or losing supporters. Most prevalent among the oppositional discourses is that of religion, which demands to be included in any commentary on sexual orientation. Following the 1993 March on Washington by an estimated one million gays and lesbians (at the time, the largest demonstration ever to be staged on the mall), a group of activist leaders were invited to appear on *Nightline* to elucidate the agenda for the march. The activists were confounded to find that a single preacher had been invited to the show and had been given equal time to state his objections. Larry Kramer, author and founder of ACTUP, appearing on the show, refused to be coerced into a dialogue with the preacher. Arguing by analogy, he complained that if there were a march by Jews or African Americans, the media would not insist on including a nazi or a klansman on the agenda. He reminded the host that nearly a million people had rallied in support of gay and lesbian rights, yet *Nightline* had offered a mere handful of moralists an equal voice. The plurality of such discursive moments is ubiquitous within the queer struggle for equality. Whenever a gay man or woman seeks to portray him/herself as healthy, moral, normal, unoffending, or benign, the opposition demands the opportunity to offer contradiction. When one says "gay," one must say "fag." The politically expedient virtue of the term "queer" is that it says "gay" and "fag" in a single utterance. Thus it invokes sympathy for sexual diversity at the same time it acknowledges that gay and lesbians are cognizant of their detractors' objections, yet they are not injured nor are they dissuaded from their self-promoting objectives.

Just as the term "queer" recognizes that there is no politically neutral language that can invoke sexual diversity, queer film is written, produced, acted, and viewed within this dynamic political culture and language, and, accordingly, it captures this ongoing social debate even as it is trying to remain gay friendly. Through its utterances and silences, its challenges and compromises, queer film perpetuates both homophobia and affirmative social progress. The loosely related essays that follow within this text attempt to expose the dynamics of the political moment as it is played out in the most accessible forms of media —film, video, and television. It observes the oft unacknowledged homophobia of mainstream male action films, the strategies of inclusion requisite to gay themed programs on network television, and the simultaneous promotion and denigration of gay socio-political agenda as it is represented in independent and Hollywood studio dramas. Contemporary film and television thus becomes an eloquent register of what mainstream America does and does not want to hear, and what it does and does not want to accept, within the struggle for gay and lesbian equality.

1
Queer and Self-Loathing: The Gay Male Conversion Fantasy

In his book about queer cinema, entitled *What Are You Looking At?*, Paul Burston observes that there are "no gay men in commercial gay porn films" (1). Of course, he is speaking hyperbolically of the gender coding of gay pornography in which the players impersonate straight men who have no real erotic desire for each other, but who have been inadvertently thrown together in a confined space (Burston, *What Are You Looking At?*, 2). The encounters that ensue between these untutored novices, of course, involve an expert knowledge of the erotic practices of gay men with none of the inhibition and moral reticence common to the "bi-curious" who "have never done this before," but who are "not getting enough attention from their girlfriends" or who are "too drunk to know what they are doing." As gay men have attempted to clean up their image and show themselves to be practical members of the broader community, they have sought to erase their fascination with straight men since such desire can be construed as promiscuous: Even if the straight man is drunk enough to mess around, in all likelihood he cannot use that excuse a second time with any credibility; therefore, such encounters cannot be interpreted as leading to a safe monogamy. In addition, the late dispute over gays in the military taught us that homophobia is fueled in large part by the fear that straight men may be the recipient of the unwelcome leer of gay men desiring them in the shower or the barracks. It seems then prudent to conceal gay men's prurient interest in straight men if for no other reason than to demonstrate that the desire is not universal. However, the efficacy of this effort is questionable. We reveal this continued longing for the "Other" in many subtle and sometimes not so subtle ways. One need only observe the titles of man websites or internet porn sites: *Real Men, Real Straight Men, Real Straight Amateurs, Straight Men Can Be Turned, Married Men, Drunken Frat Boys, Straight Guyz 1-17*, etc. Of course, one should not forget to mention those now ubiquitous and over-exposed Marine polaroids, in which our fighting men so graciously render their "chaste treasures" up to our "unmastered" gaze.

I believe, however, that a minor modification of Burston's thesis about gay porn is warranted: "Frequently, there is at least one straight man in gay pornography." Gay porn often dramatizes the seduction or pursuit of straight men by gay men, and even when all of the participants are playing straight, their activities are conducted for the benefit of the gay male erotic gaze. The imagery invites the vicarious participation of the audience in the onscreen sexual athletics. Yet often the content of the encounter includes a presumed straight man and a gay man, the latter of whom constitutes a surrogate for the viewer who imaginatively places himself in the same position. In one such film, whose title is unworthy of recollection, two men are undressing on a bed when one participant makes a remark that is unmistakably heterosexual, thus eliciting the incredulity of his companion, "What, are you straight?," to which the former replies, "Well, yes I am actually." This precedes thirty minutes of uninhibited queer sex, leaving the viewer wondering, "What kind of straight male does it without even asking for money?" In gay male porn, the "straight male" is code for the dominant partner, whose presence signals the often disavowed desire of some gay men to be feminized by a willful, insistent, and impenetrable partner (the total top), the male who only ever plays the insertive role in sexual encounters. This aspect of queer desire has led to the creation of the ridiculous straight/gay porn star. The actor who participates in hundreds of films involving gay sex, but who is actually straight, preferring his girlfriend and playing the gay porn star exclusively for financial considerations. Now either his presumed heterosexuality is a pose for the benefit of his submissive fans, or he is the most deluded man in the world. How does a straight man remain aroused in the presence of gay men toward whom he is not attracted — and this day after day while shooting sex films? Surely he is not drunk and confused all that time. Of course, the money may allow him to ignore his moral inhibitions, but unless he has a very curious fetish, the money is not likely to evoke the arousal requisite to the grueling film shoots. It should be clear by now that the "straight man" of gay pornography is an invention calculated to appeal to the submissive faction of the gay male population, and the desire for a dominant and fetishized "Other" that he elicits from his audience is an important factor within more conventional cinema, particularly the gay "coming out romance" of the new Queer Cinema.

A standard convention of many successful love stories is the overcoming of an obstacle that stands between the potential lovers and inhibits the growth of their affection. This may be a mutual animosity or indifference (*You've Got Mail*), the intrusion of parental authority (*Romeo and Juliet*), social class conflict (*Dirty Dancing*), infidelity, etc. The obstacle guarantees dramatic tension within the narrative and rescues the story from excessive sentimentality, at least until the inevitable reunion. The couple must decide that their bond is stronger than the hindrances, and in the process of overcoming, they become worthy of each other's devotion. Similarly, in the gay "coming out romance" the obstacle to be surmounted is real or perceived heterosexuality, as well as shame and violence. Inevitably, a physically underdeveloped, effeminate male becomes infatuated with a more masculine individual, and despite the ostensible heterosexuality of the latter, a romance ensues which then leads to a public revelation of their affection (or a threat of the same) and a rejection of the effeminate by the masculine partner who has a greater investment in the closet because his masquerade is more believable. Of course, the two eventually reconcile and, in most cases, embrace their love publicly.

The most interesting facet of this formulaic drama is the conceptualizing of the gay/straight binary. Paradoxically, the coming out romance necessitates both the dissolution and the maintenance of a distinction between homosexual and heterosexual. The existence of the boundary generates desire within the gay subject for the phallic other, the real man, but the existence of the romance requires that the partner be either a closeted homosexual or merely a willing bisexual. In a process of possessing the desired object, the heterosexuality that made one partner appealing is destabilized. The character is ironically coded as both gay and straight, as in the above pornographic narrative. He must become the homosexual's private heterosexual, remaining ostensibly straight while engaging in queer sex and romance.

The point-of-view of the male conversion fantasy is that of gay [post]adolescent who has already come to terms with his alternative desires and who has been the subject of abuse from his peers. He discovers, to his delight, that a former object of his admiration, a presumed straight male, harbors secret queer fantasies and has chosen the equally youthful and untutored protagonist to initiate him into this new experience. The tension within these narratives hinges upon the necessity of secrecy. The so-called straight male has participated more successfully in the gay masquerade (the ability to conform convincingly to the gendered behavioral codes stipulated by the dominant culture), and has more to lose by discovery, since no one suspects his hidden desires; his masculinity includes more overt manifestations of those codes commonly associated with heterosexuality (i.e. success in sports, success in attracting women). In order to maintain the respect of his peers, he cannot appear to have any private association with the gay male. The eventual public revelation of the relationship leads to panic and the temporary rejection of the effeminate male by the masculine. Eventually, this particularly unlikely romance resumes, both partners having overcome fear of parental recrimination and public scorn.

The "fantasy" of this chapter's title is not only the occulted desire of the closeted masculine male, but the gay wish-fulfillment manifest within the coming out plot structure. The narrative point-of-view is a convenient surrogate for the likely audience, gay males, who, viewing the film, will experience some level of personal validation, both in the sense that they see their own prurient interests indulged by the movements of the camera that lingers lovingly over the impressive physique of the desired subject, and in the sense that they see their own adolescent experiences validated through the complicity of parallel lives. Of course, these narratives retain a significant level of unreality. Each of the four films central to this discussion—*Get Real, Beautiful Thing, I Think I Do,* and *Billy's Hollywood Screen Kiss*—feature the fulfillment of a young gay man's romantic fantasy involving a convenient and exceptionally handsome straight male who will not only return his affection but parallelism develop a deep emotional attachment—one that compels the previously unobtainable male to become the aggressor. The above films illustrate the seduction of four traditionally sought after social types within a gay adolescent male's immediate environment: the athletic classmate, the neighbor, the college roommate, and the casual acquaintance. The unreality of these narratives and the means by which they pander to the collective longings of the gay audience lies in the improbability that the love interests of a gay man are so conveniently located that one could attain the ideal mate without venturing beyond one's usually narrow scope. Such stories entice their audiences by making romantic fulfillment seem accessible and easy, encouraging people to pursue love interests that in all probability are unobtainable and perhaps even emotionally unhealthy.

Get Real

Get Real, the recent British film (1999), may be more appropriately titled than even its writer, Patrick Wilde, and director, Simon Shore, understand. The title of the movie is also the name of an essay within the film, written by the protagonist for his high school's literary contest. The essay is a response to a designated topic: "Growing up in the New Millennium." The protagonist wins the contest, not for his essay about growing up gay, which he does not have the courage to submit, but for an essay that he has written imagining what it must be like to grow up as a straight male. Thus the title of the essay encourages the readers—parents and classmates—to face the possibility that their children and friends, respectively, may not be straight. It invites parents to stop assuming that they have a typical child, an assumption that is specific to the father of Steven Carter (Ben Silverstone), the gay male protagonist. The father refuses to see what has become increasingly apparent to the mother—the alternative sexual identity of their son. The title also applies to Steven and his lover John Dixon (Brad Gorton), who cannot continue to masquerade as straight males leading conventional lives. John is paralyzed by the fear of discovery. Of course, the most important recipient of the title's rather "cheeky" enjoinder is the film's audience. The climactic scene of the film takes place at an Awards Day assembly in the local high school. The scandalized audience who listens to Steven's coming out speech, his appeal to their compassion and understanding, is a trope for the audience of the film and for society at large. The audience metaphor and the directive "get real" illustrate the social project of the film, which is to generate support for the unique predicament of gay teens who have no guidance and few role models, and who do not conform to the expected heterosexual paradigm. Refusing to acknowledge a problem does not make it disappear.

In a more cynical reading, the title is an invocation to the gay audience to examine the content of its fantasies. For this author, the admonition of the title is a critique of the content of the film. The love affair that is central to the narrative is, in my opinion, implausible in the extreme—not that the high school athletic hero could not be gay, but that he, despite his commitment to his own physical development, could become not only attracted to but also enamored of an whiny, underdeveloped, effeminate intellectual who previously has been the object of his constant ridicule and scorn. I am also not suggesting that this type of match never occurs, but that it does not occur with the level of frequency in reality that it does in gay fantasy and cinema. Rather than lending credibility to the valid assertion that any body or personality type can be gay, the romantic match within the film illustrates the widespread longing of gay men for straight men who will reciprocate their affections and yet, paradoxically, remain straight. The unreality implicit in the title interrogates the premise of the love story, expressing the improbability that the effete gay male, who in the perspective of the film signifies the gay audience's point-of view, could discover the most masculine man at his school is picking up "tricks" in the local "tearoom." Finally, the admonition "get real" is directed at the gay audience in yet another context. It is a subtle urging of gay men to abandon their longing for ostensibly straight males, or those unwilling to acknowledge their desires publicly, and it perpetuates the default position of the gay community that it is always better to be "out of the closet," that gay relationships require openness to generate stability.

Certainly, the film *Get Real* recognizes the fascination of gay men with straight men as a self-defeating impulse. The same qualities that make John Dixon desirable also make him unavailable. He represents the physical side of the mind/body dichotomy very plainly represented within the characterizations of the film. The two male protagonists are constructed to represent the spectrum of male types among high school students, occupying opposite ends of this simplistic personality spectrum: Steven is the most intelligent student in school and John the most athletic. Both individuals win recognition for their respective successes at the conclusion of the film — Steven for the essay contest and John for "continuous sporting achievement throughout the year." The choice of superlative personality types guarantees a level of allegorizing that renders the romantic union still more improbable. This very unsubtle effort to demonstrate that gay desire can exist within any manifestation of masculinity defeats itself with its own generalities. At the same time that it attempts to dismantle common assumptions about who may or may not be gay, it reinforces others, suggesting, for example, that athletic males are not as smart and socially courageous as more uncoordinated males, or that effeminate and intelligent males cannot be socially successful in high school. The dichotomy created by the antithetical personality types does not generate any inclusive perspective on the redemption of teenagers from gender construction, and although such a pat conclusion would seem to be an additional over-simplification, it also seems requisite to a narrative structured upon oppositions and motivated to demonstrate the shared disabilities imposed by traditional gender roles. What is the point of creating allegorical representations of traditional masculine types if not to deconstruct them; otherwise, they reinforce butch/femme stereotypes as well as essentialized views of gay relationships and gender.

Get Real follows an expected paradigm for the gay conversion romance, moving from fear and secrecy to communion, to discovery and betrayal, and finally to acceptance and self-affirmation. The two lads of *Get Real* are distrustful of each other, as one might expect, since they meet initially in the stalls of a public lavatory and are both embarrassed to find their secret desires are compromised by someone who could divulge them to the school population. Of course, the concern is more pronounced for John Dixon, since he has been more convincing in his performance of traditional masculine gender roles. He has more to lose, at least in his own mind, since no one suspects his inclination. Steven, on the other hand, has already been the object of homophobic ridicule by the athletic bullies at school, particularly by Kevin (Tim Harris), an exceptionally cruel and abusive member of John Dixon's circle of friends. Kevin repeatedly attacks Steven verbally, calling him a "queer" and making a general nuisance of himself, once by throwing Steven's book bag onto the roof of the school. Kevin offers the perspective of the hysterical homophobe whose role is not so much to ferret out alternative sexual identities but to police compliance with traditional gendered behavioral codes; he acts as a vehicle of social control through his mockery. He does not know that Steven Carter is gay; he abuses his classmate because Steven does not exhibit those traits associated with hegemonic masculinity, which are those behaviors a culture adopts as definitive of masculine gender performance (Connell, *Gender* 111). These traits may include, but are not limited to, athleticism, sexism, homosocial bonding, anti-intellectualism, and roughhousing. Steven is a frail intellectual whose best friend is an overweight and stylish neighbor girl, so he is certainly not compliant with culturally determined notions of adolescent masculinity.

Steven assures his friend Linda that he has never told the school bullies that he is gay, and even Kevin is incredulous when he confirms Steven's orientation: "You really are queer." Until that moment Kevin's verbal assaults upon Steven have been acts of self-definition as much as social regulation. Kevin hurls insults at Steven whenever his own masculinity is called into doubt. When Wendy refers to Kevin as a "perv," the latter deflects the accusation onto Steven who is in his terms a "queer fuck." When Kevin's attempted seduction of Linda is rebuffed with the slight "take it up your bum," Kevin gestures toward Steven, "I thought that was his department." Kevin defines himself in opposition to those traits and those people who could be construed as gay and/or unmasculine, and Steven becomes the repository of all those behaviors Kevin rejects. His attitude toward his classmate is a form of protest in which he affirms his own masculinity, revealing that he is not gay, and to offer this assurance through repudiation is more decidedly his objective than to prove that Steven is gay.

Kevin's assumption that there is an inevitable parallel between the masculine/feminine and the heterosexual/homosexual binaries is deconstructed by the erotic desires of John Dixon, who conforms to all of the obligatory male gender codes but who, nevertheless, experiences homoerotic desire. Kevin's effort to regulate Steven's behavior has a broader impact. The marginalizing of Steven serves to ensure broad compliance with obligatory heterosexuality and accepted gender practice. His actions caution others to avoid similar humiliation by maintaining an accepted masculine image. The character who is the most likely recipient of this object lesson is, of course, John Dixon. He harbors same sex longings but is afraid to pursue them out of the fear of humiliation, of compromising his masculine persona. Even when he is discovered at a public restroom by Steven, he refuses to accept responsibility for his actions, offering multiple excuses for his presence, all of which are intended to suggest that he is only curious about the behavior of gay men. In this vulnerable position, he continues to deflect all aspersions of deviant desire onto Steven, even after trying to unbutton the avowed gay man's pants. John feigns incredulity, asking if Steven is "dodgy," and finally runs away from their first encounter, refusing to speak to or even acknowledge Steven for some time thereafter. When John, unsolicited, follows Steven home after a school dance, he secures the latter's assurance that he will maintain the secrecy of their relationship, stating that he, John, will break it off if anyone "even suspects" they are intimate. At school he continues to ignore Steven, only in private are they even friendly. When defending Steven against Kevin's abuse, John tells his buddy to "leave the girlies alone."

Gradually John becomes more friendly toward Steven in public, and Kevin becomes increasingly suspicious of their connection. The gay male conversion narrative generally includes a betrayal of the effeminate figure by the masculine when their intimacy is publicly compromised. The unraveling of the secrecy surrounding the romantic alliance in *Get Real* begins with the circulation of the unpublished essay about growing up gay, which John correctly guesses was penned by Steven. He admonishes the latter's recklessness, reminding his friend that a public revelation of Steven's sexuality will cast aspersions upon John's masculinity, since their friendship has become increasingly well known. This complaint is ironic in the context of the conversation which takes place on a racetrack immediately following John's success, both in winning the race and in breaking a track record. The context suggests that the categories of masculine behavior are so fragile and hysterically homophobic that they can be erased by the smallest taint of queer desire (Klein 218). John Dixon has affirmed his masculinity in a dramatic performance of his athleticism, yet he fears accusations of unmanly behavior more than ever. The revelation of the connection between himself and Steven is further advanced by the inquiries of the respective parents who recognize that the boys have given conflicting reports of their activities on the previous weekend. The accumulated pressure of these compromising events leads to John's repudiation of Steven in the locker room, where he indicates that he will not continue the relationship if it means public exposure.

After John storms out of the room, Steven vents his anger on the contents of John's abandoned gym bag, unaware that he is being observed by Kevin and another athletic thug. Kevin's resulting abusive rage involves an effort to force Steven to state openly that John Dixon is not queer. A disavowal is important to Kevin, who wants to hear his suspicions invalidated, particularly since any revelation of John's queer desire would compromise Kevin's simplistic understanding of sexuality and gender roles: Gay men are effeminate and straight men masculine. Moreover, the recognition that gay desire can exist in a conventionally masculine male constitutes a threat at still other levels. Kevin would be forced to accept the taint of association just as John has. Kevin has defined his own masculinity through a refusal of gay desire, and yet he finds himself confronted with the possibility that the person who, for him, most clearly signifies his perception of masculinity may be gay as well; such a revelation would dismantle the apparatus of gender performance that is central to Kevin's self-recognition. He would be forced to acknowledge that even he could harbor gay desires, and he would bear the public stigma of having been close friends with a gay man, the same stigma that John fears.

Returning for his bag, John interrupts the confrontation between Steven and Kevin and ends his friend Kevin's inquiry by faking a physical assault on Steven, but only after inviting the other two boys to leave the room. The playful assault, however, becomes earnest when the others reenter. John actually injures Steven in a desperate effort to make a more convincing show of his disassociation and difference. This, of course, creates a greater emotional injury for both men than any physical injury and leads to the demoralized, but determined, state in which Steven decides to come out to the entire school at a public awards ceremony.

The school environment is a typical setting for the gay male conversion romance, perhaps because school is an often rigorous and normalizing environment in which traditional gender roles are strictly policed and where those who are unable to play these roles convincingly are ruthlessly suppressed, literally pummeled into normative behavioral categories. The school that Steven and John attend is even more complicit in the enforcement of gender performance than might be expected. The school's administration refuses to allow the student newspaper to print Steven's article about growing up gay, stating that such a work has "no place in a decent school." Ironically, the institution rewards Steven for lying about his adolescent experiences, while refusing to countenance the truth that is represented in his essay about growing up gay. The gay experience is invisible, and only those who can conform to arbitrary codes of respectability are acknowledged. There is the additional absurdity that the administration refers to the institution as "decent" even as it permits the constant abuse of the weaker students by a collection of sadistic jocks. The collusion of the school in this gender coercion can be more subtle in other incidents. For example, the students study *Romeo and Juliet*, and Steven is asked by his teacher to comment on the tragedy, a work that validates all of the experiences of adolescent heterosexual romance but which says little about Steven's own experience. The same skills that he must employ in imagining what it is like to grow up straight are necessary in the analysis of the drama. When Steven fails to respond coherently to questions about the tragedy, his teacher asks him if he is having "girl trouble." The film illustrates the willful blindness of the educational system to the concerns and needs of gay adolescents. The problem is perhaps most clearly illustrated in the British school system's mandatory dress codes, which suggest both sartorial and behavioral normativity, the uniform revealing the system's program for the imposition of conformity.

Of course, the inflexibility of the school environment both at the administrative and at the social levels parallels the programmatic response of Steven's father who will not even entertain the possibility that his son is gay. Steven's father, Graham, is yet another version of the bullies at school, expressing his disapproval of his son's behavior: "Why can't you see something through for once? What's your problem?" Knowing that his son has decided not to participate in the contest, the father, when he finds the discarded essay about growing up in the new millennium, sends it in without Steven's knowledge. The father's actions signify the effort to promote a conventional lifestyle for his son, as well as the willful blindness that leads parents to the default assumption that their children have normative sexual longings. Graham ignores the clues that could lead him to an early recognition of his son's orientation. When Steven is brought home by the police because he was caught in a wooded area where homosexuals frequently meet, the father does not assume the event says anything about his son's sexuality: "What were you doing in those woods? He could have been molested by some dirty old queers." Even after Steven responds, "Where else are we supposed to go?," Graham refuses to see the obvious: "You don't think it's drugs, do you?" The normalizing elements of the home environment resemble the same at school. The father attempts to compel his son's compliance with traditional gender codes through scolding and constant pressure to perform. Graham's urging of Steven to become competitive in the writing contest is a similar impetus to that which governs the athletic culture at school. The male child is expected to be ambitious, aggressive, and competitive even in intellectual endeavors. The father's complicity with the athletic bullies is realized in his encouragement of Steven's ostensibly platonic friendship with John Dixon, and when the two boys offer conflicting accounts of their activities over one weekend, Graham immediately assumes that Steven is the liar. Perhaps the most glaring example of the father's disappointment in his son is manifest in the failure of the father to attend the awards ceremony where Steven is honored. Shocked and demoralized by the revelation of his son's sexual orientation, Graham is unable to leave the car until the ceremony is almost over. He enters after Steven has made his public coming out speech, a convenient metaphor for the father's refusal to hear and to accept the inevitable. While the father was unable to enter the awards ceremony, he was present at the athletic competition, an endeavor that he can support, a wholly masculine pursuit.

Despite his father's faintheartedness, Steven does have support, predictably from the women in his life — his friends and his mother — all of whom were fairly quick to recognize that Steven is gay. The mother became conscious of Steven's orientation immediately following the incident of police harassment. She is supportive during and after his coming out speech, while the father is completely absent. Moreover, she takes an aggressive role in the defense of her son, promising to have Kevin's "bullocks for earrings." Steven's female friends, Jessica and Linda, are also available to comfort and support him after his confession, while predictably his platonic male friend Mark is not; his absence may suggest that he is fearful of the stigma of having a gay friend, fearful of the assumption that he may be gay too, the same paranoia that motivates John Dixon, who, not surprisingly, is not available to console his lover, but is thrown into a panic over the public revelation. The punishment for his cowardice, both in refusing to support his friend and in failing to own his sexuality, is evident from the circumstances of the film's final scene, which includes an encounter between Steven and John at the now empty athletic field. The lonely, demoralized, and desolate state in which Steven finds John serves as a visual counterpoint to the reassurance and support offered to Steven by his friends. The empty track and field signifies the assurance that John will receive no succor from his friends or from the male culture within which he has struggled to excel. His shame and self-loathing guarantee that he will lose not only his lover but also his straight friends.

In the final images of the film Steven crosses the field to join his friend Linda in her car, and they drive off (very stylishly) with the radio diva singing, "Think! Think about what you're trying to do to me, Oh

Freedom...." The images suggest that the young male couple have broken off their relationship, and it further implies that self-respecting gay
men should not subject themselves to aggravating relationships with partners ambivalent about their sexual orientation. Popular wisdom informs
Steven's decision: Such relationships, while exciting for a while, are also
frustrating, demeaning, and doomed to failure. *Get Real* illustrates the same
principles in other aspects of its narrative. Steven's first erotic encounter
in the film is with a very friendly married man named Glen. While Steven
does not know Glen is attached, there is no evidence that the knowledge
would have altered the former's behavior. The film does not depict the
two men having sex, but the dialogue indicates that they have an erotic
encounter in the woods, the same area that figures into the story later.
Upon hearing of the encounter, Linda calls Steven a "tart," a word commonly used to signify loose women. Steven's defense of his actions includes
ecstatic tributes such as "stunning, witty, gorgeous, and dangerous." He has
made plans to meet Glen again, and this time invites Linda along to inspect
this new love interest. Predictably, Glen does not appear. Perhaps Glen
never intended to show up and was only being polite when he agreed to;
or maybe Glen experienced guilty pleasure after his liaison in the woods;
or, most likely, Glen saw from a distance that Steven had naively brought
another person, and discretion dictated that he not approach. Unfortunately
for Glen, he has an unexpected encounter with Steven at a very inoppor-
tune time. Steven's father is a photographer, and Glen, with his wife and
newborn, unwittingly decides to have the family portrait on a day when
Steven is helping in the studio. At first, Steven sees only Glen and begins to
question him, despite Glen's obvious alarm. This is understandably the closeted bisexual's greatest fear. When he sees Glen's family, Steven does at least
have the sense to abandon his questions and any hope of a relationship.

The same subject is developed in a parallel episode of the film. It is
thematically appropriate that Steven joins Linda in the car before they
drive off into the film's credits. A subplot of the narrative involves Linda's
vexed efforts to attain her driver's license. While she practices for this rite
of passage, she begins an affair with her driving instructor, of whom she
becomes quite enamored, only to find out that he is married. Driver's Education becomes a trope for the growing experiences depicted elsewhere in
the drama. The protagonists are learning to navigate and control the vicissitudes of life and love. Both Steven and Linda have abandoned affairs
that were meaningful to them but doomed to secrecy and shame.

One character type common to the romance genre (particularly those
that depict doomed relationships) that is missing from *Get Real* (perhaps
with good reason) is an alternative love interest for Steven, someone who

is not as exciting and good-looking, but who is sincere and at least willing to own his sexual orientation, someone who constitutes a better romantic choice. Perhaps the reason for omitting such a character is to emphasize Steven's painful isolation. If he had a gay friend who was open about his sexuality, his own self-overcoming and courage would not have been so prominent within the development of the narrative. He has to learn through trial and error; the lessons more dearly bought become more meaningful. The inclusion of the alternative romantic interest would also have de-emphasized the prominence of John's experience within the narrative, more roundly condemning his predicament. Although the story is told from Steven's point-of-view, John's own lifestyle choices, while coded as unproductive and self-destructive within the framework of the narrative, are, nevertheless, common and legitimate. His pain reveals the alienation of gay men within straight male cultures (here athletics), as well as the considerable pressure to conform. His point-of-view from within this masculine enclave more acutely criticizes the normalizing and exclusionary practices of such institutions than Steven's complete absence from the same.

In *Get Real* Steven's decision to walk away from his relationship with John Dixon is perhaps more courageous than his public coming out. It is a repudiation of the fascination of gay men with ostensibly straight or unavailable men. When I use the word "straight " here, I use it in the same way that it is employed elsewhere in queer culture and queer cinema. Gay/straight is a lifestyle choice, not exclusively determined by sexual object selection. In this film, and elsewhere, gay or straight involves an individual's decision to embrace particular cultural values. Thus a person can have sex regularly with someone of the same gender and still publicly and privately disavow any association with gay identity and gay culture; this is a description of John, who in his own mind can acknowledge that he loves Steven but still maintain he is not gay because he refuses to self-identify with gay culture; he is frightened of public scorn. This is not to say that he does not make substantial progress in accepting his own desires, but that he cannot take that final and important step toward openly and unblushingly acknowledging his emotional and physical needs. Unlike Steven, John cannot shuffle off self-loathing, and there is little doubt that Steven will be happier for his decision.

Beautiful Thing

A far more believable film, and yet one that remains a gay romantic fantasy, is Hettie MacDonald's *Beautiful Thing* (1996). Here the protagonist and his mate do create a lasting bond, but there is, nevertheless, a significant difference in the level of knowledge and acceptance of the two partners, and that level, as in the previous film, is directly related to the ability of each individual to blend in with and conform to traditionally straight male cultures. The adolescent romance of *Beautiful Thing*, like that in *Get Real*, retains a quality of gay male wish-fulfillment. Here the protagonist Jamie (Glen Berry) has a crush on the boy next door, who turns out to be a willing recipient of affection. Jamie is considerably less masculine and perhaps more sensitive than his neighbor Ste (Scott Neal), yet the two are an altogether more likely match than the partners in *Get Real*. Jamie and Ste do at least have consistent interaction with each other before they become lovers, are similar physical types, share comparable domestic environments, and are brought together in a more plausible fashion.

As in *Get Real*, the two boys' relative abilities to perform traditional masculine gender roles (particularly in athletics) determine their social position within the school environment. However, the action of *Get Real* revolves primarily around the school setting; *Beautiful Thing* begins at school and moves into the home, where it remains. The film opens in the familiar setting that traumatized so many adolescent gay men — the high school gym class. Jamie, from whose point-of-view the story is told, is the predictable outsider, the object of ridicule and bullying by the more physically aggressive males in his class. His aversion to P.E. is clearly longstanding; he does not even dress for the class. When the new gym teacher inquires, McBride, the most aggressive and abusive of the athletic males, pleads sarcastically on Jamie's behalf: "Don't make him play, sir." Taking their cue from McBride, the other athletic boys begin to toss Jamie's book bag in a circle until McBride, receiving the package near the fence, drops it outside of the playing field, effectively expelling Jamie from P.E. and from the homosocial bonding that is at the center of exclusive male cultures. As though she is stipulating that the narrative is not going to detail the clichéd problems of adolescent gays in school, director Hettie MacDonald allows Jamie (retreating from his humiliation) to lead the camera, crew, and narrative across the asphalt terrain of central London to the apartment he shares with his mother Sandra. From here the narrative encompasses brief forays into the outside world, the impact of each measured in the home environment.

The same detachment from male social groups that Jaime experiences at school is reiterated multiple times in the film. His neighbor and future lover Ste is one of the soccer hooligans who toss his bag in a circle, so Jaime's disconnection from the athletic bullies is not as complete as

Steven Carter's in *Get Real*, and Jaime is clearly more capable of defending himself. He counters the verbal abuse of his peers with his own invective: "Fuck off, McBride!" In many ways, his disconnection is self-imposed, and the bullies' behavior is a semiconscious effort to patrol gender role compliance among their peers, an endeavor aimed primarily at the other members of their own group, since those who do not wish to be included cannot be manipulated by the threat of exclusion. As in *Get Real*, the narrative concentrates on the separate experiences of the two male protagonists in relation to the all male social institutions. While Jamie leaves gym class to watch television romances, Ste is depicted in the company of other boys returning from practice. Jaime attempts to mend this social breach several times, no doubt to share the experience and company of his increasingly intimate friend Ste. Jamie, seated on the grass, observes while the more athletic and aggressive boys kick around his soccer ball, finally landing it in a nearby pond. His scolding initiates a collective lunge for the water where the boys ignore the ball while playing and roughhousing in the water. McBride tries to include Jaime by pushing him in the water; however, the latter is unable to enjoy the moment, recoiling from the splashes that the other boys savor. He clearly experiences anxiety in the presence of strenuous rough and tumble adolescent activities, here revealing his inability to distinguish roughhousing from abuse. Jaime has difficulty forming male bonds; when he explains to his mother that he is going to a party with his mates, Sandra reminds him that he does not have any mates. At the party Jaime keeps the company of the same people who previously excluded him until his mother intrudes to revile the slanderous neighbor girl Leah (Tameka Empson). His mother's actions redound upon Jaime's head, initiating recriminations against him where previously there had been peaceful co-existence among the party members. Jamie leaves the gathering on his mother's heels, and the fact that Ste sides with Jamie in the subsequent argument over Sandra's actions and follows him out of the party suggests a growing bond between the two boys. Ste abandons his school friends in favor of Jamie's company. However, this connection is quickly, but only temporarily, severed.

The circumstances that bring Jamie and Ste together are related to their home environments. Both boys live with single parents in adjacent flats in East London. Jamie resides with his mother, who is immature, self-centered, and reluctant to assume a traditional maternal role. When the school calls to inform her that Jamie has cut gym class, she, while staring into a mirror and applying her lipstick, remarks, "I don't want you to think this is any reflection on me." The image of vanity is reinforced by Sandra's love life, which involves a younger male whom she retains mostly as a convenient sex partner. He is, nevertheless, good natured and sensitive to a fault. Indeed, his nurturing qualities become a source of continuous humor within the film. Clearly influenced by the mid–twentieth century counter culture, Tony drives a VW van, maintains no job, and offers the boy his harebrained, pot-induced observations about life that leave the other characters rolling their eyes. Sandra and Tony sport their affection openly around the boy, to his intense irritation. After the adults speak explicitly about oral sex in front of Jamie and Leah, the boy lashes out, urging his mother to "try being a bit more of a mother to me." Sandra confides, "I never had a mother, so what do I know about bringing up kids," and later, "So you got me for a mother, but who said life was easy." Although somewhat self-centered, Sandra is not a neglectful parent. She does show concern for her son's well-being, but as a single working mother she is often unavailable to watch and guide him. She is, however, laboring to improve the conditions of their domestic lives by pursuing an offer to manage her own pub.

Sandra and Leah, the neighbor girl, are similar personalities at contrasting stages of life. Leah is Jamie's age and is as much a "good time girl" as Sandra. The two engage in a continuous abusive repartee, the subject of which is speculation over who is the bigger "slag." This dialogue accounts for much of the humor in the film, but it finally arrives at outright hostility after Leah suggests that Sandra aborted her second child, the insult that prompts Sandra's visit to the high school house party. The smoldering animus between the two women involves an unacknowledged resemblance, one that accounts for their bitterness and competitiveness. The two eventually acknowledge how much they have in common and call a truce at the resolution of the film, and they do so through their mutual support of the boys' orientation. They acknowledge their affinity, as well as the cessation of hostilities, by dancing together alongside the boys in the final sequence.

Sandra's contentious relationship with Leah is countered by her concern for the well being of Ste, who lives with his father and brother in the apartment on the opposite side of her own. Ste's father and brother are abusive toward him, forcing him to assume all of the domestic responsibilities in the absence of the mother who is never accounted for. Ste is shown cooking and cleaning for his unappreciative family, a task which brings him no consideration when he makes minor mistakes. He accidentally burns the dinner while trying to ensure quiet during his father's nap and is subsequently forced to eat all the burned food. His brother Trevor beats him when he finds that Ste has scuffed a pair of tennis shoes. The father is a drunk and a "bar fly" who seldom speaks except to offer criticism. Ste tells of finding him passed out on the street with people stepping over him, an incident that has a permanent effect on his perception of his father whom he thereafter regards as pathetic.

Ste's home life is parallel to his life at school. His brother and father monitor his compliance with traditional male gender codes in a fashion similar to that used by the athletic bullies. The image of Ste's athletic clique leaving gym class is later reconstituted, the second group involving Trevor, Ste, their father, and some friends returning from a boxing match. Predictably, Trevor beats his brother in front of the entire group. Just like the adolescents, the adult male group polices gender roles with the threat of violence, and the characteristics that guarantee expulsion from male societies are softness, passivity, and homosexuality, characteristics which in the mind of homophobes are coterminous. After he begins to develop a relationship with Jamie, Ste lives in fear of his father and brother discovering his secret. Leah indicates that Trevor already knows where Ste has been sleeping, and to prove her point she draws a parallel between Ste's last beating and the most recent evening he spent in Jamie's room. Later, when Sandra finds out about the relationship between the two boys, she promises not to tell the father because she does not want to be responsible for a child's murder.

The relationship between Jamie and Ste results partially from the degradations of the latter's home life. When Ste is beaten by either father or brother, he spends the night with Sandra and Jamie to escape further abuse, and because there are only two bedrooms, the boys are forced to share a bed. The affection between the two emerges from the growing intimacy associated with the sleeping arrangements. Typically, within the conversion romance, one partner is more comfortable with and more knowledgeable about his sexuality than the other. Jamie is altogether more intellectually mature than Ste, while Ste is the more masculine and able to pass undetected within straight male cultures. While Jamie is not entirely effete, Ste is clearly the partner coded as straight, the object of a gay male's seduction. Prior to the boys' trysts in bed, there are no indications that Ste has any homoerotic tendencies. There are no unusual shots that reveal Ste's hidden desires, no lingering gazes, nor any doubtful curiosity or attentiveness toward Jamie or any other male. The camera and dialogue offer no evidence to suggest that he is not heterosexual before the first bedroom encounter. Of course, the narrative is one of self-discovery and acceptance for both of the adolescents, yet Jamie seems to be more inclined toward the lifestyle even before his first sexual experience. He also has less fear of public disclosure, perhaps because he already endures many of the abuses associated with coming out, and his open acceptance will not, in all likelihood, make him any more socially marginalized than he has been.

The erotic aspect of the narrative is clearly filtered through Jamie's perspective, and his lascivious gaze is the audience's own. The film assumes its audience is primarily gay males who will share Jamie's desires. The viewers are allowed a brief glimpse of Ste's bare ass as he stares in the bathroom mirror. Within the narrative of the film, the gaze belongs to Jamie. Ste is objectified physically, shown semi-nude several times. He is the passive recipient of the gay male desire. He only acquiesces to Jamie's advances; he does not instigate, at least not initially. These qualities signify that he is straight, or at least more straight, and his reticence is designed to make him more desirable.

One of the signs purported to signify the heightened influence of gay males on the dominant culture is the increased objectification of the eroticized male body within the media (Simpson 97, 104–105), and while this may seem to forget the impact of women's willingness to embrace their desires publicly, the representation of the nude male form as an idealized sexual object is indeed a nearly universal feature of gay iconography, and gay men are willing to revere these images unabashedly. The idealized form is invariably that of the muscular athletic male, frequently depicted along with the trappings of traditionally straight male professions or pursuits—construction worker, soldier, athlete, etc. When have we seen such images depicting florists, decorators, actors, waiters, choreographers, etc.—dancers being a notable but infrequent exception? This observation is not intended to deny the diversity of professions, skills, or pursuits within the gale male community, but to acknowledge that there are certain pursuits and certain physical types coded as heterosexual and others designated gay. Furthermore, those professions that seem the most likely to signify crossover interests of the male heterosexual/homosexual communities are also seldom invoked as objects for the erotic gaze, i.e. lawyers, doctors, professors, bankers, etc. Thus, those forms that compose the iconography of gay male veneration are overwhelmingly represented as heterosexual, and the erotic gaze of the gay male reveals a longing for the attainment of the straight male body. The gaze assumes a level of passivity on the part of the individual who is commonly represented as aggressive, both to facilitate seduction and to ensure that the straight male remains straight even while engaged in queer sex. The heterosexual male overly willing to pursue gay sex is no longer recognizably straight and is, thereby, less desirable.

Ste does not return Jamie's stare, nor is he given the opportunity within the imagery of the film. Jamie's is not a sexualized body. He looks

but is not looked at. The series of bedroom scenes prior to consummation depict the progressive seduction of Ste, the first involving only friendly
conversation, the second including the application of soothing lotion on
Ste's bare and bruised back, and an invitation to sleep head to head, a
request which is initially rebuffed by Ste. When he does acquiesce, moving to the opposite end of the bed, he disavows responsibility, indicating
that he has only moved to accommodate Jamie's wishes. Of course, this
alteration in the sleeping arrangements leads to intimacy and, predictably,
to guilty pleasure on Ste's part. The situation is aggravated further by
Leah's indiscreet accusations about the sleeping arrangements. Angry at
Jamie and, in all probability, at himself too, Ste lashes out, labeling Jamie
a "queer" and, thereby, denying his own collusion in the affair. The temporary rejection of the more effeminate partner by the masculine is a routine feature of the conversion romance. The masculine individual
perceives the behavior or reputation of the effete partner as a threat to his
own heterosexual masquerade, and this is the case even when there is an
equal responsibility for their intimacy and for the threat to their
anonymity. There is a public disavowal in which the masculine partner
poses as the unwitting victim of the effeminate male's sexual aggression.

Rejection is closely followed by reconciliation and both public and
private acceptance. The self-acceptance of the couple is facilitated by the
appeal to community. The boys visit "The Gloucester," a local gay bar
where they discover that there is a support system for them, an alternative to both Jamie's isolation and Ste's participation in hostile straight
male social groups. The Gloucester is a refuge from the universal scorn
in their living and educational environments. However, even this positive
experience would not have been sufficient to bring the boys out into the
open had Sandra not followed them to the pub and subsequently confronted her son. Although the revelation brings temporary hysteria, it
eventually leads to greater understanding and acceptance on the part of
everyone involved.

The juxtaposition (both spatially and philosophically) of the two
households that have produced gay sons is an effort to obviate Freudian
theories of homosexuality. Freud blamed distant fathers and domineering mothers. When the male child fails to abandon its Oedipal fixation
on its mother in order to identify with a father who is distant, absent, or
unworthy of emulation, the child may model his attractions on his
mother's, thus developing a homoerotic predisposition (Sedgwick,
Between, 23). Jamie is closely bonded with his mother. While she displays
maternal affection, she also treats her son more like a friend than a child.
Their fights resemble lovers' quarrels, replete with mutual recriminations

and even light violence (i.e. slapping). It is obvious that they have only each other to rely upon; the mother's boyfriends come and go. While there is no sustained discussion that characterizes Jamie's father in the film, there are a few details that may or may not be descriptive of him. Jamie mocks his mother when she makes light of Ste's daily beatings, telling her that "it was not so funny when that bloke of yours beat you up." This, in all likelihood, is not a reference to Jamie's father but to a more recent affair, one that Jamie was able to witness himself. However, it is certainly a comment on the type of man with whom Sandra becomes involved. While the current boyfriend is not abusive but ridiculously sensitive (even trying to raise Sandra's consciousness about women's issues: "I wish you wouldn't use words like 'bird.' It really disempowers you."), he may be a rebound lover, one whose appeal is behavior antithetical to that of the former abusive partner. It is clear from the dialogue that Jamie has either never met his father or was too young to remember him. He asks his mother if his personality resembles his father's; she counters, "You're like me." The exchange suggests that he has never had a paradigm upon which to model his romantic attractions except that created by his mother, and the resulting imitation of Sandra's sexual attractions is represented visually by the alternating shots of the two bedrooms and the two sets of lovers.

The fact that Jamie has no male role model is further reinforced by the presence of Tony, who is at best a parody of fatherly wisdom. While Sandra is at work, the two men become acquainted, and the only fatherly advice Jamie can get out of his mother's boyfriend is ridiculous platitudes about the unimportance of names and ages, advice so simpleminded that even a teenager recognizes its uselessness. Moreover, Tony is a kept boy who walks around the house all day long in Sandra's bathrobe, an appropriate image of androgyny. Since he is fairly attractive and serves no practical purpose except to satisfy Sandra's romantic needs, Tony's role clearly represents the reversal of erotic spectatorship. While it is traditionally the male gaze that eroticizes and objectifies the woman's body in film, *Beautiful Thing* inverts the hierarchy of subject and object within the filmic gaze by allowing the male body to be the central figure in the prurient interests of the audience and the dramatis persona. While there is certainly no harm in such portrayals, it is also easy to conclude that such a lifestyle is not what Sandra would wish for her son. Instead, her own desires become the pattern for her son's. Jamie, too, selects the idealized male form upon which to project his loss and the resultant longings.

Ste is in an altogether more aggravated situation. His mother is not even mentioned in the film, and, as the youngest and the least physically powerful member of the household, he is thrust into the feminized role of the domestic facilitator: cooking, cleaning, and facilitating the comfort of others. It would be an understatement to say that Ste's father is unworthy of emulation. As a drunken bully, he offers no guidance to Ste, only punishment and indifference. More often detached than abusive, the father is unresponsive to his family, an example of what one contemporary sociologist refers to as "male autism," an inability or unwillingness to express one's emotions (Horrocks, *Crisis* 107). The father is the subject of his son's contempt. Ste dismisses his father as "pathetic" and offers the observation to parry Jamie's request for his companionship, suggesting that he does not need external support or comfort. The fact that Ste has no mother or father upon whom to model his erotic desires may explain why Ste is much more confused about his sexuality than is Jamie. The absences in the lives of these two boys translate directly into their respective desires. In Lacanian terms, "desire is a lack," a need to heal the psychic wounds created when the child was separated from the mother or abandoned by the father (Ragland-Sullivan 75). Ste longs for a feminized male to replace his absent mother and to represent his own symbolic emasculation, while, like Sandra, Jamie desires an individual who possesses traditional masculine qualities. Ste is more masculine than his neighbor because he has a pattern for male social behavior in the house, but is emotionally incapacitated by the absence of a model for male affection and sentiment.

The conversion and emergence of the boys in the narrative is mirrored by other difficult, even impossible, transitions. These parallels to the central tension of the film are intended to unveil the longings that are a part of every person's character. Leah is a black woman who develops an obsession with Mama Cass (Cass Elliot of the *Mamas and the Papas*), a fixation that Sandra labels "unnatural," a term often employed to denigrate homosexuals. Leah's love of Mama Cass goes beyond an interest in her music. She impersonates the singer, sporting white face and carrying a hair brush for a microphone. In the crisis of the film, she identifies so fully with her idol that the others cannot get her attention unless they call her Cass. In addition, she emulates Cass' self-destructiveness, threatening to jump from the balcony and wandering into traffic. Through her longings, Leah attempts to rupture racial, temporal, and class divisions. Tony represents a similar form of code breaking. His behavior suggests an unspoken desire to cross gender boundaries. His hyper-sensitivity toward women's issues, his willingness to be treated as a house boy and sex object, and his comfort with women's bedroom attire suggest gender bending. These two characters represent the ubiquitous and even obligatory presence of "camp" humor in gay art. They offer comic relief that punctuates the more sentimental and even maudlin portions of the narrative. But camp plays a more pivotal role in the film. Camp reveals the artificiality and the performative qualities of gender and sexual roles (Meyer 4–5), as well as of other social codes that are created as much by environment as by nature or genetics. The desire of others in the film to breach the seemingly stable boundaries between social categories suggests that camp and masquerade are not exclusive to the gay community, and through the universalizing of the longing to break free from normalcy, the vexed process of coming out is less stigmatized. Among this collection of eccentrics, Jamie and Ste seem comparatively conventional. Indeed, the decision to abandon the straight masquerade appears in this context to be a declaration and affirmation of stability and mental health.

The conversion fantasy of *Beautiful Thing* follows the paradigm laid out in the discussion of *Get Real*. Here, however, the social separation between the participants in the burgeoning romance is less stark. There is, nevertheless, a distinction in gender coding between the two boys, one more queer than the other, and the latter consequently more neurotic, despite the image of stability resulting from the capacity to disappear into normative society. Both films suggest ostensibly that conforming to traditional gender codes and desires is not the pathway to mental health for gay teenagers. Freud indicated in his letter to an American mother that her gay son was not mentally ill, that homosexuality is not pathology unless it is accompanied by neurosis, and that pathology can result from the subject's effort to conform in a fashion that is contrary to his inclination (Ablelove 381–383). Mental illness is not inherent in homosexuality, although it can result from the stigmatization of and discrimination against gays and lesbians. The boys in both films are separated by their level of acceptance. The one coded straight is a great deal more conflicted about his desire to engage in same sex eroticism because he has a greater investment in the praxis of heterosexual male cultures, which are defined in large part through the repudiation of homosexuals (Klein 218, 221). He is identified with a social group that cannot countenance homoeroticism or even a small measure of effeminacy in men.

In *Get Real* Steven Carter is unable to bring John Dixon from a private willingness to engage in homosexual practice to a public affirmation of desire. Dixon is willing to abandon the relationship altogether, losing the little support that he has for his longings, before he will accept a gay public image. It would be difficult to maintain that such a person is better off disavowing his sexual inclinations and embracing neurosis (a conflict between desire and actuality) rather than facing social stigma associated with those who will not conform. Jamie is more successful in bringing his partner, Ste, to an acceptance of his orientation. The concluding image of the film depicts the two slow-dancing in a public square, surrounded by the tall, sterile housing projects of central London, buildings that emphasize the boys' breach of cold conformity. They are joined by Sandra and Leah, who suggest the support of family and friends, the two at odds are unified in their mutual support of the boys' coming out. Ste's willingness to dance, in spite of the probability that his father, brother, and mates will find out, constitutes a refusal of the behaviors stipulated by straight male cultures. The two boys cling to each other against the scorn and disapproval of the outside world. With a public avowal, Ste ceases to be straight in a way that is far more profound than can be created by queer sex.

I Think I Do

The low budget comedy *I Think I Do* (1999) offers an illustration of the conversion fantasy as it is played out among young adults. The narrative focuses on a group of students graduating from George Washington University and later reuniting for a friend's wedding. The conversion romance is played out against the backdrop of this traditional wedding that is mocked at every level, even by the bride and groom. The resulting counterpoint between the conventional and the irregular exposes the artificiality of romantic conventions, particularly through the subversion of gender codes associated with a gay relationship. The action of the film takes place within a progressive social environment, so the struggles that the gay protagonists endure are related exclusively to the psychology of self-acceptance and self-overcoming rather than to the potentially violent manipulations of heterosexism and homophobia. The induction and reconstruction of the ostensibly straight male includes exclusively internal obstacles to an acceptance of his hidden sexuality. The fear of shame and ostracism does not operate to coerce the reticent party into collusion and compliance with conventional gender constructs. Instead, the potential lovers are zealously encouraged to pursue a lasting relationship, their friends often more hopeful than they are.

Whereas *Beautiful Thing* and *Get Real* illustrated the conversion fantasy among neighbors and high school classmates, respectively, *I Think I Do* reveals the pattern of wish-fulfillment within the college dormitory. The film opens with a sequence of vignettes intended to illustrate initial intimacy (platonic, of course) and progressive estrangement of roommates Bob and Brendan. In the first twenty minutes of the film the degeneration of this friendship is played out over the principle holidays in a single academic year — Halloween, Christmas, Valentine's Day. Each segment reveals an alteration in the evolving interpersonal dynamics of the same group of seven friends. The mood of each holiday sequence and the decline of intimacy in the friendship between Bob and Brendan is captured icongraphically by parallel shots of a neighborhood street. In the Halloween segment one of the men is depicted pushing the other down the street in a shopping cart, an activity that suggests traditional collegiate homosocial bonding through the loss of inhibition, an intimacy that grows out of close quarters and alcohol consumption. The obvious sexual tension between the two men is further elaborated in the subsequent party sequence. They cannot keep their hands off of each other, although the touching is within the parameters of the socially acceptable. Generally, men can touch each other only in violence or parodies of violence, unless, of course, the context in which they act is one involving extreme emotional or physical distress, or unless the subjects are related. In such cases, the behavioral codes can be slightly more permissive. Bob and Brendan roughhouse, slapping each other with their caps, revealing their mutual affection in non-threatening displays of mock violence. After the party breaks up and the boys return to their room, they continue the same display of intimacy through feigned combat, wrestling on the bedroom floor and grabbing at each other's underwear to deliver that dreaded locker room humiliation — the wedgie. The meaning of this intimacy is differently interpreted by each roommate. Brendan has clearly become an object of sexual desire for Bob, who watches him out of the corner of his eye as Brendan undresses for bed. Bob resists the cessation of mock hostilities between the two because they are a justification for touching, which could lead to sexual intimacy. He tries to dissuade Brendan from his inclinations toward sleep by offering another pretense for playfulness; this time the wrestling concludes with what could be construed as a moment of romance: Brendan lying on top of Bob, the two staring into each other's eyes. If the imagery itself is not enough to convince the audience of the unfulfilled sexual tension between these two, the musical score, the Partridge Family's "I Think I Love You," helps to define the action. While Bob is clearly prepared to embrace the moment, Brendan recoils, upset by the near breach of the decorum and prohibition that regulates interaction between men. However, the audience is left with a clear impression that Brendan also harbors some repressed affection for Bob that he cannot act out. Inadvertently commenting on the action in the next room, Carol and Matt, the couple whose marriage is the occasion for the reunion after graduation, complain about the noise of roughhousing: "We are trying to have a little romance here," words with an application to the activities in both bedrooms.

The Christmas sequence exposes the disintegration of erotic potential in the interaction between the two men. Brendan becomes increasingly preoccupied with women. The image that begins the episode defines the growing antagonism and distance between the two men. Bob and Brendan are shown arguing rather than sporting in the street, as in the Halloween segment. At the ensuing celebration, Brendan is occupied with pursuing women while Bob jealously observes, favoring his broken arm, obviously a visual metaphor for his emotional wounds. Carol recognizes that Bob is in love with Brendan and encourages him to look for a companion at a local gay bar because he will never possess his roommate. Auspiciously, Carol observes, "... you're a funny talented guy, and sooner than you think, you're going to meet a fucking prince"—words that accurately predict the success Bob has after college.

The Valentine's Day episode recounts the final unraveling of mutual good will between Bob and Brendan. This time Bob wanders down the street all alone, abandoned by his former companion. At the subsequent party, Brendan is once again occupied with his date. This time, however, Bob has company in his misery—the mutual friend Sarah, who had been Brendan's love interest at Christmas but who has now been cast aside for another woman. When Brendan ejects everyone from the couch to make a bed for his drunken date, the celebrants are too inebriated to be helpful. Brendan directs his irritation toward Bob and a playful bout of wrestling ensues. This time Bob grabs Brendan's ass in a feeble effort to resurrect some of their long-stifled familiarity, and Brendan responds to the violation by hitting him in the face. The segment concludes with Bob shut out of their room while Brendan occupies his bed with a woman. The image concludes the progressive displacement of Bob within Brendan's emotional priorities, and the three holiday episodes together illustrate the process whereby straight males gradually substitute women for the emotional homosocial bonds of adolescence.

The bulk of the narrative is consumed with events subsequent to college. The reunion of the classmates several years later is motivated by Carol and Matt's marriage, another of life's celebrations and the only one, aside from a funeral, capable of bringing a group of former classmates back together en masse after graduation. Interestingly, the relationship central to this gathering is not Matt and Carol's, but the bond between Bob and his boyfriend Stirling, a soap opera heartthrob from the show on which Bob is a principal writer. The group's preoccupation with Bob's new relationship is intended to suggest that he has managed to catch the perfect man. Of course, the ripple in this harmonious reunion is the return of Brendan, who, unbeknownst to the wedding party, has decided that he is gay and has become nostalgic about his former friendship with Bob, secretly hoping that they can develop a new bond. The subsequent reversal of affections and aggressions is the fantasy of all spurned romantics. Those who have been rejected long that someday the recipient of their former devotion will change his or her affections and will pursue his or her former devotee, but only after the spurned lover has lost interest. This turnabout is so infrequent and improbable that it gives the narrative a quality of unreality. When one couples this with the idea that plain-looking Bob could have roped in the ultimate hunk for a boyfriend with whom to make Brendan jealous, the story strains credibility still further. The narrative becomes a variation on the revenge fantasy in which the unrequited lover inflicts emotional distress on the person who formerly imposed the same. Thus the story assumes the qualities of wish fulfillment; the film performs the repressed fantasies of both characters and audience, a practice that vicariously salves the emotional wounds of both.

The wedding preparations and celebrations are structured upon a semiotic counterpoint between gays and straights, and most of this subject matter involves the gender bending and subtle ridiculing of Stirling Scott, the primary outsider at the wedding. Stirling's treatment within the narrative suggests the objectification of the male form and the queering of the film audience. Laura Mulvey's seminal article on cinematic voyeurism genders the film audience as heterosexual white males and the object of the camera's concentration as the eroticized female form (11–17). The queering of the camera and audience's look involves the displacement of the female as the object of the voyeuristic concentration; thus the audience members are titillated and aroused by the brief glimpse of the unveiled male form. In *I Think I Do* the only exposed bodies are those of men, most prominently Stirling's, but also Brendan's. As a soap opera sex symbol, Stirling's role in the film is to offer the primary example of the desired male body. He is so constantly the subject of comment and concentration by the wedding party that Sarah irritably urges the group to move on to another topic. Bob, as writer for the soap in which Stirling is the main love interest, repeatedly places his character in the hospital where he can be shirtless on camera.

The objectification of the male form within the gaze of the cinematic audience is also coded as a feminization of that object. The regulation of masculine gender roles tends to dissuade excessive attention to appearance among men. Although men may be expected to look neat and clean, the process of attaining this condition, the ritual of grooming, is generally not the appropriate focus in narratives featuring men. On the other hand, in a culture that values women as sex objects, the process of their beautification is a commonplace thematic even in narratives intended to emphasize their intellectual and professional achievements. *I Think I Do* both ridicules and reveres Stirling as a male sex object and as an androgynous, vain man. He is depicted engaging in those observances generally reserved for the males in a wedding. He spends the evening with the groom, Matt, looking at the D.C. monuments while Bob attends the bridal shower; he catches the garter at the reception; and he proposes marriage to Bob. However, simultaneously, his own beauty preparations are an analogue to the bride's. Bob sarcastically compares Stirling's bathroom to the "Clinique counter at Macy's," and Stirling reveals that the chemicals are intended to stave off aging, as he is about to turn thirty. All of his beautification is intended to prepare him for nothing more substantial than a tour of Washington. A parallel process to his own takes place in the bride's chambers before the wedding. Unwilling to finish her preparations for the ceremony and emerge from the bathroom, Carol dons a facial mask and a bathrobe. In parallel shots, Stirling is shown applying a cream mask to his face as well. Just as Stirling complained about turning thirty, Bob must reassure Carol that marriage does not accelerate aging. In a parody of the male bonding that is part of the groom's rituals in preparation for the wedding, Stirling is depicted sewing up the groom's trousers as the two discuss their mutual marriage plans. Almost as though he is jealous of the bride, Stirling insists upon upstaging the straights by announcing his own plan to marry Bob.

Stirling's androgyny makes him a foil to Bob's other love interest, Brendan, who even after his conversion is nevertheless coded as straight. Brendan's sober, earnest, and self-effacing manner makes him a meaningful counterpoint to Stirling's vanity and flamboyance. Brendan is offered to the audience as the more sensible choice for Bob, despite Stirling's classic good looks. Brendan's appeal is not limited to his appearance. His manner is more masculine. He aggressively pursues Bob as a straight man would a woman, with pleas and romantic overtures intended to win the affections of the love interest, while Stirling's interest in marriage seems to be more about his own personal fulfillment; Bob is only the convenient and imminently replaceable recipient of his affections. Stirling is the center of his own world, while Brendan, by contrast, focuses on making Bob happy and hopes his own emotional needs will be filled along the way. Bob and Brendan also seem to have more common interests and behavioral patterns. They enjoy staying out all night drinking, while Stirling, like the housewife who disapproves of her husband's late night activities, returns to the room and complains bitterly when the men wake him upon their return.

Bob's occupation as a writer for an overly sentimentalized soap opera becomes a trope for the fashioning of an idealized romantic partner that is the project of the film *I Think I Do*. A portion of the dialogue confirms the parallel between Bob's show and the action of the film. Just as Bob transforms Stirling into a straight male sex symbol for the show, a construction contrary to reality, writer/director Brian Sloan manufactures an idealized masculine partner for Bob, an individual formerly straight who, having rejected and humiliated Bob, later regrets his actions and returns to plead for reconciliation and love. In both the film's central narrative and its internal analogue the amplification of sex appeal is achieved through the framing of an ostensibly straight male, and that appeal is not aimed exclusively at heterosexual women. There is little doubt that Bob's infatuation with Brendan is in part intensified by his initial disinterest and inaccessibility. Even between the two men masquerading as heterosexual, the preferred choice is the one whose imposture is most convincing — Brendan, whose masculinity is reinforced by its former authenticity. Regardless of his conversion, he is portrayed as a more genuine man than an individual referred to as a "dreamboat" by the women in the film. Despite his classic good looks, Stirling is finally too androgynous to compete with Brendan, the formerly straight gay man.

I Think I Do is a gay variation on the interrupted wedding thematic. The lack of enthusiasm of the bride for the conventions of the wedding day undermine the romance of the rituals. Indeed, the action suggests that marriage is the death of passion. Carol and Matt are the only ones who do not have sex on their wedding night, but, instead, go to bed fighting. The sexual dynamics of the wedding party are far more interesting than those of the married couple. However, the traditional marriage is not the only one being disrupted. Bob and Stirling have also decided to marry, and it is this arrangement that is completely destroyed. The interrupted marriage involves the introduction of a former and more passionate love interest who draws away the bride or groom. Brendan's interference in the happy couple's plans serves as the gay analogue to this traditional romantic theme. Bob arrives in the company of Stirling and leaves alongside an old flame. Perhaps the reason the wedding that frames the narrative is not Bob and Stirling's is because heterosexist politics have ensured that such narratives will continue to strain credibility far into the future.

Billy's Hollywood Screen Kiss

No recent film more directly addresses the attraction of gay men to straight men than writer/director Tommy O'Haver's comedy *Billy's Hol-*

lywood Screen Kiss (1998), which examines the infatuation of Billy Collier (Sean P. Hayes), a struggling young photographer, for Gabriel (Brad Rowe), a straight male model. As in *I Think I Do*, O'Haver's film identifies the movie industry itself as the contributory cause of the gay men's romantic preoccupations. Yet while Brian Sloan's characters in *I Think I Do* are troubled when they recognize the ways in which their relationship has come to resemble a soap opera, Billy consciously attempts to relive the romance of old Hollywood movies, both in his emotional and in his professional life. The content of his fantasies and his photography is drawn directly from classic romances, i.e. *From Here to Eternity*, a work that becomes a recurring motif within the film. However, unlike the previous films listed in this chapter, *Billy's Hollywood Screen Kiss* is conscious of itself as a gay male fantasy, analyzing the self-destructive ramifications of doomed affections and flirtations. Billy does not, as in the other films, attain the unavailable yet convenient man, but instead finds that his fantasies have once again condemned him to a failed and self-indulgent relationship.

The unwise and unproductive romantic choices that Billy repeatedly makes can be partially explained by the deconstruction of a rigid gay/straight binary within the film. The repeated references to the "Kinsey

In *Billy's Hollywood Screen Kiss,* Sean P. Hayes (*left*) plays Billy, a gay man with an unrequited attraction to the sexually ambiguous Gabriel (Brad Rowe, *center*).

Scale" suggest that the division between heterosexuals and homosexuals constitutes a continuum rather than an impermeable boundary. In the Kinsey Scale, sexual proclivities are rated with a number between one and six, these numbers signifying the degree of one's reliance upon a single gender for sexual arousal. If the Kinsey Scale can be assumed to have some validity, then most people, whether they are self-identified as straight or gay, can be expected to have some measure of same sex desire and such an assumption encourages the pursuit of those who would otherwise seem unavailable. In the most intimate scene between the two protagonists, Billy describes the Kinsey Scale and labels himself a "perfect six," which is completely gay, but when he asks Gabriel how he would describe himself, the companion changes the subject. Much of the dialogue and action of the film is devoted to speculation about the true answer to this query.

The scenes that punctuate the progressive effort to seduce Gabriel involve the tedious speculation of Billy and his friend Perry (Richard Ganoung) over the [im]probability that Gabriel has some or does not have any romantic interest in men. Billy's hopefulness is countered by Perry's cynicism and practicality. Both Perry and George (Meredith Scott Lynn) attempt to dissuade Billy from his self-destructive infatuation with Gabriel, reminding him that he is prone to infatuations with "unavailable men." Perry even equates Billy's current preoccupation to "repetition compulsion." The conversations between photographers Billy and Perry take place in the photo lab and involve an over-examination of the interaction between Billy and Gabriel. Perry speculates on the three potential outcomes of the flirtation:

> One is that he is most or at least somewhat gay, and he does actually want to screw around with you. Two, he's gay and not attracted to you, and you're merely projecting. Three, he's straight, enjoys the attention and you're merely projecting, and may I remind you, you have a history of merely projecting.

Even Perry's hopefulness that Gabriel could be interested in Billy is undercut by the additional assertion that Gabriel would be "coming out of the closet," to which he adds, "you know what we boys do when we come out of the closet."

Billy's history of frustration with straight men began early in life. He offers two brief accounts of the formative experiences in his childhood and adolescence, both of which resulted in his rejection by a friend to whom he reveals his same sex interests. As a child, he confided in a friend, Kent Bartlett, that he liked to look at naked men. The boy was subsequently forbidden by his mother to keep Billy's company. In another seminal experience, this time in high school, Billy is temporarily snubbed by another adolescent with whom he shares a similar interest in music. Following a Violent Femmes concert, he makes a play for his friend, who does not appreciate the gesture but who does eventually decide to forget that it ever happened.

The representation of straight men in the film is occasionally unkind and is frequently hyperbolic. There are two representations of exclusively heterosexual males, and these individuals are boorish, classless, and stupid in the extreme. The first is George's boyfriend Andrew, whom Billy refers to as "too straight to appreciate fine camp," this because the man objects to the dialogue in the film *From Here to Eternity.* Andrew seems to be simultaneously harmless and clueless, not even sure when he is being insulted. He is sufficiently lascivious to satisfy George's lust, but is incapable of romance. After George dumps Andrew, she rebounds with a "stoner" who has a boat at Catalina Island and who announces with pride that he drops acid every Saturday night. Gundy is even less romantic than Andrew. Although he tries harder (sings to her, etc.), he is too vulgar in both language and taste to be a serious romantic companion. George begins to recognize her mistake when Gundy is unable to remember her name accurately and identifies sex with her as the single adequate replacement for his Saturday night "dose." She spends most of the evening trying to escape from him and is reduced to taking a romantic stroll down the beach with Billy at sunrise.

The potential for romance among gay men seems to be equally unpromising. Billy's boyfriend Fernando is appropriately enthusiastic and insists, as they make love, that Billy is "special," yet Fernando's promiscuity undermines his protestations. It is clear that many people are "special" to Fernando, especially his lover Peter, with whom he has an "open relationship." Paradoxically, romance necessitates the potential for the failure of love: the initial reluctance on the part of one or both partners and the subsequent chase, as well as the sexual tension generated by the possibility of continued hostility or indifference. The overcoming of reticence and the exhilaration of the chase create the emotions requisite to a powerful romantic union. Thus, imminent accessibility nullifies passion, which needs more than the union of bodies. For Billy, the pursuit of straight men is romantic because it involves a potential re-creation of the defining stories from Hollywood's Golden Age, in which all of the movie stars and their characters are at least ostensibly straight, and the pursuit of them involves the possibility, indeed the probability, that the seduction will never achieve consummation. Out of this challenge is born the tension that generates romance. When Billy finally spends the night with Gabriel, the sentiment and anticipation is intensified because of the uncertain intentions of the participants and because the accumulated energy of all the former speculation is "forced to its crisis." The reality of Gabriel's orientation will be revealed, and the continued association between the two men hangs in the balance. For Billy, the moment is virtually intolerable: The enterprise in which he has a sustained emotional investment stands or falls upon the first touch. He will either gain a lover or lose a friend, experiencing elation or despair. The immediate availability of the sex object or the perception that relations are only physical are anathema to romantic love.

Billy's preoccupation with the conventions of courtship are revealed in both his artistic/ professional life and his dreams, a parallel which is explainable in Freudian psychology, since both impulses rise out of the unconscious. Billy's professional enterprise, for which he first recruits Gabriel, constitutes a visual metaphor of Billy's emotional life and his infatuation with straight men. He is attempting in his photographs to recreate famous Hollywood kisses by using straight male models and drag queens. The creative enterprise entails an effort to insert the gay male erotic consciousness into the screen romance. Just as the audiences of the cinematic conversion fantasies discussed in this chapter observe the enactment of their own desires and longings for inclusion and gratification, Billy literally tries to posit a camp representation of his own erotic/romantic interest within the re-enactment of the seminal scene. The subsequent images reveal the important role that Hollywood has played in constructing the conventions of romance for gays and straights alike. Using an ostensibly straight male model, Gabriel, and a drag queen, Billy reconstructs the famous imagery of lovers frolicking on the beach in *From Here to Eternity*. Of course, drag queens are commonly indicative of the gay man's alter ego, an amusing surrogate for the gay man's libido and his feminine self. Thus the image of Gabriel rolling in the sand and waves captures iconographically the wish of many gay men to love the straight male in the way the woman does, to be inserted imaginatively and vicariously into the heterosexual conventions of love and courtship. The drag embodies Billy's role in the central relationship of the film and, more broadly, suggests the fulfillment of romantic fantasies for many gay men. The production of the Hollywood Screen Kiss series becomes a metaphor for Billy's pursuit of love.

The influence of Hollywood on Billy's romantic fantasies extends into his subconscious. The film includes four dream sequences in which the possibilities created by the advent of Gabriel in Billy's life are experienced imaginatively. However, these sequences also reveal Billy's gradual recognition that his romantic fantasies are unattainable, that a man like

Gabriel lies beyond his reach. These segments include romantic music, begin with an image of an aged movie reel counting down to its first shot, and reflect the content of the most recent interaction between Billy and Gabriel.

In the first dream the potential lovers, dressed in Tuxedos on the beach, stare directly into each others eyes (so close as to be uncomfortable) and offer the clichéd dialogue of the cinematic melodrama, i.e. "I never thought it could be like this," etc. This meaningless talk continues at such length and is delivered with such overblown passion that it becomes an effective parody of the romantic genre. Of course, this is the same dialogue that both Andrew and Gabriel complained about after viewing *From Here to Eternity*, and that Billy previously defended as "fine camp."

The second dream sequence suggests Billy's gradual recognition that Gabriel is unobtainable. Here the two men dance in a rather lengthy sequence reminiscent of Fred Astaire and Frank Sinatra movies. Behind them a film reel is running, depicting drag queens singing "This Is My Song." Eventually a woman is introduced into the reel, and Gabriel disappears from the foreground and reappears dancing with the woman onscreen, a reminder of his inaccessibility. This dream immediately follows Billy's uncomfortable visit to Gabriel's apartment where he (Gabriel) receives a call from his girlfriend in San Francisco, and although it is clear they are breaking up, it also confirms that Gabriel really has a girlfriend, a fact that Billy had previously questioned.

The third sequence follows the abortive effort at intimacy between the two men and reflects the embarrassment and panic that Billy experiences after having been rebuffed. The sequence is drawn from Hitchcock's *Vertigo*. Billy is running in front of the traditional hypnotic spiral while he hears all of the voices of warning that were a prelude to the uncomfortable moment, voices that told him what a mistake it was to pursue Gabriel. He, of course, wakes up screaming, only to find that Gabriel has left without warning.

The final dream follows Billy's discovery that Gabriel has left town with photographer Rex Webster and other models to conduct an advertising shoot on Catalina Island. Here Billy's subconscious reflects this separation, as well as the conclusion of their flirtation. Once again the shot includes a film of the beach projected in the background. The sequence depicts Billy in the foreground while Gabriel is represented on the screen behind. As Gabriel runs into the surf, Billy cannot follow. The image suggests that potential romance between Billy and Gabriel resulted from the combined influence of Billy's imagination and his love of Hollywood romantic melodramas. The image of Gabriel running into the surf once again invokes *From Here to Eternity*. However, Billy does not get to play Deborah Kerr to Gabriel's Burt Lancaster; he is left out of the scene altogether, reminded once again of the unreality of movie scripts. The image is also appropriate to the subject matter insofar as Gabriel left for a shoot on Catalina beach, and Billy has not been invited to accompany him.

Perhaps the most unexpected twist in the film's narrative, and one shared by Billy and the audience, is the revelation that Gabriel really is ready to convert and is comfortable with the decision, but, nevertheless, is not interested in Billy romantically. Instead, Gabriel has become involved with another model on the Catalina shoot. Billy has been excluded from Gabriel's affections in a way that he never considered. They are not inhibited by the formidable gap between alternative sexual orientation, but instead between the still more rigorous separation of the pretty and the plain. The disclosure must be more emotionally devastating than the belief that Gabriel is entirely straight. Billy realizes that he has seen too many "Goddamned movies," and reminisces about his dream of a perfect kiss between himself and his obsession, a kiss that links the cinematic and the real. To emphasize the irony that romantic fantasy involves the union of those who in reality will not bond, Perry confesses that he has retained a romantic crush on Billy for years. The idea that Billy has been oblivious to this sentiment, absorbed by pursuit of an unobtainable man, reveals the universal disappointments of love. The perfect kiss was within Billy's compass, but he had no interest in the person who offered it. The revelation of this fact limits the resentment Billy and the audience are allowed to harbor towards Gabriel for his disinterest, suggesting that all those engaged in the pursuit of love are equally guilty of disappointing others. In a resounding irony, Perry departs with "Catalina's only homosexual," and Billy has his romantic stroll along the beach with his girlfriend George.

The repeated allusions to the conventions of the Hollywood romance and to the film as cultural object may be intended to literalize a rhetorical device involving the homonym reel/real, thus suggesting a semiotic juxtaposition of antithetical ontologies. The events depicted on the film reel are unreal, and the real is exclusive of the reel. However, to his peril, Billy has confused the reel and the real and must learn to separate them. For Billy, Hollywood-inspired fantasy intrudes upon the authentic, and his problems arise when he assumes others will share his cinematic idealism. The film *Billy's Hollywood Screen Kiss* as an object addresses the same issues by undercutting the romantic expectations of the moviegoing audience. The audience expects a traditional conclusion in which the protagonists of the gay male conversion fantasy come together in a fashion reminiscent of the heterosexual love conventions, one that offers hope and renewal to those who share his preoccupations. Instead, the film's interior action is intended to disabuse Billy of his unreal and unhealthy expectations for love, and as a cultural artifact the film accomplishes a similar task for the movie audience, reminding them that even if the presumed straight man turns out to be convertible, that does not mean he will have an interest in the gay man who hopes to initiate him. To assume he will is to obfuscate, once again, that boundary between the reel and the real.

Conclusion

The gay male conversion fantasy involves a paradoxical union of the reel and the real. While such infatuations do maintain a uniform presence within the gay male sexual dynamic, the frequency of their success is grossly exaggerated within the productions of the new queer cinema, and, with the exception of *Billy's Hollywood Screen Kiss*, the above films offer little caution against embarking on such an emotionally perilous course, and this in spite of the almost universal popular wisdom within the gay community that such pursuits are self-destructive and self-defeating. One may argue that the content of the reel is dependent upon the unreal, but that the reel is intended to impact the real. Fantasy shapes reality. Film as an art form relies upon wish-fulfillment to captivate its audience, whether it be through the display of erotic conquest, the triumph of justice through resolute action, the restoration of order through explicit violence, or the privileges of extravagant wealth. The movie audience wants to experience lives better than their own, and they are regenerated by a display of success beyond their own scope, a pageant that offers hope for the transformation of their own lives. The same is particularly true of the romantic genre in which there is a union of ostensibly incompatible personalities, an exhibition of conquest and self-overcoming intended to invigorate the oft demoralized participants in the real pursuit of love.

If the Hollywood romance is, by its nature, instructive fantasy, it is certainly useful to examine those directives and codes offered to condition desire and action within the conversion fantasy. This genre within the new queer cinema assumes a passive gay male audience, a group paradoxically defined as desirous of their own sexual subordination but determined to achieve it through aggressive action. The audience is invited to identify with the passive partner in this desired relationship. Gay sex is seldom — as it is touted — a union of equal partners, but, as with heterosex, it is often a dramatization of unequal power relations, and this is particularly true in situations where the gay man desires a straight man, where the objective is the conquest of a dominant male (as is the case in the conversion fantasy). In this context, the longing of the gay male is the subconscious wish to be, at least temporarily, disempowered. The fascination for straight men then constitutes a desire for subordination to that group traditionally coded as superior and dominant within heterocentric culture. This yearning is a capitulation to the same power differential against which the gay community rails. Thus there is an unspoken collusion between homosexuals and their oppressors. The image of the gay man infatuated with the straight man is politically counterproductive. However, people do not generally choose their partners on the basis of political expedience. Ironically, the reticent straight males who chafe against homoerotic desire, particularly that directed toward them, because it signifies their own feminizing or emasculation, might be well advised to consider the extent to which the queer look reinforces their masculinity. Rarely is the gay man, pining for the het male, motivated by the desire to subordinate and feminize him — quite the opposite; so the much dreaded shower room soap scenario is a heterosexual fabrication, not because gay men would ignore the naked straight men, but because in such a situation straight men would generally have only each other to fear. The scenario is a projection of the straight male desire onto gay males — a preoccupation with penetration. The lust of the gay male as it is represented in the conversion fantasy is often the active pursuit of passivity. The individual coded as the social penetrater of gender boundaries is nevertheless the sexually penetrated. Straight male bravado and sexual self-satisfaction is at some level reinforced by the capitulation to gay desire. This is how the participant in gay male pornography can be designated straight.

Despite the implicit submissiveness of the conversion fantasy protagonist and his audience, this sub-genre of the new queer cinema offers them an entirely different type of empowerment, an empowerment that goes beyond the recognition that the stories of gays and lesbians have finally been deemed worthy of a place within American pop culture. Regardless of his implicit sexual subordination, the gay protagonist of these films is constructed as socially and intellectually heroic, at the same time that he is physically insubstantial. The gendered contrast between the two principle characters in each of the above films is dismantled. The masculine is frequently constructed as brave and forthright within the traditional gender binary, yet in the above films the characters coded feminine are more courageous in their willingness to face down public scorn by "coming out" than are the masculine characters who find it easier and more expedient to hide their sexuality, perhaps because they invariably blend in better. The feminized protagonists are the more sexually aggressive (at least in their pursuit of their love interests), while the masculine characters are content to remain the passive objects of admiration. The cinematic couples listed above also share a didactic relationship with the feminine male, the more knowledgeable and mature partner, the one who initiates the masculine partner into the mysteries of their new sexuality. The character performing the straight male is emotionally weak and irresponsible, confused by his queer desire and inclined to blame others for his predicament.

The veracity of the above gender reversals would in most cases be taken for granted by the gay male audience familiar with the social and gender politics of the typical gay bar, where the more masculine patrons are often the more passive, satisfied to stand apart, posing, flexing, and waiting for the less impressive physical specimens to admire them. Those who dare approach are immediately presumed effeminate; otherwise, they would never show so much interest in another man. (Sometimes it seems almost a miracle that anyone gets together.) Such behavior, of course, reverses the sexual dynamics of the straight bar where the most masculine men are the most aggressive, at least in theory and particularly in the popular, romantic imaginations of the gay men.

Conversion fantasy films also reinforce the default assumption of gay liberationist theory that it is always better to be "out of the closet" (Vaid 57), a postulate so universal that it is seldom ever interrogated. This assumption does not seem to include an appreciation of the extraordinary hostility of many populations within the country toward gay men and lesbians, and this in spite of the fact that violence against gays is one of the premier platforms of the movement's political agenda. Nevertheless, everyone in these films is expected to come out, and they are coded as cowardly and irresponsible if they do not. Thus it is clear that the audience of the conversion fantasy film are also "out of the closet" and predisposed to sympathize with others who are. Jamie, Steven, Bob, and Billy fulfill their duties as gay men by living openly and by helping others do the same. While gay liberationist theory assumes correctly that hiding our heads for so long allowed the most absurd lies about us to proliferate, I am not sure that the veracity of that assumption leads inevitably to the conclusion that everyone should come out, in spite of circumstances, and that everyone who does is assured emotional health and a more fulfilling life. In many parts of the South the only thing that such a person could be assured of is abuse, either physical or emotional. In all of the above films the action is set in a progressive environment: London, L.A., and D.C. Where are the coming out stories of the American South and Midwest? I suspect the conclusion of such narratives would more closely resemble that of *Boys Don't Cry* than of *Beautiful Thing*.

Another curiosity of the gay male conversion fantasy is the implicit assumption that straights can be converted but gays cannot. Now this supposition may be a satiric reversal of church rhetoric, which maintains gays are ruined heterosexuals who only need Jesus to turn them around. However, as much gratification as these satiric barbs bring, we need to acknowledge that straight men are no easier to convert than gay men. Moreover, the conversion fantasy does not advocate the polymorphous perverse that identifies all people as bisexual. The gay male is firmly committed to his orientation, and the straight male is simply confused, waiting for the right gay man to "turn him around." Of course, paradoxically, the gay male desire for the heterosexual includes the presumption that the straight male will still be straight after his conversion; he will simply desire sex with and become devoted to the homosexual who initiated him — hence the straight star of gay pornography. The danger of the conversion fantasy is that it seems to reinforce the recruitment myth. For religious and conservative hysterics, heterosexuality is a condition from which people are drawn away; it is the default erotic predisposition of all humanity. Thus the conversion of an individual who displays any heterosexual inclinations is a recruitment, because, left to their own devices, such people would never deviate. I, of course, recount this position with a great deal of irony. What has been labeled recruitment is actually de-programming. In an environment where the only sexual conditioning that a person can hope for is heterosexist, never referring to homosexuality with anything but the most vitriolic denunciations followed by the threat of social sanctions and physical reprisals, the person who did not need a little encouragement and emotional support in order to embrace his or her queer potential would need to be extraordinarily strong willed, self-confident, and resolute.

Regardless of the emotional fortitude requisite to coming out, the fascination of gay men with straight men is at some level an exercise in self-loathing, and I do not refer to the willful pursuit of emotional pain, but to the desire for self-obliterating through the embracing of that which, by its nature, is repudiation of the self. Homosexuality is the "repository of all that is excluded from hegemonic masculinity" (Connell, *Gender* 78), and the repudiation of homosexuality is an act of self-definition for straight men and adolescents (Dollimore 218). To embrace that which constitutes an institutionalized refusal of one's own humanity, of one's place within gender and society (for decades, even spoken discourse), can be nothing less than self-annihilation, a capitulation to all that is most hostile to one's nature. The gay man's desire to possess the straight man is a celebration of all that one is not.

French psychoanalyst Jacques Lacan has argued that "desire is a lack" (Sarup 13, Ragland-Sullivan 172). Simply put, the desirous long to obtain through coupling that which they perceive is missing in themselves, and in each case it involves some misrecognition and representation of the Phallus. Women misconstrue the penis for the Phallus, and men the mother. Lacan altered Freud's vexed theories of "penis envy" and "castration anxiety," adding to them with the idealized representation of the Phallus (which signifies the symbolic — language) of which all humanity, male and female alike, are deprived. All individuals are castrated twice, once within the family romance and once by language. The desirous long to replace what they perceive is missing — the Phallus — or to be inserted into the Symbolic order. Gay men's futile desire to possess the Phallus through the sexual conquest of the straight male is a desire to be inserted into the social discourse, both in language and in social institutions, which are perceived to be the possession of heterosexual men. However, as with all other longing, the desire of gay men to acquire Phallic authority through the pursuit of straight men is to misunderstand the place of straight men within the symbolic. They do not possess the Phallus either; their own desires are yet another manifestation of the same emptiness. Perhaps subconsciously, gay men yearn to obtain cultural legitimacy from the pursuit of het males or to have a place in the hegemonic cultural institutions from which they have been traditionally excluded, but as with all other sexual longing, this practice, by its very existence, ensures its failure. Paradoxically, the desire to love the straight man is the desire to become straight, to occupy a position within cultural institutions that are by their nature heterosexist.

For the audience of the cinematic conversion fantasy, the wish fulfilling pageant played out on the screen exceeds the satisfaction to be derived from the representation of sexual conquest. While the actual possession of the ostensibly straight male is not sufficient to create a place for gays within social institutions, since the process only serves to marginalize the desired object as well, the reel has its place within the real. The reel allows our stories to be written into the public discourse, and as the audience watches in the dark, yearning to see the union of gay and straight played out on the screen, the act of watching verifies that such a union has already taken place, but not without compromise and capitulation.

2

Courage Teacher: The Portrait of an Aging Artist with an Angry Young Man

As a young man of 19 years I traveled from Illinois to Florida to join my brother, already residing in West Palm Beach, mostly to escape Illinois winters and the oppressive environment of an Illinois farming town. At the time, my brother worked for a decorator on Palm Beach's Worth Ave., one of the most exclusive streets in America, the cultural equivalent to Rodeo Drive in L.A. and Fifth Avenue in New York. Arriving in West Palm, I, of course, needed work, so my brother put me in contact with an aged man whom he had met on Worth Ave., a decorator who had just arrived in town and needed an assistant for a job he was completing in a condo on the beach. I accepted the opportunity and was for a couple years gainfully employed by Eugene, a talented decorator who never went to college but who had managed to convince clients to trust his judgment in design despite of his lack of formal training. They were certainly well advised to do so; his interiors were frequently extraordinarily beautiful, a marriage of the elegant, costly, and refined with the rustic and sometimes even vulgar, a combination that in some ways described Eugene's person as well. The single action that defined his style for me involved his placing of a ragged side chair with a straw seat and chipped paint next to an ornate, inlaid, and petite French desk in the master bedroom of a condominium penthouse on Worth Ave. It was a bold move; I cannot remember if the client kept it. When she returned, her first action was to remove many of the items he had introduced to the residence, but overall she was very pleased.

While working together, Eugene and I struck up an uneasy and unequal friendship; he was my employer, benefactor, and mentor, and I his house boy (platonic) and assistant. I say "uneasy" because we were not always happy with each other, and "unequal" because he never left any doubt that we were not friends or peers. He was a talented, critical, and aging designer, and I was a hostile, directionless, and confused boy, filled with rage at myself and most everyone else. When it became evident to Eugene that I was wrestling with an alternative sexual identity, he offered his guidance and wisdom, derived from a lifetime of experience as a gay man, and he never expected (nor wanted, I suspect) any sexual favors. The advice that Eugene offered to me was simple enough, the default position of the gay and lesbian movement since Stonewall: "Don't be ashamed and don't hide." I am not sure how much this information helped me to cope with the outside world, but I certainly appreciated the reassurance. He explained that no one had been available to help him through his struggle with his own identity issues and that he hoped to help me avoid the same isolation and self-loathing. In retrospect, his advice revealed the necessity of the oral transmission of gay and lesbian culture. In the past, unless one was fortunate enough to glean the support and insights of an older and wiser member of our community, one was forced to navigate the vicissitudes of "coming out" with little comfort or encouragement, and this was and still is particularly true for adolescents who are insulated from the necessary information by aggressive and puritanical efforts to protect them from knowledge about sex.

The lessons that Eugene taught me were ongoing and included subjects such as sexually transmitted diseases (at a time when the like was easily eradicated with penicillin) and relationships, which for me were little more that neurotic attachments to unavailable men (a pattern that has not changed much in the past twenty years), and, of course, art and design. In some ways he had become my spiritual father. I cared a great deal about him, but we never completely approved of each other. I was rash and angry, and he, in his declining years, was disinclined to abide me. Moreover, I found him hypercritical and imperious. We did not part on the best terms, but we were civil and were able to meet in subsequent years to reminisce. I, of course, returned to show off my marginally impressive education, while he very graciously acknowledged those of my personal advancements that flew in the face of his expectations.

My periodic returns to West Palm were initiated by the necessity of my testimony in a lawsuit brought against one of Eugene's clients who was unwilling to pay. I noted the decline in his hygiene, his growing depression, and his excessive consumption of wine. He had become one of those frequently inebriated men in the pub whom everyone finds amusing and annoying. Eugene used to tell of his former battles with alcoholism and of his recovery through Alcoholics Anonymous. He complained that when he was a degraded alcoholic he had been forced to stay with his family and that they had sold all his property, an act for which he had never forgiven them and had broken off contact. I have no idea if this story was a fair assessment of events; they may have sold his property to finance his maintenance, or perhaps he had fabricated that theft because he could not face the idea that he had squandered his property in pursuit of the bottle. However, at the time, I naively assumed its veracity, and it is certainly the case that he had no love for his family — except some distant nephew — and in the time that I knew him he had no contact with any of them. The focus of such narratives in conversation with him was usually to reinforce the point that he had once been much more successful. He even bragged of having once decorated the President's yacht (I never thought to ask which president). In the months before I left West Palm, Eugene had begun to consume wine at dinner. At the time, I did not know that this practice was a very bad sign for a former alcoholic, but it did become evident that his consumption was steadily increasing. Alcoholism reintroduced itself into his life like the loving embrace of a new wife "hardly to be shaken off."

My infrequent returns to West Palm revealed him to be increasingly debilitated. He would sit in his living room filled with antiques and Pekinese. He had acquired a boyfriend who was plainly exploiting him financially. By this time, Eugene was too debilitated to work. He lived off of the property he had amassed before his most recent decline, hocking his accumulated antiques at local shops to keep himself in food and shelter. The combination of alcohol, disappointment, and fifteen years with a colostomy bag had diminished his strength. I do, however, remember one conversation on his porch in which he expressed horror and fear over the newly named and rapidly proliferating AIDS epidemic. I remember being rather callously incredulous that a man his age (over 70 by this time) would waste his energy concerned about an illness that could take as much as ten years to develop. I now realize my response was indicative of how easily the young dismiss the sex lives of the aged. As it turns out, he was never in much danger of contracting AIDS anyway, because the same circumstance that necessitated a colostomy bag made transmission of the virus to him unlikely. In the final years of his life, I fell out of contact with him, but my brother continued to see and hear about Eugene periodically as the aged man went about town plying his overpriced antiques and periodically getting fleeced.

I remember when my brother called me to tell me that Eugene had been found murdered because I was a doctoral candidate who at that moment was tutoring a younger boyfriend on Greek culture for his Humanities class at the community college. In the weeks that followed, the sordid tale of Eugene's death came out. It was not entirely surprising to me that he had been undone by violence because he had for many years resorted to patronizing hustlers. However, this implicit assumption turned out to be hasty. The young man who was charged with his murder claimed that Eugene had paid to be murdered, a defense so odd and unlikely that it was probably true. He had been caught because he had bragged to other vagrants at a local shelter that he had killed an elderly man in West Palm. His companions did not believe him until he took off his shoes and revealed the blood on his socks, at which time they reported him to the police. When he was picked up, he was driving Eugene's Jeep Wagoneer.

The improbable account that the murderer gave for his actions was eventually verified. Eugene had spoken to several acquaintances in the proceeding weeks, including my brother, to whom he had expressed a wish that euthanasia were not illegal, and he indicated that he would hire someone to kill him, but that he was afraid of pain. Evidently, he overcame this fear. He was found stabbed and rolled up in a rug on the floor of his bedroom. The murderer was a vagrant whom Eugene had hired to work on his lawn and probably, although I do not know for sure, in his bedroom as well. In the subsequent weeks there was a *Volpone*-like scramble to claim the remainder of his property, and although they were not in his will (at least not while I worked for him), the family was allowed to go into the house and carry out what remained. The most interesting example of the desperation with which his friends pursued his antiques involved a previously estranged boyfriend who was found by police cowering in the bedroom closet of the sealed off crime scene. He had broken in hoping to seize property that he claimed Eugene had promised him. I have always believed him because Eugene would consolidate people's loyalty and express his gratitude by naming them in his will. I know this because I was once a part of that legacy.

"What thoughts I have of you tonight," Eugene, "lonely old courage teacher." The end of Eugene's life is a composite of many issues pertinent to the aging of gay men and to the community as a whole: isolation, violence, substance abuse, illness, and inheritance. For many years I have been provoked by the thought of him sitting in that house with antiques piled to the ceiling, antiques that increase in value with each passing year, while his life became valueless, both to himself and to others. The role he played in my life as a sponsor, both emotionally and financially, is a rare vestige of the once more prevalent practice of inter-generational mentoring, a practice that has been a familiar and accepted part of homosexual bonding since the Greeks. Whether motivated by loneliness, lust, or even vanity, the effort to offer guidance to a new generation of gay men and women is a noble endeavor, particularly in an environment that explicitly stipulated there would be no direct public discussion of gay men and women, even in the midst of an epidemic directly affecting that community. The collective wisdom of the gay community has been passed along in an oral tradition, but perhaps this worthy preoccupation has been replaced more recently by the growing social visibility of the gay community and the general public's willingness to tolerate explicit depictions of our lives, particularly within the independent film industry.

Two recent films directly address the issues of aging among gay men, *Love and Death on Long Island* and *Gods and Monsters*. Both focus on an aged man's longing for youth, vitality/health, and social relevance. The central character of each film is an individual who, injured by loss and/or ill health, has embarked upon a desperate course to validate his own life through communion with a young man who signifies personal and cultural values in opposition to his own. In each film the protagonist is a highly successful European artist in his declining years who seeks to influence another through the transmission of his memories and his craft. Moreover, each film is organized through the semiotics of antithetical masculinities. In both movies the aging homosexual is British and is associated with the European aristocratic traditions of high art, high culture, and male gentility/effeminacy (Sinfield 3, 137); is well-mannered and well-spoken; and is attended by a devoted and concerned maid who has mistaken her charge as a domestic servant for the task of a wife and mother. The young men are clearly middle class with a heavy investment in mainstream heterosexist values. They are virile and physical, more so in *Gods and Monsters* than *Love and Death*, and they signify the ascendancy of the American values of pragmatism, simplicity, wide-eyed credulity, and democracy over the decayed esoteric and aristocratic traditions of the old world. The Europeans long to embrace American brawn, while the Americans yearn for the validation of the European intellectual culture.

Love and Death on Long Island

Writer/Director Richard Kwietniowski's *Love and Death on Long Island* is a film that retains as its principle subject matter the aesthetics of proper filmmaking. The story focuses on the professional and personal crisis of an aging and highly successful, yet antiquated, British writer, Giles De'Ath (John Hurt), who, having been described as an "erstwhile fogey" in the press, and having suffered public humiliation in a radio interview because of his unfamiliarity with the technological revolution, embarks upon a desperate effort to reconnect with the world around him. His pursuit involves both an effort to understand film as well as a desire to find a person who can reacquaint him with the modern world. In his poem "The Palace of Art," Tennyson captures the paradoxical necessities of the artist who must maintain isolation in order to be creative, shaping and structuring his life, building the palace of art around him, but who must also periodically dismantle this construct and reunite with suffering humanity for the sake of his subject matter. This conflicted state is the predicament of Giles De'Ath at the beginning of the film when he realizes that his art and creativity have drawn him away from the world.

Giles' desperate journey of renewal is initiated by a film, a very bad film which he mistakenly attends through his ignorance of the multiplex structure of the theater venue. He believes he is going to see a film based on an E.M. Forster novel, *Eternal Moment*, but instead ends up in *Hotpants College II*, a teenage saturnalia. Cognizant of the film's degraded subject matter and poor production quality, he is nevertheless transfixed by the image of Ronnie Bostock (Jason Priestly), occupying a minor yet memorable role within the context of the bad acting and the childish subject matter. An obsession with the young actor ensues. Bostock becomes the vehicle and the leitmotif for Giles' survey of modern culture, compelling him to obtain teen magazines and to familiarize himself with television and video, purchasing a VCR and the acquiring of a video rental membership, actions which reveal Giles' ineptitude with contemporary consumerism and technology. Giles also begins a scrapbook, entitled "Bostockana," in which he meticulously documents his fascination with the actor. The title of the memorabilia is reminiscent of the expression "Americana," sharing the same unusual suffix, and is obviously intended to invoke Bostock's symbolic association with American culture in the mind of Giles De'Ath.

The audience is left to speculate on the true impetus for Giles' obsession. It is clear that Ronnie is not as promising an actor as Giles believes. Indeed, his maudlin expressiveness seems comically inappropriate within the context of *Hotpants College II, Tex Mex* and *Bernie's Pizza*. The audience of *Love and Death* is left to speculate that Giles' admiration for Bostock's work may be misleading, either the result of his unfamiliarity with the medium or the first manifestation of a homosexual longing that he unconsciously seeks to validate and dignify, disguising it as professional admiration. Ostensibly, Giles De'Ath is heterosexual; his much older wife has recently died, and he is childless. Thus he is associated with sterility, embodying the stereotype of the stuffy, aristocratic Englishman, uncomfortable with warmth or passion. His interest in Ronnie does have its homoerotic dimension, but it is even more indicative of the homosocial, the longing for male companionship. When Giles draws male nudes of Ronnie, attaching cut out heads from the teen periodicals, he catches himself in an impropriety because he scribbles out the drawing and apologizes to the absent young man. The incident reveals an erotic interest but also a desire to elevate the imaginary relationship above the physical. It is true that he eventually tells Ronnie that he loves him "desperately," but his love could be both self-love and/or paternal love. Giles characterizes Ronnie as "all that I myself have never been," perhaps that which he might have been had he been born later, the hope and expectation that most fathers have for their sons, the opportunity to live vicariously a second life with all new choices. The love could also be the attraction of opposites, not in gender, but in age, orientation, interests, and nationality.

When he senses that he is going to lose Ronnie to a woman and to America, De'Ath makes him an offer that helps to define the nature of his intentions toward the young actor. He promises to devote his life entirely to Bostock's career if the young man will accompany him to England where, in Giles' view, he will have better opportunities to become a serious performer. He offers precedent cases for such bonds between men, including the homosexual relationship between Rimbaud and Verlaine, and between Cocteau and Marais. Giles explains to the increasingly alarmed Bostock that there is a lengthy European tradition of the young man aligning himself with an elder who assumes responsibility for the young man's guidance. He, of course, obliquely alludes to the Greek paederastic tradition in which an older warrior was the sponsor of a younger, teaching him the art of war, protecting him on the battlefield, and embracing him in the bed. The relationship extended to other forms of education and usually crossed class boundaries, as it was considered an extreme humiliation for the young man if he were of the same social rank as the elder and/or was beyond early adolescence (Greenberg 143). The relationship was a reciprocity, the young man receiving instruction and the fellowship of an adult, and the elder receiving companionship and sexual gratification. The same alliance is subtly alluded to in the references to Shakespeare and Whitman, the former having exemplified such a relationship in the personas of his sonnet sequence, and the latter having defined fraternal affection in his *Calamus Poems*. Of course, Bostock is unmoved by historical precedents for De'Ath's proposition, and, without anger or vitriolic words, he departs, but not before he reveals his mature affection for the elder man with a comforting gesture.

In her seminal work *Between Men,* Eve Sedgwick's rethinking of the Freudian Oedipal drama reveals that the young male child must reject the attachment to the mother in order to be worthy of the company of men. The contest over the Oedipal mother, who literally stands "between" father and son, is the prototype for all male relationships, which are negotiated over the bodies and finally through the exploitation and rejection of women (Sedgwick 22–27). For Giles, women are paradoxically the potential inhibitors and the facilitators of relations between men. As he becomes increasingly obsessed with Ronnie Bostock, his maid's intrusions into his study become more troublesome, and he incrementally excludes her from his study, perhaps fearful she may uncover some embarrassing artifacts revealing his secret life. Finally he dismisses her from her duties in the afternoon. Moreover, Mrs. Reed (Elizabeth Quinn), who convinces Giles to lift his moratorium against interviews, is responsible for his reintroduction to the world of men, the first event in a process that leads him to his love for Ronnie. The best example of the manipulation of women for the furtherance of homosocial and potentially homosexual bonding is Giles' treatment of Ronnie's girlfriend Audrey, whom he courts in order to gain access to her boyfriend. Following her to the grocery store, he intentionally engineers an encounter by crashing his cart into hers. He woos her with talk of Ronnie's career and affects an interest in her (one that can even be construed as sexual) so that she will introduce him to Bostock. Giles attempts to usurp her position in Ronnie's affection, systematically excluding her from the interaction between men. As the relationship develops, she is depicted more and more in the role of servant, cooking and cleaning while the men lounge and confer. When she realizes she has been exploited to engender the bond between Giles and Ronnie, she responds by planning a trip that will consume the remainder of Ronnie's free time before his return to L.A. Consequently, Giles urges Bostock to choose between the company of men or the company of women. Through its implicit homosexual agenda, Giles' proposition for Bostock breaches the etiquette of homosocial bonding and guarantees that Ronnie will choose Audrey.

The meta-cinematic feature of Kwietniowski's *Love and Death on Long Island* offers the most compelling window on the film's content. Giles De'Ath's effort to embrace the modern world involves the creation of a screenplay, and one that illustrates his own transition form 19th to 20th century values. The film opens with the image of Ronnie and his dog walking on the beach, while a voice-over reveals that this beginning is actually a conclusion: "This story began with the end of another, far far from the surf of Long Island." The end of the story is its own inception as the narrative circles back to its origin. The image of Ronnie on the beach will be repeated at the conclusion of the film, and the opening statement is the first line of Giles' screenplay, depicting his pursuit of love on Long Island. However, the screenplay's screenplay creates a logical paradox since the action of the narrative goes beyond the confines of Ronnie's script reading. Is the film *Love and Death on Long Island* the script that Ronnie reads, or does the film contain an internal second script reading? When Ronnie tears up the screenplay, despite Giles' assumption that he will treasure it, are his actions Giles' creation or are they a reactionary response to Giles' over-confidence? Where does the screenplay actually begin and end? And do any of the characters actually exist outside of Giles' imagination, or are they merely an allegorical fabrication exemplifying his need to refashion himself for the modern world, to embrace Americanized technology and commercialism? These questions are unresolved within the film.

Love and Death contains an extensive, yet subtle, commentary on the qualities of fine cinema. The inclusion of embedded video clips within *Love and Death*, particularly clips of movies whose virtues are beneath consideration, creates a revealing contrast to the central action. The audience needs little encouragement or direction to recognize the artistic superiority of the framing narrative to those embedded; they occupy opposite ends of the cinematic spectrum. The childishness and hilarity of *Hotpants College II* and *Bernie's Pizza* foil the sober and somber subject matter of the central narrative, and yet they exist only as a portion of *Love and Death*. The video clips are the filmmaker's cunning means of introducing and exploiting the commercial success of such subject matter for his own film at the same time that he ridicules and rejects the teenage saturnalia as a genre and an artistic form. The film *Love and Death on Long Island* then becomes an artifact substantiating its own narrative philosophy. It is a film unlikely to have any success at the American box office at the same time that it contains commentary repudiating the commercialization of art. Giles remarks, "In Europe, we have a much stronger tradition of work with, what you call, a message." The film as artifact justifies its own predictable lack of success and identifies this failure as a virtue.

The professional philosophy that would justify the simultaneous exploitation and degradation of base subject matter is included in the film as well. Giles explains to Ronnie that Shakespeare used bawdy humor to "please the mob in the pit," but that he had the capacity to elevate the subject matter. Following Shakespeare, Giles De'Ath, in his pursuit of new and more contemporary subject matter, appropriates low art for the advancement of high art. One must compromise with the low in order to

generate an audience for the high, and such a project is Giles' quest on
Long Island — to negotiate an alliance between the lofty and the base. His
pursuit of Ronnie Bostock is a thinly veiled allegory of his flirtation with
the contemporary and the commercial. Giles is ready to degrade his artistic vision, and Ronnie hopes to elevate his own. They are men primed for
a settlement; however, their negotiation fails because neither is prepared
to sacrifice his professional vision permanently. Ronnie will not abandon
his contacts in Hollywood for the uncertainty of a more serious career in
Europe, and De'Ath cannot abandon the European commitment to serious art for American commercial values, yet each man has had a temporary impact on the other. The adventure on Long Island has resulted in
Giles' first film script, and the inclusion of Whitman's eulogy in *Hotpants
College III* offers Ronnie an opportunity at serious acting.

The contrast between the video clips of the teen movies and the events
of *Love and Death*'s narrative offers two distinct visions of male bonding
that signify the respective European and American interpersonal and educational values. Giles tells Ronnie that the tutorial bond between an elder
and younger gentleman is much more common in Europe than in America: "In Europe, it is often the case that a young man benefits from the
wisdom and experience of an elder. There's almost a tradition of such
experiences." The bond in Giles' vision includes intimacy between two
men, an intimacy that may not be entirely platonic, but which is designed
for the mutual physical and intellectual uplifting of those involved. The
close male relationships illustrated in the video clips of the bad teenage
movies are fraternal bonds common to the American university system
and to other all-male cultures that are devoted to the enthusiastic pursuit
of women, practical jokes, and alcohol; however, unlike the European tradition — as Giles defines it — the single criteria requisite for inclusion in
the homosocial relations among American men in male cultures is the
refusal of homosexual longing (Connell, *Masculinities* 40). In each of
Bostock's films he is cast as an outsider, the victim of violence or practical jokes, and he suggests the sensitive male artist's exclusion from the
company of other men; thus his filmic roles are an incentive to De'Ath's
romantic longings. In his mind, Giles elevates the suffering and sensitivity that Bostock displays in his films to the melancholy demise of the
promising 19th century, Romantic poet Chatterton, who killed himself
for love. The pre–Raphaelite painting of Chatterton hanging in the Tate
Gallery in London becomes Giles' idealized conception of Ronnie's professional and personal persona.

The casting decisions for the male leads in *Love and Death* reinforce
the film's content. John Hurt is a seasoned and respected actor who

frequently plays an effete gentleman, artist, or intellectual, and who also plays in Independent Films that retain a high amount of cultural prestige. Even in his role in the blockbuster *Alien*, he is a scientist, the first to die, and feminized by having gestated the monster in his belly. It is easy to imagine Hurt as incompatible with the youth market, his age and his genteel masculinity makes him an unlikely choice for the frequently overly simplistic gender construction of mainstream films. The courting of Ronnie Bostock/America may suggest an aging actor's struggle for relevance in a youth oriented profession. He strives to make his work current by appropriating contemporary issues as well as the star power of the youthful. Like Anne Rice's aging vampires, he longs for a youthful companion who can reacquaint him with an increasingly alien world. Ironically, Hurt's appearance in the film *Love and Death on Long Island* is not likely to alter the type of career opportunities that are already his expectation. The film draws few of the youthful consumers often responsible for the success of so much Hollywood cinema. He confesses: "I don't exactly write for the youth market."

Priestly, of course, was initially a teen actor starring in *90210*, where he became enormously popular, but since leaving the television show, he has been unable to break into mainstream films, although he has starred in several low budget independents. Perhaps it is his intention to make quality alternative cinema as opposed to blockbusters because of the prestige associated with such projects and the personal gratification of being taken seriously as an actor, or perhaps they are the only scripts he is offered because he was overexposed on television and typecast as a teen heartthrob. These problems are similar to those of Ronnie Bostock, who is "sick of playing a dumb kid" and who thinks that, "you can't be a teen idol if you're going to be a serious actor." He hopes that De'Ath will write a serious script in which he can play the lead, and when he is forced to reject the British writer, Bostock, nevertheless, takes his advice and introduces the Whitman eulogy into *Hotpants College III*, hoping to be recognized for his serious talent. The irony of Ronnie's predicament is that even the promising association with a serious writer such as Giles De'Ath turns out to be little more than a clichéd stalking of a teen idol. Whether or not he is willing to acknowledge it, Giles' interest in Ronnie has little to do with his acting or his career, both of which have become mere excuses to get close to the teen star. His pursuit of Ronnie becomes an allegory of the casting of a low budget, independent film that has little chance of generating much financial return unless it includes a well known star who agrees to work cheaply for the credibility s/he will receive by acting in a serious film. Priestly/Bostock is pursued, no doubt, for his star power rather than for his powerful acting, yet, paradoxically, while the script of the film includes Bostock's rejection of Giles' proposition and fails to inspire any faith that Bostock has the talent Giles sees in him, the film *Love and Death* includes Priestly as a serious actor acting well in a serious role.

The title *Love and Death on Long Island* seems enigmatic since no one dies, and the fact that Giles' surname is a homonym for "death" does not entirely explain the allusion to the same, although it does suggest the amusing sojourn of Giles on Long Island where he is very much the outlander, acting out his British assumptions and routines in a foreign setting. Certainly Giles' effort to reinvent himself personally and artistically when he has become laughably antiquated, and his desperate pursuit of love, constitute a struggle against aging and death, "mixing memory with desire," a consciousness of his own mortality born in upon him by the recent death of his wife. The film contains a number of allusions to death, particularly in the subtle conjunction of the images of the sea with references to Walt Whitman. For Whitman, the sea signified spirituality, the hereafter with which we merge when we die and from which we are separated when we are born: "I too had been struck from the float forever held in solution./ I too had receiv'd identity by my body" (*Crossing Brooklyn Ferry*). In *Love and Death* the image of the sea recurs most notably and obviously in the beach scenes where Ronnie frolics with his dog. In this case the sea suggests loneliness and isolation, facing the unknown future, an overwhelming, inevitable, and inscrutable natural force. Giles longing to join Ronnie on that beach suggests his wish to face the future and the unknown with a like-minded companion. They first meet and shake hands on the beach, and Ronnie invites Giles to accompany him to the Hamptons. The Whitmanesque eulogy that Ronnie delivers in *Hotpants College III* captures the union of death and sea: "Now finale to the shore,/ Now land and light finale and farewell./ The untold want by life and land never granted./ Now voyager sail though forth to seek and find." The speech can announce the death and rebirth of Bostock as an actor, but it can also be a literal allusion to Giles, whose name De'Ath is implied in the graveyard scene. In this case the eulogy is a tribute to his mentor as they both embark on new phases of their lives.

Giles' effort to connect with the young American may have been misguided, but at some level it seems to be an effort at self-validation, both through the desire to reconnect with the modern world and through the need to justify his own life by educating what is, in effect, an apprentice. However, it is also a sign of his willingness to embrace life after an extended period of symbolic death and withdrawal. Despite his failure to acquire the permanent companionship of Bostock, De'Ath's adventure is a repudiation of death and withdrawal, a renewal signified by his donning of the sunglasses (given to him by Bostock) as he taxis to the airport. He may have failed in the pursuit of love, but he has succeeded in resurrecting himself and, at the same time, has had a positive influence on Bostock's career, urging him toward the elevation of his craft by offering him the speech designed to get him recognized as a serious actor. In *Love and Death on Long Island* the homosocial/homosexual bond signifies the potential union of the high and low art, of young and old, of British and American, of the refined and the vulgar, and of the contemporary and the antiquated.

Gods and Monsters

Many of the same binary oppositions that structure and define *Love and Death on Long Island* are reiterated in Bill Condon's *Gods and Monsters* (1998, based on Christopher Bram's novel *Father of Frankenstein*), which ruminates upon and fictionalizes the death of legendary Hollywood

In *Gods and Monsters* Ian McKellen plays James Whale, the famed director of *Frankenstein*. The serenity of this introspective image belies the torment that the character suffers as a result of a stroke, a torment that causes him to long for death.

director James Whale, whose most famous work is the film *Frankenstein*. The screenplay of *Gods and Monsters* is a complex fusion of ideas related to sex, death, and war. The friendship that arises between James Whale (Ian McKellen) and Clayton Boone (Brendan Fraser), Whale's gardener, constitutes a re-allegorizing of his horror film narratives, with the two protagonists taking turns as the monster.

The interaction between Whale and Boone is defined by opposing representations of manhood. Whale is the accomplished, refined, and effete artist who has no pretenses to traditional masculinity. He is open about his homosexuality and possesses a self-assurance that could only be derived from a long residence in a very permissive environment (Hollywood); he flaunts his effeminacy and his orientation, speaking openly about his former lover David as well as his many sexual conquests, revealing none of the shame that his maid Hannah expects from a "bugger." When he is interviewed by the flamboyant Mr. Kay, he unblushingly promises to tell him anything he wants if Mr. Kay will remove an article of clothing for each answer. When he attends the reception for Princess Margaret at a rival director's house, he identifies Mr. Boone as his lover and later explains that it was just "two old men, slapping each other with lilies."

Boone's strident manhood reveals the insecurity of the "masculine protest." He has to prove his masculinity constantly with exaggerated displays of hardiness, roughness, disapproval, and, most of all, heterosexual longing. He becomes enraged by Whale's stories of his sexual escapades, remarking, "Isn't it bad enough that you told me you're a fucking fairy, but now you've gotta rub my face in it?" Masculine protest is defined by the boisterous denial of femininity in the male, and particularly any femininity that might reveal homosexual interests. Masculine protest is the idealization of macho bravado, and it is an identity that is very fragile because so many behaviors can damage it. Merely crossing one's legs in the wrong fashion can compromise the convincing performance of manhood. Boone is rough and hardy among his friends at the bar. He is ridiculed for his vanity in agreeing to sit for Whale's drawing, a consciousness of appearance being anathema to "real men." The anger of masculine protest derives from the fear that the revelation of homosexuality is an assault on the virility of the individual who hears the confession. Boone denies homosexual interests whenever the issue is broached and whether or not the conversation impugns his virility. Implicit within his denials is a vanity that assumes any homosexual will desire him. Boone is surprised when Whale disclaims any interest in the young man's body.

Boone epitomizes the virulent homophobia of American culture, and his association with James Whale constitutes his re-education on many issues. There is an assumption that the audience will identify at least in part with Boone's harsh judgments of Whale's life, but will also recognize the irrational fears implicit in his position and will eventually repudiate them. Boone and Hannah signify two separate responses to Whale's sexual orientation. Boone is the angry and violent homophobe who feels that physical coercion is justified in the suppression of homosexual behavior, while Hannah's homophobia is tempered by tolerance and compassion. They represent two oppressive traditions aligned against the advancement of homosexual interests: male gender norms and religion. Hannah loves Whale, but her religious conditioning will not allow her to condone his lifestyle: The "sins of the flesh" will deprive him of heaven. Boone cannot abide Whale because the old man's behavior undermines simplistic, binary constructions of gender.

Clayton Boone's re-education is specifically directed at his reductive views of acceptable masculine performance. Most notably, his idealization of military service is subverted. When Whale asks if he knew any gay men during the war in Korea, Boone denies the presence of homosexuals in the service. Whale insists that, "there may be not atheists in the foxhole but there are occasionally lovers," and offers his own experience as confirmation to the incredulous Boone. He explains that he was an officer in World War I and recounts his affair with a young soldier. Whale's story is intended to interrogate Boone's (and perhaps America's) heterosexist idealization of masculinity and military service. Boone claims to have developed his macho swagger in the Marine Corp. serving in Korea; however, as it turns out, his war experience is a ruse. His disapproving father had missed service in World War II because the conflict was over before he could embark, and the son very much wanted to prove his own manhood by contributing in a way his father was unable, but his appendix ruptured, leaving him with a medical discharge and a grudge. His bravado is a hyperbolic response to his failure to prove himself in battle. The scene involves an ironic reversal of expectations: The effeminate homosexual is a war hero, while the blue collar, heterosexist thug is physically unfit for duty. The scene deconstructs socially constituted codes of masculine behavior, revealing that heterosexuality cannot be a coherent factor in the determination of an individual's fitness for military service. The obvious national implications of the contrasting characters suggests the openness of the British to the military service of gay men and lesbians as opposed to the exclusionary policies of the Pentagon. Moreover, it suggests that under a threat of war a country cannot afford the luxury of excluding able bodied men on an irrelevant pretense.

The film also dismantles class assumptions surrounding homosexuality, often mis-recognized as aristocratic decadence (Sinfield 137). Whale suggests the same when he remarks that Mr. Boone "has never met a princess, only queens." Hollywood's elite, a group, according to the film, inundated with gays, are often characterized as America's royalty, yet *Gods and Monsters* reveals a gendered stratification of which the characters are only dimly aware. Whale remarks that everyone is equal in Princess Margaret's eyes; they are all commoners. Whale compares the class consciousness of Britain to idealized American values of equality in which "everyone is middle class." However, he does not acknowledge the various ways in which people are classified and excluded in America. American homophobia is so vitriolic that queer sex can disqualify an individual from recognition as a viable and productive member of society; it consigns masses of people to second class citizenship. For Boone, a groundskeeper can be assured of his social superiority to his own employer based entirely upon sexual object choice. Boone can conclude that a rich, famous, and successful film director is worthy of scorn because he has the audacity to talk about his alternative sex life. The title *Gods and Monsters* may intentionally invoke class stratification, signifying the tendency of any society to idealize some and demonize other segments of its population. In this case, the assignment of the appellation "god" or "monster" to each of the two protagonists would be determined by which character's perspective one embraces. Whale views Boone's hyper masculinity as monstrous, yet noble, while Boone recoils from Whale's monstrous sexual longings, yet retains a fascination for Whales talent and celebrity. Whale defines the "great gulf" between the two men as "disgust" and "fear of the unknown."

In his book *Monsters in the Closet*, Harry Benshoff discusses the frequent parallels between homosexuality and monstrosity in horror films. *Gods and Monsters* first acknowledges and then attempts to subvert the same equation. Increasingly, Whale's life resembles his horror movies, with Boone cast as the young protagonist who unwittingly ventures into the habitation of a mad scientist. Many common features of the horror film are included, such as Hannah's ominous warning of the "master's" perversion, the dramatic revelation of the master's monstrous sexuality, and the final battle with the madman who turns upon his unsuspecting companion. The imagery of a thunderstorm punctuates the film, and the traditional association of the storm with madness is included as well. When Whale learns of the damage caused by his stroke, he describes it as an electrical storm in his brain, and on the evening of his death he acknowledges the menacing weather: "A perfect night for mystery and horror, the air itself is filled with monsters." Of course, the film is punctuated with clips from *Frankenstein* and *Bride of Frankenstein*, images that comment on the action. The intertextual quality of the cinematic allusion is a product of Whale's growing madness, the effect of his stroke. Memories torment him unchecked and unfiltered, but there is a method in the madness. The horror clips provoke a response from the viewer, offering Whale a solution to his degenerative illness. He will create a "second monster" who will liberate him from his suffering.

Whale's madness reveals the content of his subconscious. His reveries interpret the Frankenstein films as an artistic response to the horrors of the great war. The subtle wit of *Frankenstein* and *Bride of Frankenstein* reflects the gallows humor that made the trenches of World War I tolerable. The creation of Frankenstein's monster and the monster's bride are the efforts of Whale to resurrect artistically his dead lover whose body hung in full view of the trench for weeks. The dead soldier on display became the object of ridicule for the living who could only face their own mortality through humor. The wasteland that the monster traverses in the classic Frankenstein imagery is the battlefield of France leveled by the destruction of war. The imagery of the monster also signifies the masculine bravado and brutality that leads nations to war, and this authentication of masculinity through violence is what motivates the character of Clayton Boone. The warring nations create a monster that will turn upon its maker.

The imagery of Frankenstein's monster is also occasionally associated with Boone, both in the confused mind of James Whale and in the imagination of the film's audience: Boone is depicted gazing over the shoulder of Boris Karloff, the original monster, at a Hollywood cast party; Whale comments on Boone's perfectly architectural skull, a reminder of the monster's notorious flat head; and the lightening flashes simultaneously on Whale's original sketch of the monster and on Boone's head and shoulders in the penultimate scene of the film. The audience is thus directed to equate the primitive intellect, the social marginality, and subsequent brutality of the monster with Boone's own qualities and with masculine protest in general. The narrative suggests that such masculinity must be softened by the presence of femininity, either through the civilizing agency of a wife or through the internalization of feminine qualities within the individual male. The Monster desires a wife, and Boone, at the conclusion of the film, has been completely domesticated by his own family and is able to cope rationally and affectionately with his memories of James Whale, proudly demonstrating the original Frankenstein sketch, the image of his former self.

The crisis of the film reveals the extent to which Whale has literalized his own art. He has sought to harness the masculine brutality of Boone to create a new monster, one that will turn upon and destroy him. He is certain that Boone's heterosexuality and hysterical homophobia will be sufficient to goad him into violence, a frenzy that will, in essence, euthanize Whale. However, Whale unconsciously becomes the monster through his demonizing and objectification of Clayton Boone and his callous effort to compromise the young man's future in order to achieve his own artful and timely death. In his assumptions about Boone, Whale fails to recognize that Boone's masculine bravado is a ruse to obscure his own physical failures, his inability to earn his manhood in war. Whale nevertheless shames and outrages the young man by groping him, hoping to incite his violence. Interestingly, the ensuing struggle is an analogue for sex, the young aggressive male struggling on top of the elderly effeminate gentleman, their fury mimicking the frenzy and excitement of the sex act. However, Boone is not able to perform, particularly when he finds out that his violence is a consummation for which Whale has been in lengthy preparation. Boone recoils, displaying real grief over the betrayal. The scene dramatizes the assumption that gay men and straight men can only ever embrace in violence, the heterosexual seeking to exorcise the demon he fears in himself, and the homosexual celebrating the masculinity of another and castigating his own unconscious and socially constituted shame. In the penultimate scene the "great gulf" between the two men has been narrowed. The revelation of Whale's violent longings and Boone's sensitivity deconstruct the binary suppositions implicit within any comparison of straight and gay men, of gods and monsters. Whale's longing for death is guilt that he did not join his dead lover on the battlefields of France, and Boone's hope to become a model and his effort to befriend his gay employer demonstrates his desire to evolve beyond the insecurities of his school boy bravado. In one imaginative re-creation of Whale's Frankenstein imagery, Boone, portraying the monster, conducts Whale, his creator, across the desolate landscape of France to a trench where the famous director can join his former wartime lover in death.

Gods and Monsters and *Love and Death on Long Island* include comparatively positive images of gay men, revealing successful, fairly well-adjusted, intelligent, artistic, and harmless (except perhaps to themselves) elderly gentlemen. However, both films raise a compelling question about aging and homosexuality. In *Gods and Monsters* Boone dismissively and perhaps naively remarks that Whale is too old to be thinking about sex and, therefore, has no plans for Boone's seduction. In the language of conservatism, homosexuality is a series of poor choices. With each sex act the gay man or woman consciously chooses to deviate from normative sexual relations, and a lifetime of such choices are no indication of any fundamental biological drive for same sex bonds. For example, that great moral authority and demagogue Trent Lott, Senate Majority leader from Mississippi, has likened the condition of homosexuals to kleptomaniacs, driven entirely by compulsion and poor judgment. In the context of such ruminations, it is questionable whether aging gay men are actually still gay. If at some point within one's geriatric convalescence one ceases to desire or practice queer sex, does one then become straight? The vitriolic rhetoric of the religious right maintains that gay men and lesbians exist exclusively at the moment of queer desire and the individual sex act, and are imminently reformable through the refusal of deviant lust. This insistence upon the invisibility of gays and the refusal of our humanity and culture may be yet another ineffectual loophole through which we can invalidate persecution and discrimination. Since we are only gay at the moment of the sex act, we cannot be considered deserving of discrimination in the interim; we do not exist as gays at any intervening moment. The films included in this chapter invalidate such assumptions by revealing that being gay includes memories, desires, preoccupations, talents, and point-of-views, all of which can be passed from one generation to the next. *Love and Death* may even suggest that one does not have to have queer sex in order to be gay, since prior to his fascination with Ronnie Bostock, Giles De'Ath may never have had any interest in same sex relations.

Ostensibly, De'Ath and Whale are reasonably positive images of gay men, particularly considering the artistic necessity of creating well rounded, believable characters, as well as the long history of intentionally unflattering and even reprehensible portraits. Nevertheless, the depictions of Giles and James are not above reproach, leading to somewhat ambiguous conclusions about the potential reaction of the cinematic audience. The depiction of lecherous old gays in hot pursuit of virile young heterosexuals is, of course, troublesome. The fear that gay men find heterosexual men irresistible activates homophobia. Even the rhetoric of institutionalized gay bashing fears that straight men may become the object of the gay male gaze. Following the dissolution of the nation's most vitriolic and punishing sodomy laws, courts in the state of Georgia have consistently concluded that it is no longer a felony to have queer sex, but it is still a crime to ask for it, a law that institutionalizes straight men's fear of queer propositions. Moreover, the national discussion over the integration of the military with openly gay individuals focused on the impracticality of creating separate facilities for straight and gay men, because the knowledge that one soldier may openly desire another in the shower or the submarine barracks was too great a burden for the national imagination. While both films reveal the troublesome relationships revolving around gay male desire for straight males, they also negotiate a settlement in which gay and straight men can coexist peacefully. Despite Clayton Boone's hysterical homophobia, he learns to appreciate James Whale as a person of considerable talent and accomplishment, and even after Whale's outrageous treatment of him, and perhaps because of it, Boone is able to develop a sincere affection for the man who previousl "disgusted" him. Boone is forced to face his worst fears regarding his friend ship with Whale when the elderly man gropes him and even threatens to reveal the act to Boone's heterosexist friends. The sobering aspect of the incident for Boone is the realization that Whale does not want his physical love, but his violent embrace, the single condition under which heterosexual men are allowed close bodily contact. Following the incident, Boone becomes unexpectedly tender and affectionate toward the old man. Ronnie Bostock is startled to discover that Giles De'Ath is interested in his romantic companionship more than his career, but he is not overly concerned by the revelation. His manhood is not compromised, so he does not resort to a histrionic display of rage in order to disassociate himself from the idea of homosexual attraction. He leaves the old man sitting in the restaurant, not because he is too offended to keep De'Ath's company, but because Giles will not accept the idea that Ronnie is a heterosexual male devoted to his girlfriend. Later, when he receives the screenplay fax, he reads it calmly and with great interest until the final paragraph presumes to know him better than he knows himself. The representation of heterosexual men patiently suffering the company of gay men is counter to the unacknowledged social conditioning of American adolescents who are programmed to respond to the revelation of gay men's sexuality, and indeed to gay men themselves, with disgust and violence. This revolutionary strategy has been duplicated throughout the American media, constantly exposing the audience to images of straight and gay non-sexual alliances.

The depiction of the aging gay men in *Gods and Monsters* and *Love and Death on Long Island* creates another equivocal reading. The loneliness and desperation of the two protagonists (not to mention the suicide attempt of Whale) reinforce the infantilizing rhetoric of heterosexists who seek to dissuade gays and lesbians from their innate sexual proclivities by reminding them that homosexuality is a solitary and depressing life, and, frequently, upon this patronizing foundation rests the legitimization for discrimination and exclusion. Of course, such an argument taken to its logical conclusion could deprive all unhappy people of their civil rights; moreover, it strips gays of personal responsibility just before it blames them for making the wrong choices. Indeed, the appellation "gay," suggesting lightheartedness, was adopted to combat the image of the unhappy homosexual. De'Ath and Whale may be desperate, but there is no indication that they have always been. Indeed, both men have experienced enormous professional success in the past and have only recently departed from long-term relationships. Whale's stroke-induced flashbacks reveal a happy prime filled with supportive friends and lovers, as well as a permissive environment where gay men were allowed to act out, i.e. camping it up on the set of *Bride of Frankenstein*. De'Ath seemed to be completely oblivious to his own loneliness until he was reminded of his seclusion by a radio host. The hateful rhetoric of the clergy invariably includes conjectures and accusations of mental illness, this in spite of the fact that they are not qualified for such a diagnosis and that the American Psychiatric Association disagrees, the latter having concluded that most unhappiness among gays and lesbians results from persecution rather than unwarranted shame and self-loathing (Bayer 52–53). The isolation of the two protagonists is mitigated by the presence of loving companions and servants. Moreover, the predicament of each man could not be assuaged by family, since Giles was married for many years and, as far as the audience can tell, developed homosexual tendencies only after his wife died. The absence of children results from his wife's advanced age rather than his inability or unwillingness to propagate. Whale's misery and desperation results entirely from his advanced illness. There is no indication that he would desire suicide if he could expect a full recovery from his stroke. Indeed, Whale's suicide can be viewed as liberating, since he, unfettered by convention and morality, took control of his life by electing to die rather than to decline any further.

There is an insidious element to the nationalistic binary constructed in each film, where the gay man is British and the straight man American. The association of the aging gay man with the sophistication and wisdom of the old world could be construed as somewhat becoming; however, it also serves to represent gays and lesbians as outlanders, inconsistent and unfamiliar with American working class values. The cultural didacticism implicit in such portrayals is not likely to inspire the support and approval of a mainstream audience who frequently loath the pretense of aristocratic posturing. While Britain is regarded fondly by Americans for its perceived cultural sophistication, Americans nevertheless have a strong sense of national superiority, of social, moral, and ideological righteousness, the inevitable arrogance of a rich, young nation that has enjoyed much success on the world stage and is now virtually unchallenged in its influence. Thus the association of the gay men with European cultural values may be effective in inspiring consideration based upon an appreciation for cultural relativity, but it may also inspire intransigence and cultural bravado by portraying gay men as particularly un–American, alien to our social values of hard work, democracy, and materialism. Much of the dialogue in both films is dedicated to the comparative analysis of Britain and America. In *Gods and Monsters* the comparison flatters the Americans, but here Whale has lived in the U.S. for a long time and has become accustomed to it, although he has remained little more than a resident alien culturally, still preferring the English aristocratic pretense. In *Love and Death* the comparison is to the detriment of the new world, Giles unable to acclimate himself to American culture and desiring to return to England with his American companion; however, he is, nevertheless, left looking like a foolish old man. It is difficult to say which portrait would be more disparaging, the outlander who remains to poison Hollywood with his decadence or the one who cannot abide residence in the U.S. and desires to abscond with and convert one of its brightest sons.

The appearance of *Gods and Monsters* and *Love and Death on Long Island* in the same year seemed something of a curiosity. Each deals with an aging gay gentleman who befriends a young man chosen to rescue him from desperation. In each film the elderly gentleman offers a lifetime of wisdom, experience, and opportunity, while the young man offers companionship, physical beauty, and vitality. The relationships are structured upon the ancient tradition of didactic bonds and alliances between aging and youthful males. Moreover, through casting, each film allegorizes the bond between Britain and America. Britain enjoys the wisdom and prestige of a long history, while America retains the energy and promise of youth. The aristocratic class consciousness of Britain is contrasted with the middle class uniformity of American culture. The didacticism which is implicit in the relationship between the elder and the younger is a vehicle for the transmission of cultural knowledge between generations and between the filmmaker and the audience. The pedantry of the dialogue is meta-cinematic, educating the audience of the film as it educates the characters. The aging artist becomes a metaphor for the film industry in its project to pass on our cultural history — in this case the collective history and wisdom of gay men — and in its confidence that cinema can have a positive influence upon society.

3

"Naught's Had, All's Spent": Shakespeare, Queer Rage, and *The Talented Mr. Ripley*

In the aftermath of Jeffrey Dahmer's killing spree, a public debate ensued within the Milwaukee community addressing the supposed violence of the gay men. From the pulpit, unprincipled and hypocritical preachers argued that Dahmer's crimes were yet another indicator of gay decadence, this time signifying violence. Gay leaders responded by reminding the public that Dahmer's violence was perpetrated against gay men. Dahmer admitted that his murderous activities were revenge against black males for the jailhouse rapes to which he was subjected. His subsequent rampage, in all likelihood, misunderstands the sexual orientation of those who assaulted him, insofar as he assumed that prison rape is a gay crime rather than the desperate substitution for hopelessly isolated and gender segregated heterosexual males.

The image of a queer serial killer who kills gay men captures a compelling cultural paradox: gays are violent victims. At one level, such a representation is a means of blaming the violence against gay men on gay men. Thus the heterosexual community is allowed to appreciate the violence against the homosexuals without actually taking responsibility for it, an alternative solution to denying that violence against gays happens at all. Gay men are simultaneously constructed as ineffectual sissies, because they presumably cannot match the physical prowess of straight men, and as super-villains, because they must constitute a sufficient threat to mainstream society in order to warrant continued discrimination. Amusingly, the accusations of gay violence are leveled by that segment of the population responsible for all war and virtually all rape, murder, theft, child abuse, spouse abuse, and assault.

Anthony Minghella's *The Talented Mr. Ripley* (1999) examines the behavior of a gay serial killer who is motivated not by a secret gratuitous obsession for blood, but by a desire to improve his station in life, to hide his secret desires, and to strike back against persecution. The film draws a parallel between the notorious ability of serial killers to walk among us undetected and the similar ability of gay men to blend into mainstream society, a quality that accounts for Mr. Ripley's talent. The portrait would be offensive were it not for the screenwriter/director's ability to direct the sentiments and support of the audience toward Tom Ripley, who — although he goes too far — is more likable than most of the people he kills. Minghella succeeds in winning the audience's sympathy by generating and exploring a Shakespearean connection to his subject. The portrait of Shakespeare's most villainous hero, Macbeth, as an angry gay man may, however, be less homophobic than it at first seems. Tom Ripley constitutes a resurrection of the villainous, cinematic homosexuals identified in Vito Russo's *The Celluloid Closet*. The character retains many of the stereotypical qualities of the gay rogue, but, at times, he seems to be as much "sinned against" as "sinning."

Only a few direct references to Shakespeare are included in the film. The most important of these occurs in a conversation between Tom Ripley (Matt Damon) and Dickie Greenleaf (Jude Law). Tom invites Dickie to copy a passage from the book that the former carries with him through much of the film; that passage is an important thematic verse from Shakespeare's *Macbeth*:

> Stars hide your fires;
> Let not light see my black and deep desires [I.iv.50–51].

In case the film audience does not recognize the passage, the dialogue identifies the book from which it is copied. Dickie comments: "I love that you brought Shakespeare, but no clothes." Tom can be seen reading the same book at various times within the film. In one notable scene, Dickie, who has become increasingly distant from Tom, is shown swimming and roughhousing with his friend Freddie (Philip Seymour Hoffman), while Tom, dejected and resentful, sits reading and sunning himself on Dickie's yacht. Marge (Gwyneth Paltrow), Dickie's girlfriend, characterizes the behavior of the two in the water: "Why do men always play at killing each other?" The comment refers to both the swimmers and the murderous events of Shakespeare's violent tragedy. The images of Tom reading at such key moments, particularly ones intended to reveal his growing estrangement from Dickie, suggest that the Shakespearean text is a pattern for Tom's ambitious murders.

Within *Macbeth*, the passage, "Stars hide your fires;/ Let not light see my black and deep desires," signifies a pivotal moment for the villain-hero. Having fought ferociously to protect King Duncan's throne from rebels and invaders, Macbeth, nevertheless, finds himself passed over in the royal succession: Duncan's son Malcolm will inherit. Slighted and furious, Macbeth vows to seize the crown. His invocation to the stars initiates a continuing image motif in which he and his wife summon the darkness to hide their crimes from God, society, and their own consciences. While Macbeth seeks the power and affluence of the Scottish throne, Tom Ripley desires his friend's wealthy lifestyle. Tom kills Dickie only after it becomes apparent that the latter plans to exclude him from his company and his prosperity. Tom confesses that he has become accustomed to affluence. Of course, Tom also desires his friend physically (an idea that is more subtly developed in Highsmith's novel), and Ripley is jealous because he perceives himself as having been displaced in Dickie's affections by Freddie Miles. These are the forbidden sentiments and longings Tom desires to hide from himself and the world.

The most striking appropriation of the Shakespearean paradigm lies in the structuring of the film. Obviously the screenwriter had to simplify the byzantine plot of the novel, stripping it to a succession of real and attempted murders, each subsequent crime born out of the necessity for concealment. In the psychological preparation for his murder of King Duncan, Macbeth's chief concern is safety. He is particularly troubled by ramifications such as exposure, punishment, and revenge:

> But in these cases
> We still have judgement here, that we but teach
> Bloody instructions, which being taught return
> To plague the inventor [I. vii. 7–10].

Macbeth's subsequent killings can be explained by his paradoxical desire to gain safety through murder (Campbell 222–239). With each killing, a new threat of exposure arises requiring yet another murder until he is abandoned by everyone save mercenaries. After Duncan's murder, Macbeth fears Banquo: "To be thus is nothing,/ But to be safely thus. Our fears in Banquo/ Stick deep…" (III. i. 48–50). He believes that Banquo alone can expose his crimes, and his concerns are echoed by his wife:

> Naught's had, all's spent,
> Where our desire is got without content.
> 'Tis safer to be that which we destroy
> Than by destruction dwell in doubtful joy [III. ii. 4–7].

With this resolution Macbeth suborns the murder of Banquo and Fleance in order to gain security and peace. However, the belief that only one person threatens their success proves shortsighted. Even before Banquo's body is cold, Macbeth identifies his next rival, and concluding that he has already "stepped" so far into a river of blood that to return "were as tedious as go o'er" (III. iv. 136–138), he elects to silence Macduff by murdering the latter's family.

While Ripley lacks Macbeth's paranoia and predilection for violence, he, nevertheless, is driven by a desire for safety. In the film, each of the three killings for which he is responsible arise from his fear of exposure. While the killing of Dickie is clearly Tom's plan in Patricia Highsmith's novel, Minghella alters the circumstances of the first murder to mitigate Tom's responsibility. Like Macbeth, Ripley reacts to provocations that include slights against his manhood. When Dickie compares him to a "little girl," Tom lashes out, striking him in the brow with an oar, yet the aggressor's initial reaction is remorse, including an attempt to reconcile with and comfort his friend. Only after Dickie attacks him in retaliation does Tom commit murder. While such an act can hardly be characterized as self-defense, it is not premeditated, although it may be a knee-jerk reaction to the fear of losing his newfound prosperity. Like Macbeth, Tom becomes the traditional tragic overreacher, the individual who aspires above his place in the social and cosmological hierarchy, a place to which he was not born (Levin 23).

The second killing is tragic necessity. Freddie Miles discovers that Tom is impersonating Dickie, and before he can confront Ripley with the specific accusation, the latter dashes him in the head with a blunt object and disposes of the body. This killing is motivated by a desire to safeguard the fruits of his first murder. By impersonating Dickie, Tom has attained financial and social success, both of which he stands to lose if he is exposed. As with Macbeth, Tom has, in effect, usurped the title of his first victim, and it has brought him influence that he was not born to and did not enjoy formerly. Before Tom left America, he was advised by a chauffeur that the name Greenleaf "opens many doors." Dickie's wealth and political power is dynastic, the advantage of name. Thus Tom need only assume the name in order to enjoy all of the benefits of family, and since the law and social custom (not to mention Dickie's own objections) forbid his attainment of name through marriage, Tom must kill Dickie and assume his identity if he wants to enjoy the latter's familial title. When Freddie discovers that the surname has been appropriated, Tom acts to protect the integrity of this newly acquired identity. While Macbeth complains that his "genius" is "rebuk'd" in Banquo (III. i. 55), Tom fears Freddie's capacity to expose his machinations. Although Ripley hopes to gain peace through the second murder, ironically, it has the opposite effect, arousing the suspicions of the Roman authorities and forcing Ripley to suspend his profitable masquerade.

The attempted murder of Marge (an event that does not occur in Highsmith's novel) is also motivated by Tom's need to hide his crimes from the world. Marge discovers that Tom is in possession of Dickie's rings, the same that Dickie promised never to remove. These, of course, direct her suspicions toward Tom who, when confronted with the evidence and her obvious suspicions, determines that he must kill her to safeguard his secret. In a clear example of cinematic metaphor, Tom, who has been summoned from his bath by the accusation, is so stunned he momentarily drops his towel, exposing himself. Quickly covering up again, he excuses himself to put on a robe and selects a razor with which to execute his next murder. In the traditional cinematic gesture of the psychotic killer, he moves slowly toward his potential victim, speaking in a reasonable and conciliatory tone that is, nevertheless, full of menace and revelation for the individual in retreat. Of course, the attempted murder is interrupted by the advent of the mutual friend Peter.

The final killing is the invention of the screenwriter and director, Minghella. Peter Smith Kingsley (Jack Davenport) is briefly mentioned in the novel but plays no substantial part in the plot. However, in the screenplay Peter becomes Tom's lover, the man who can show him the attention and affection that Dickie will not, yet Tom is, nevertheless, forced to kill Peter at the end of the film in order to maintain the integrity of his secrets, one more killing for safety's sake. As with Macbeth, Tom's last murder provokes the most regret. The final images of the film depict Tom sitting in his cabin stunned and isolated, remembering the circumstances of his most recent homicide. For Macbeth, the final murders are entirely punitive; Macduff's wife and children have committed no offense and are not in a position to expose his secrets. He kills them because he cannot reach Macduff himself who has fled to the English war party. Ripley is faced with a similar dilemma. He cannot allow Peter to encounter Meredith (Cate Blanchett) and her aunt on the boat from Venice to Greece, since each party knows him by a different name. Thus Ripley is faced with a bitter irony. He must kill the one person he loves rather than the two for whom he feels nothing simply because he has easier access to the former, and Peter's death will be easier to conceal. The filmgoer is left with the impression that Tom may have to continue killing indefinitely. Each murder, intended to remove the final obstacle to his security and to conceal his secret forever, creates yet another rival who must be put down.

Macbeth, out of a sense of injured merit, seizes the throne to which he has no legitimate claim. He sacrifices everything to maintain this imposture, to remain wealthy and powerful. The symbols of his office are the robes of kingship, and Shakespeare develops this image motif thoroughly. When he is addressed as Thane of Cawdor, Macbeth responds, "Why do you dress me/ In borrowed robes?" (I. iii. 108–109). When Macbeth urges his wife to abandon the plot to kill Duncan, he explains: "…I have bought/ Golden opinions from all sorts of people,/ Which would be worn now in their newest gloss" (I. vii. 33–35). As Macbeth's defeat seems imminent, Angus describes his predicament: "Now does he feel his title/ Hang loose about him, like a giant's robe/ Upon a dwarfish thief" (V. ii. 20–22). Vestments signify social status.

The imagery of clothing plays an equally important role in *The Talented Mr. Ripley*, where it represents wealth, identity, and social class; indeed, such imagery helps to organize the film. The narrative opens with a voice-over: Ripley interpreting events that have already transpired but will be recounted for the movie audience. He expresses regret for his crimes and identifies the borrowing of a jacket with a Princeton University logo as the origin of his problems. Princeton suggests the cultural and intellectual elite of the American Northeast, a social distinction that Ripley has not earned. However, the borrowed jacket catches Herbert Greenleaf's attention, motivating him to engage Tom in a venture to retrieve Dickie. The necessity of borrowing a jacket to perform at a cocktail party reveals Tom's lack of status and resources, and the subsequent observation by Dickie that Tom has brought no clothes to Europe further reinforces the idea that Tom is without identity and position. One of the initial gestures of Dickie's affection involves an offer to buy Tom a jacket on their trip to Rome, and Dickie's breach of this promise signifies the beginning of the men's alienation. Dickie abandons their plans for a shopping trip in order to entertain Freddie Miles. Returning early to Mongibello, Tom decides to sample his friend's clothing and is discovered admiring his reflection in the mirror when Dickie returns unexpectedly. The image of Ripley in borrowed clothing, of course, anticipates the impersonation of Dickie that follows the murder. When discovered by Freddie Miles in Rome, Tom is forced to explain why he is wearing Dickie's jacket. Even after Ripley is forced to assume his former identity, he is better dressed than before his trip abroad. It is difficult to tell if he still retains Greenleaf's wardrobe. As with Macbeth, Tom's usurpation of another man's clothing signifies the appropriation of his identity and an improvement in social status that arises only through murder.

Ripley persistently denigrates his former life, revealing his ambition.

Several additional image motifs in the film reveal Tom's effort to create a new self-image, one with which he is comfortable. The recurring images of mirrors within the drama are the most obvious of these filmic metaphors. Ripley is repeatedly depicted searching his reflection in the mirror, as though he expects to find clues to a new or former self. The mirror is associated with a his role-playing from the beginning. In the early cases, the mirror serves to signify and even facilitate Ripley's fantasy life, but, increasingly, it becomes the object of torment, a mocking reminder of his fraud and impersonation. Tom rides his scooter through a narrow alley lined on both sides by mirrors, and imagining that he sees Dickie Greenleaf lurking behind the reflections, he becomes disoriented and collides with the glass. Moreover, Tom briefly stares into the bathroom mirror after he selects a razor with which to kill Marge. Perhaps the most powerful repetition of this motif occurs in the final shot of the film when Tom sits, staring at his own reflection, while remembering Peter's voice before the murder. This is the moment when the mirror retains the clearest association with self-evaluation. The audience is reminded of an earlier conversation with Peter in which Tom generalizes about those with guilty consciences, "You never meet anyone who thinks they're a bad person." Before he kills Peter he reveals the regret arising from violent and fraudulent actions:

> I'm lost.... I'm gonna be stuck in the basement ... terrible, alone in the dark. I've lied about who I am and where I am. Now no one will ever find me.... I always thought it would be better to be a fake somebody than a real nobody.

Of course, the mirror imagery is not unique to either literature or cinema, but is a commonplace device often employed to signify the process of self-evaluation and self-understanding. In the context of *The Talented Mr. Ripley*, the image motif may be intended to invoke the dramatic tradition of the "mirror for magistrates." In early modern tragedy the practice of self-evaluation, particularly that inspired by a decline in personal fortunes, is occasionally illustrated by the introduction of a mirror into the scene, a mirror in which the tragic figures reevaluate their identity and social status. The most memorable example from Shakespeare occurs in the deposition scene of *Richard II* : "Let it Command a mirror hither straight,/ That it may show me what a face I have,/ Since it is bankrupt of his majesty" (IV. i. 266–268). Another instance of the same can be drawn from the closet scene in *Hamlet*. In his effort to shame his mother into repentance and reformation, Hamlet calls for a glass that will reflect her corruptions: "You go not till I set you up a glass/ Where you may see the inmost part of you" (III. iv. 20–21). In *Ripley* the mirror images alternate in their signification — from encouragement to mocking to accusation. They facilitate Ripley's fantasy life, his ambitions before he kills Dickie and his guilt after the commission of his crimes. Macbeth does not call for a looking glass, but despite his effort to kill his own conscience and to act without remorse, he has clearly engaged in self-evaluation at the end of the drama. He first refuses to combat Macduff: "My soul is too much charged with blood of thine already" (V. viii. 5–6). Like Ripley, Macbeth is compelled by the momentum and consequences of his former crimes to kill those whose deaths cannot be rationalized. Both men have regretfully "supp'd full with horrors" (V. v. 13).

Macbeth's soul-searching obviates a curious duality, and one that has led some scholars to question the unity and believability of his character. He moves rapidly from a patriot, risking life and limb in defense of his king, to a regicide, and from a warrior who can "unseam" his enemy "from the nave to th' chops" without compunction (I. i. 24) to a murderer, distressed by his inability to get the blood off his hands. These shifts can be explained by Macbeth's ambition and disappointment, the intervention of supernatural forces, and his wife's cunning, as well as the arbitrary social distinctions between state sanctioned violence and murder. A similar disunity can be observed in Tom Ripley, but here the duality suggests that he is a sociopath, a psychotic killer. Because of insult and rejection, Tom pummels the person he loves with an oar until the latter is dead, lies with the corpse in a romantic embrace, and shortly thereafter assumes the dead man's identity and social position. The film repeatedly suggests that Tom has a dark half, an ambition, which overrides all his better motivations and prevents him from feeling remorse for others. He often appears to be mimicking the emotional responses of others. This duality in Tom's character has a visual equivalent in the imagery of the film: the constant use of side and bottom lighting in the closeups of Tom's face creates a sense of his mystery and menace. Frequently, one side of Ripley's visage is heavily shadowed, suggesting that he is hiding something from the world, perhaps his forbidden desires, his ambitions, and/or his crimes. Even the promotional posters for the film reinforce the lighting motif that is Ripley's signature; Tom is depicted in the foreground, one half of his face in darkness, as he stares jealously and longingly at the happy embrace of Dickie and Marge. The couple, through contrast, define Tom as the outsider who looks on a happiness that he will never enjoy. The side lighting suggests that he harbors resentment and is plotting against the serene couple.

Minghella reinforces this motif by altering the relationship of Dickie and Marge for the film to allude to Tom's hidden homosexual desires. In the novel, Dickie and Marge are certainly emotionally involved, but they have not slept together as in the screenplay, and Dickie maintains that they never will. They certainly are not planning to marry as in the film. Ripley is deprived of the socially sanctioned union that Dickie and Marge will enjoy, and, interestingly, it is the knowledge of the impending nuptials, combined with the dismissive insults, that instigate Tom's murderous rage. Tom longs for a valid and lasting indication of his connection with Dickie, one that he initially tries to achieve through fraternal associations: "the brother I never had."

Tom admits to Peter that he has secrets he cannot share, that he must keep locked in a room in his basement. He longs to "fling the door open, let the light in, and clean everything out," but those secrets are damaging to his personal and public persona. The room in the basement and the partially shadowed face are metaphors for the memories of destructive acts buried in his subconscious, as well as for the homosexual closet. There is a part of himself that even he cannot openly embrace. However, in the expected Freudian fashion, his hidden life emerges in his dreams. In the film's single dream sequence, Tom's crimes are compressed into a montage, after which he wakes in horror. Of course, unpleasant dreams are a commonplace representation of a guilty conscience. Macbeth's peace-of-mind is similarly disrupted by nightmares, the intrusion of fear and guilt. He regrets that he and his wife must "sleep/ In the affliction of these terrible dreams" (III. ii. 19–20).

The image of Tom sitting alone in his cabin at the conclusion of the film is the culmination of the process of isolation and alienation associated with his tragedy. The final image emphasizes the irony of Ripley's buried life. He is forced to kill his last companion for safety's sake, and he, as he feared, is finally alone: "I am gonna be stuck in the basement ... terrible, alone in the dark." Whenever he emerges into the public, his secrets are compromised; some know him as Dickie Greenleaf and others as Tom Ripley, and the most recent incident on the ship bound for Greece is the most troublesome because he believed that he had escaped from potential discovery, only to find that his secrets must now be kept in still closer quarters. Only when completely isolated can Tom be secure from discovery; he is literally bound in his cabin. Macbeth's lament for the escape of Banquo's son Fleance from the hired killers could easily be inserted into this scene of the film:

> I had else been perfect,
> Whole as the marble, founded as the rock,
> As broad and general as the casing air,
> But now I am cabin'd, cribb'd, confin'd, bound in
> To saucy doubts and fears [III. iv. 21–25].

Macbeth becomes increasingly isolated as a consequence of his reiterated crimes and the suspicions aroused by his actions. He complains that he cannot look to have troops of friends in his old age as others do. In Roman Polanski's film version of *Macbeth*, the tragic hero's alienation is so extensive that he is alone in the castle Dunsinane when the English invade.

The juxtaposition of antithetical representations of space in the above Shakespearean passage characterizes the settings of Minghella's film as well. The locales chosen for the early portion of the film, particularly those in Mongibello, include broad expanses created by the wide angle lens and the large field depth that encompasses both the action of the players and the surrounding scenery. The frequency of broad camera shots leading up to the first murder signifies the openness and sincerity of Ripley's demeanor, as well as improvement in his prospects and social status. However, as he becomes the object of suspicion for the various murders, the settings become increasingly claustrophobic. He moves to Rome to escape the prying eyes of Marge, and the labyrinthine city streets become the site for much of the action. The looming buildings suggest enclosure and menace, the narrow circuit within which Tom must perpetrate his fraud. Briefly following the first two murders, the interiors of the building become more spacious as Tom enjoys his newly appropriated affluence; however, at the same time, they lack the brightness and warmth of the Mongibello sites. The interiors are dark and cold, even vault-like; this is particularly true of Tom's lodging in Venice. Of course, the final scene on the boat to Greece ironically combines the antithetical concepts of space developed in Mongibello and Rome. The shots on deck reiterate the broad expanse of the early scenery, signifying the renewal of Ripley's expectations. He believes he is finally free from scrutiny and suspicion and that he can enjoy his new life with Peter. However, the sudden intrusion of Meredith demonstrates that he still cannot come out into the light and broad spaces, at least not in the company of Peter. Thus the final cabin images in the film reveal the abrupt reversal of Tom's expectations: He laments, "I'm gonna be stuck in the basement," a complaint that characterizes his spatial and social prospects, an allusion to his lodging at the beginning of the novel.

It is clear that Minghella has decided to film Highsmith's novel in order to cash in on the explosion of gay subject matter in cinema. The casting of Matt Damon as a character with homosexual longings virtually guaranteed the film's commercial success, a fact that exposes a change in Hollywood's construction of masculinity. The events of the novel have been altered for the screen in order to obviate the homosexual desires of the main character. The Tom Ripley of Highsmith's novel is much more

Matt Damon in *The Talented Mr. Ripley* plays an ambitious sociopath who hides his latent homosexual longings from his friend Dickey Greenleaf (Jude Law) and from himself.

reluctant to accept his alternative desires than is the Ripley of the film, who acknowledges that he loves Dickie and desires to develop a relationship. Moreover, he embraces Peter and they openly cohabitate. Of course, he is not entirely comfortable with his sexual orientation. He will not admit it to the Italian authorities, a reluctance that may be merely pragmatic.

What does Shakespeare's *Macbeth* have to do with the film's gay thematic? The most obvious connection is the necessity of secrecy, of hiding one's desires: "Let not light see my black and deep desires." Macbeth is preoccupied with protecting his secrets and his newfound affluence from the suspicions of his peers and subjects. The atmosphere of Minghella's film is certainly not one in which an individual can openly flaunt an alternative lifestyle. Tom makes several real and implicit denials of his sexual orientation, even pretending to have a fiancée back in the States. Shakespeare's *Macbeth* also asks pertinent questions about the nature of manhood, exploring the significance of gender constructs (Waith 265–68), an issue that is obviously relevant to the gay dilemma, since many conceptualize homophobia as the hysterical fear of finding feminine passivity in a male and/or male aggression in a female. However, most importantly, *Macbeth* explores the dangers of social and political ambition. Macbeth feels he has been unjustly deprived of the position of affluence to which his personal virtues entitle him. Similarly, as a gay man, Tom's longing for a permanent relationship with Dickie is frustrated by legal, social, and emotional barriers. Like Macbeth, Tom defies social convention, grasping for the fulfillment of his desires, and the remainder of the film depicts his ongoing efforts to mitigate the consequences of his actions.

When viewed as a portrait of a gay man's struggle for inclusion, the film is somewhat troublesome. Tom is, after all, a sociopath and a serial killer, driven to desperate measures by Dickie's rejection. This pattern is a cliché within the traditions of homophobic rhetoric. The homosexual is so desperate for an unavailable heterosexual man that he resorts to violence and subterfuge. Moreover, Tom then assumes the identity of the dead man in a psychotic effort to retain that which he has lost, revealing an element of narcissism reminiscent of Freud's early characterizations of homosexual longings (Freud 11–12n). The subject becomes the object of his own desire. These potentially inflammatory subjects are, however, mitigated by the film's portrait of Dickie Greenleaf, who is unsympathetic in the extreme. He coquettishly toys with Ripley's feelings and then cruelly and insultingly rejects him. Dickie is capricious and arrogant, unfaithful to his fiancée and his friends, regarding others as amusing distractions until, like a child, he tires of them. The vilification of Dickie in the film is so complete that the audience sympathizes with his killer, longing for Tom to escape justice.

At some level the film may be exchanging one prejudice for another. Dickie, Meredith, Marge, and Freddie Miles are all members of the American monied elite, while Tom and Peter are clearly working class. The displays of class insolence by both Dickie and Freddie effectively remove them as subjects of the audience's sympathy. Dickie calls Tom a "leech" and reminds him that he cannot pay his own way to Cortina and, therefore, is not invited. Yet Dickie enthusiastically participates in the squandering of the finances with which his father sponsored Tom's trip abroad. They use the money to buy a refrigerator. Freddie Miles is equally contemptuous of Tom, calling the latter's apartment bourgeois and outwardly mocking him. The implicit condemnation of the American aristocracy, as well as the circumstances of the first murder, are reminiscent of Theodore Dreiser's *An American Tragedy*. As with Clyde Griffiths, who plots to drown his pregnant girlfriend Roberta because she stands between him and the fulfillment of his material success, Tom kills Dickie in order to maintain his newly acquired lifestyle. In both cases the crisis takes place in a boat, and in both cases the murderer's guilt is mitigated. Clyde plans the murder of Roberta, but at the last minute cannot go through with it. The boat overturns accidentally, and she drowns just as he had planned.

Tom lashes out in anger, hitting Dickie in the head with an oar, but the circumstances suggest that if Dickie had not then attacked him, Tom might not have finished him off. Perhaps the parallels between Dreiser's novel and Minghella's screenplay are an effort to tie the story into a more contemporary tragic tradition than that of Shakespeare. The same qualities that compose parallels between Clyde and Tom also invoke Richard Wright's *Native Son*. Bigger Thomas is perhaps even more analogous to Tom than is Clyde, since Bigger's predicament is directly the result of discrimination and social oppression. The alienation and exclusion of Bigger Thomas made him paranoid and volatile, and it is these qualities that draw him into murder. In all three works the remainder of the action following the first murder is an unraveling of the consequences. For Clyde and Bigger those consequences lead inexorably to the electric chair. For Tom the ramifications draw him into more troublesome murders and eventually into isolation and emotional desolation.

Author James Baldwin, in his study *Notes of a Native Son*, argued that inside every black man was a Bigger Thomas ready to explode into violence through a combination of fear and anger (38). Similarly, one might maintain that Tom Ripley is the killer inside every gay man, enraged by overt social exclusion and persecution. Minghella's portrait of the gay killer is then a warning of the potential ramifications of continued legal discrimination and marginalization of homosexuals. The social and cultural reprisals against those who reveal their orientation necessitate desperate measures in the maintenance of secrecy. If Tom could openly embrace his queer desires and attain a reasonable measure of acceptance within American society, he would perhaps not be forced to resort to such dire measures in pursuit of security. Much of the violence associated with the gay community has its origin in the social stigma constructed to police gender and sexual norms. The physical and cultural violence exacted against gays can partially account for the violence perpetrated by gay men desperate to hide their secret longings and/or eager to lash out at the population responsible for degradation and humiliation. Ripley's violence includes a still more insidious threat. The gay man, unlike Bigger Thomas, can walk among his persecutors without detection, can, indeed, impersonate them, win their trust and friendship, and exact revenge upon them. In this context, gay invisibility becomes a potent threat, because it virtually guarantees the infiltration of the perceived enemy into the ranks of its oppressor. Here, Eve Sedgwick's theories regarding the closet have a meaningful application. While the closet has been traditionally coded as a place of fearful hiding, it can also be understood as a locale of subterfuge and subsequent empowerment, the closeted individual perpetrating a fraud upon his potential victimizers (Taylor 15).

In *Macbeth* Shakespeare attempts to demonstrate how much responsibility can be invested in a tragic hero while still generating sympathy for the character. Macbeth is a villain, and yet the audience cares what happens to him. *The Talented Mr. Ripley* invites its audience to sympathize with a gay serial killer. Perhaps Highsmith and Minghella are audaciously attempting to demonstrate a similar virtuosity in character development, investing the central figure with qualities that virtually guarantee his condemnation and showing that he is, nevertheless, more sympathetic than most of the characters he kills. Of course, the potential homophobia of such portrayals is mitigated by the inclusion of Peter among the victims, an individual who is a loving and non-aggressive gay man. The film may also be a warning to its audience of the potential danger in the obligatory suppression of homosexual desire. Tom's repressed rage explodes to the hazard of those around him. The film thus argues that forced secrecy and the social exclusion of gay men is detrimental because it compels them to seek out more dire and desperate means of concealing their "black and deep desires."

4

Gladiator: Family Values and Promise Keepers in the Colosseum

The family values campaign of the past ten years has alternated between a source of amusement and a cause for outrage in the gay community. Seldom has there been a more ideologically incoherent and ill-named alliance, particularly since the movement has nothing to do with family or with values, and its ostensible source (scriptures) offers little consistent and credible validation for its principles. The family values campaign is a cynical and misdirected effort on the part of a large group of unprincipled preachers to deflect blame for the problems of the American family onto the single group who is, arguably, the least responsible. Gays and lesbians are condemned for destroying an institution from which they are legally and systematically excluded. It takes a rational person only a moment to conclude that the problems of the family emerge almost entirely from within that institution, i.e. absentee fathers, divorce, spouse abuse, child abuse, poverty, etc. Instead of facing the problems of the institution directly, the family values advocates have concluded that movies and queers, and particularly movies about queers, are the subversive threat. The projection of blame onto gay men constitutes an effort to condemn a particular version of manhood, to demonize male absenteeism (emotional or physical) by associating it with that indefatigable devil, the feminized man.

Sociologists have defined the gay male as a symbolic "repository for all that is excluded from hegemonic masculinity" (Connell, *Gender* 78). As heterosexual males collectively attempt to absolve themselves of responsibility for their failures, for the dissolution of familial traditions, they create a scapegoat that can signify, for the entire group, the expulsion of destructive elements and the creation of the antithesis of the idealized father/husband. Since paternity (represented as impregnation), under usual circumstances, requires heterosexuality, the demon created to represent the "anti-father" is the individual whose ability (or willingness) to propagate is problematic, the gay man. Since the ideal father/husband is traditionally required to provide for and protect his family, his symbolic alternative is once again the feminized male, coded as emotionally and physically incapable of sustaining a family. It is no wonder that the politically and ideologically naive "Promise Keeper" movement is so profoundly homophobic, since it idealizes traditional masculine traits and wildly oversimplifies the practices that led to the feminist critique of patriarchy, mistakenly believing the only problem has been the failure of husbands to remain loyal to their wives and to provide emotionally and physically for their families. One could almost praise such a movement since it at least places much of the blame where it belongs; however, it also comically mis-recognizes the offenses of the male dominated society. It is true that men should practice fidelity and should spend more time with their wives and children and that such behaviors would improve the disposition of the family, but the Promise Keepers also argue for the scriptural superiority of men in leadership, explicitly the leadership of the family. Moreover, the "Promise Keepers," like any group, construct their own opposition (a group I will term the "promise breakers"), the group who is excluded from the club and who, by contrast, define those included; ironically, the ostracized group does not include the husband who fails in his fidelity or his commitment, since there is no effort to bar those who do not live up to the ideals of the movement. The demonized other, the promise breakers, are homosexuals who are marginalized within the movement's rhetoric. It is no surprise that the leader of the Promise Keepers is a former NFL coach, since the concept of masculinity he advocates resembles adolescent locker room bravado in which the real men prove their manhood by abusing the sissies.

The construction of masculinity through opposition is certainly not unique to the Promise Keepers. Gay men are accustomed to seeing themselves through the eyes of prejudice. Even as the media has become more gay friendly, it has continued to perceive the issue of homosexuality as a diologic phenomenon, as a controversial issue rather than a civil rights revolution. Gays and lesbians are seldom mentioned in the media without inclusion of the histrionic voices of our devoted detractors, and despite this uniform inclusion in the public discourse surrounding homosexuality, the religious right fails to appreciate the deference shown to them by the media.

Conservatives have identified Hollywood as anathema to their ideology, one of the principle instigators in the decline of family values, but they may fail to recognize the extent to which cinema reinforces their agenda by conditioning young boys in the behavioral patterns of hegemonic masculinity (those character traits the society collectively agrees signify manhood) and by semi-consciously reinforcing homophobia. The action film that targets adolescent boys is frequently constructed upon a heterosexist binary, vilifying one form of masculinity while venerating another. I have discussed this phenomenon elsewhere in an article addressing *Rob Roy* and *Braveheart*. In each of these films the hyper-masculine protagonist is foiled by an effeminate court dandy. Rob Roy (Liam Neeson) is tormented by the mincing and lisping fop Archibald Cunningham (Tim Roth) who threatens his family, his home, and his person. In *Braveheart* the character of William Wallace (Mel Gibson) battles to save Scotland from the tyranny of the British, yet his courage, valor, integrity, masculine brawn, and heroic task are countered by the silly, sarcastic, ineffectual, and vain Prince, the future Edward II, who is repeatedly offered as the visual antithesis of Wallace and who is drawn into the comparison by the Scotsman's effort to steal Edward's unhappy and unsatisfied wife (Keller 147–151).

In the more recent film *Gladiator* (2000) there is a binary pattern of character development similar to that in *Rob Roy* and *Braveheart*, where family values and restrictive theories of masculinity are constructed and policed, where traditional masculinity is valorized as more effeminate males are vilified. The film ostensibly deplores violence as entertainment — at the same time that it dramatizes the extreme violence of the gladiator's arena. It denigrates the Roman audience that enjoyed the spectacle in the Colosseum, yet panders to the American audience's longing for bloody distractions. It moons over the restoration of democracy in Rome, and yet repeatedly disparages the judgement of the masses. It celebrates paternalism in many manifestations, and yet equates effective fatherhood with violence, militarism, and betrayal. It venerates Rome's wars of ethnic conquest, the Romanizing of the barbarian tribes, and yet ostensibly promotes multiculturalism and condemns the Roman circus for its celebrations of militarism.

Gladiator is an anachronism in its persistent promotion of American family values and American post-industrial constructions of fatherhood. Just as *Rob Roy* dramatizes the struggle of the 20th century American family in the Scottish Highlands of the 18th century, *Gladiator* laments the assault on American family values and the heroic yet vexed struggle of the American father in ancient Rome. The appropriation of stories remote in time and place in order to subtly address the politics of the present is a practice that has a long history. Shakespeare frequently adopted remote subjects and settings in order to allegorize his commentary on the Elizabethan and Jacobean courts, and to avoid the severe punishments that could follow any unflattering representation of the monarch. Of course, in the context of the American film industry the ramifications of including unpopular politics are not so punitive. The worst that can befall the moviemaker is financial failure, and while that is a fearful eventuality, the director will at least avoid incarceration and keep his tongue and/or his hand. Of course, the inclusion of American family politics in a film that defies the censorious expectations of the same may be a smoke screen to distract the audience from an outright condemnation of the violent subject matter. The film may socialize adolescent boys (the target audience of action films) in the acceptability and appreciation of violence, but it also teaches them to be devoted fathers (even when absent), homophobes, and militarists, all of which are desirable within the framework of American Family Values. However, most important, it avoids all graphic displays of sexual activity because, while the family friendly boy is supposed to love sex with girls, he is not supposed to have any instruction in the subject.

With *Gladiator* the socialization of adolescent boys begins with antithetical representations of manhood captured in the Maximus/Commodus dichotomy. In the oppositional construction of these two central characters the audience is offered a lesson in the correct actions and laudable values of hegemonic masculinity. Maximus' courage and valor are very much the subject of the film. He is a highly successful military leader whom Marcus Aurelius credits with having won the battle and the war against the barbarians in Germania. He is not a general who watches safely from a distance directing the movement of troops. Instead he engages in direct hand to hand combat without any additional safeguards beyond his own strength and swordsmanship. Of course, the opportunities for Maximus to display his valor by killing other combatants are legion, both before and after his enslavement; they are literally too numerous to catalogue. No single combatant is a sufficient challenge; thus he is featured contending with multiple opponents, human and animal. The extent of Maximus' valor can be most easily appreciated through his capacity to endure rather than his ability to inflict pain. Sociologists have recognized that masculinity is frequently measured by the individual's faculty for suffering patiently, a phenomenon known as "male masochism" (Horrocks, 42). Indeed, the image of the heroic protagonist's body wracked with pain is a staple of Hollywood's action epics. One need only recall that the image of Rambo in agony is more common and memorable than any display of triumphant elation. The action figure does not rise above the violence he unleashes; he is the chief victim of it. The wracked and suffering body is not only his own: he suffers for his family, his comrades, and his nation. Maximus survives a near fatal wound from his executioners. In the gladiatorial school, he reveals his strength by refusing to fight, allowing himself to be struck repeatedly without defense and returning to endure yet another blow. Of course, the most significant example of the same is his combat with Commodus after the latter has treacherously stabbed him before the contest. The anguish that defines Maximus' masculinity also has a social element. He does not fight for personal glory, but for the revenge of his family, the liberation of his colleagues in the gladiatorial pool, and the restoration of democracy in Rome.

In contrast to Maximus, Commodus is the pampered and effete prince who delegates all butchery to others more expendable, thus transcending the violence that he generates. Commodus is representative of the paradoxical conceptualization of queer men in a homophobic culture where we are simultaneously violent and cowardly, too physically ineffectual to inflict harm personally. Commodus' decadence is defined by his love of the tortured male body in the gladiatorial games, a slaughter that he resurrected upon his father's death, but within which he does not have to participate. While the authentically masculine Roman males combat the Germanic hordes in the opening sequence of the film, Commodus maintains a safe distance, entering only at the completion of the battle. Instead of fighting for the glory and territory of Rome, he lounges with his sister in a carriage, scheming the death of his father Marcus Aurelius. His late arrival is calculated to avoid danger, thus emphasizing not only his cowardice but also his sense of entitlement, as he expects to be named Aurelius' successor as Emperor of Rome without having done anything to create or sustain the empire. When the effeminate male, Commodus, does engage in violence, it is not with the forthright courage and determination of the soldiers and gladiators. He kills through treachery, preying upon the weak. He strangles his helpless aging father, even as the man is attempting to reconcile with him, and when Commodus does muster the courage to fight in the arena, he attempts to guarantee his victory by incapacitating his opponent in advance. Commodus' violence is always calculated specifically for advancement of his personal ambitions and for the mitigation of his personal fears.

The binary construction of the two principal characters in the film is also framed by the issue of fraternity. The traditional male appreciates the camaraderie of men, while the feminine male is excluded from homosocial bonding, the fraternity of real men. Male cultures are structured through the expulsion of homosexual interests (Sedgwick, *Between* 5), desires that cast suspicion upon the incentive for the formation of fraternal bonds. Maximus enjoys the camaraderie of the soldiers, and, despite his leadership position, conducts himself as a mere equal, celebrating with the common soldiers following his victory in Germania. The same fellowship of real men is reiterated in the gladiatorial school where Maximus quickly earns the respect and friendship of his fellow slaves, instructing them in the advantage and effectuality of teamwork. While gladiatorial games are a sport that emphasizes individual prowess, Maximus brings the legionnaire's military wisdom to the arena. The Roman legions were successful because they fought as cohesive units and consequently triumphed over the chaotic warrior mentality of the barbarian tribes, a Roman superiority in the art of war deftly illustrated in the battle scene at the beginning of the film. Maximus quickly recognizes the advantage of, and appropriates, a similar fraternal teamwork in gladiatorial combat. In his first fight he is chained hand to hand with the African slave Juba (Djimon Housou). The two effectively destroy their opponents by working with, rather than against, each other. The same practice is illustrated in their initial battle at the Roman Colosseum where they are made to combat a collection of chariot-driven archers, representative of the Roman legions of Scipio Africannus. Maximus instructs them in the collective benefit of remaining together on the battlefield. Those who venture away from the group are quickly killed, but the cohesive unit succeeds in trouncing the superior enemy. A similar camaraderie evolves socially within the group of gladiators, specifically between Maximus and Juba, who enjoy a brotherly affection, rising from their mutual longing for a restoration of their family lives. Their affection evolves from their mutually explicit protestations of heterosexual desire. In effect, they come to love each other by maintaining their love for others.

Commodus creates a visual contrast to the fellowship among lesser men, often photographed in dark, solitary, luxurious interiors with perhaps a single attendant or family member. The single most profound image of isolation in the film is Commodus' coronation ride through the streets of Rome with all of his people lining the venue to pay him homage. His physical and emotional detachment are evident. He has no peer to keep his company, not even a wife, only his sister and nephew, both of whom despise and fear him. He has no appreciation for the consultation of advisors. When he meets with the Senate, he is offended by the their presumption in speaking for the Roman people and longs to dissolve this legislative body altogether. Commodus' authority is paternal rather than fraternal, and, indeed, he maintains a cankered and insincere notion of brotherhood. Twice he refers to Maximus as "brother": congratulating him on his victory in Germania and embracing him before their bout in the arena. Each of these verbal exchanges precedes Commodus' effort to kill Maximus. Indeed, the relationship between the two men is structured upon the mythology of Cain and Abel. While the two are not actually brothers, Marcus Aurelius viewed them as such, referring to Maximus as the "son he never had" and offering him the succession to the throne, with the stipulation, of course, that he restore the republic. The contention between the two nominal sons arises out of jealousy when the father prefers the personal virtues of one over those of the other. Commodus complains of his father's failure to recognize and appreciate him, a shortcoming for which he subsequently kills his father and attempts the same with the brother. Although he becomes emperor of Rome, Commodus is, nevertheless, an outcast; he can never again appreciate the company of men because none are his equals.

The American ideal of masculine virtue, as represented in *Gladiator*, includes an unflagging devotion to democratic values. The action of the film is situated around a struggle to restore the Roman republic. The conflict between Maximus, the slave/gladiator, and Commodus, the Emperor, captures allegorically the class fissure inherent in the distinction between monarchy and democracy, with Maximus, the working class hero, triumphing over the aristocratic decadence and insensitivity of Commodus. Thus, in a tale of ancient Rome, the film reconstructs and reaffirms the social objectives of the American revolution, no doubt for the socialization and edification of its young audience. But at the same time that it reaffirms America's cultural commitment to democracy, it creates homophobic non-sequitors, reinforcing the Cold War connection between homosexuality and un–American activities. Commodus' austerity and arrogance also define his opposition to the restoration of democracy in Rome, effectively demonizing the less masculine male as retrograde to a republic, stigmatizing him as the un–American tyrant. Not only will he not honor his father's last wishes to restore the Roman republic, he longs to remove even the pretense to democracy. Like his father's, his rule is paternal, but he lacks "wisdom, justice, fortitude, and temperance," the qualities his father identified as requisite to virtuous leadership. Aurelius excludes his son from the succession because Commodus is not a "moral man," thus implicitly legitimizing the continued exclusion of those with alternative sexual desires from political and social power. Commodus thus represents the absurdist paradox commonly associated with American homophobic politics: gays are ineffectual supervillains. While gays are

systematically excluded from power, they are, nevertheless, very powerful, even indomitable. This paradox illustrates one of the mechanisms
whereby strident homophobes conveniently mis-recognize themselves as
victims rather than perpetrators.

There are a few other inconsistencies and inaccuracies in *Gladiator*'s
promotion of American democracy besides its queer-bashing structure.
The film suggests that the gladiatorial games, or violent entertainment,
are one of the principal signs of Roman decadence, and that the decadence
is a consequence of corrupt leadership, particularly that of Commodus,
who seeks to distract the masses from their innate desire for freedom by
constantly staging bloody spectacles. Yet at the same time that the film tries
to promote an ideology which relies upon a faith in the good judgement
of the masses, in their ability to participate in their own government, it
consistently disparages that same group, suggesting that they are easily led
by the nose with simple diversions, i.e. bread and circus. The dialogue of
the film offers imperious criticism regarding the vulgarity and stupidity
of the average citizens; even Senator Graccus, the man who hopes to revive
the republic following Commodus' death, shows contempt for the people
he will lead. He remarks that, "Rome is the mob.... He'll [Commodus]
bring them death, and they'll love him for it." Graccus attends the games
and is clearly disgusted with the proceedings. While it is not difficult for
the film audience to accept the idea that the gladiatorial games must end,
as they are retrograde to our own ideas of civility, decency, and equality,
the benevolent paternalism that follows Commodus' death cannot, by
implication, differ greatly from what went before, since, according to the
film, the mob requires the guidance of an enlightened leader who will
draw them away, even deprive them of their base desires. While it is easy
to agree with the necessity of eliminating the violent spectacle, it is not
very comforting to know that the masses have been stripped of their entertainment (as ghastly as it may be) through the arbitrary will of a few "ser-
monizing ... old men" who patronize the Roman people for their own
good. Such a thematic too clearly alludes to the same practice within
American culture, particularly within the South, where the people consistently have their entertainment and lifestyle choices limited by the censorious condescension of moralizing preachers and politicians.

The inclusion of Juba, Maximus' friend, confidante, and fellow family man, is intended to suggest a respect for cultural diversity within the
Roman Republic. Juba reminds the audience of the rehabilitation of American democracy through the elimination of black slavery. Through his
death, Maximus releases Juba, who is allowed to return to his family; and
in one of the final photographic sequences of the film, Juba eulogizes his

liberator: "Now we're free. I will see you again, but not yet." This conclusion inaccurately implies that slavery has been eliminated in Rome with the restoration of Senatorial influence. Moreover, we cannot forget that Rome's great general, Maximus, who dies for democracy and diversity, is a principal player in the forced subjugation of many non–Roman cultures. He is a committed imperialist, imposing Roman rule through violence, and thus eliminating cultural diversity on a much broader scale than within the city limits itself. While the battle with the Germanians is defined as a repulsion of a planned invasion by tribes lying outside the empire's boundaries, one cannot forget the cultural bravado that created the Roman Empire, the fundamental belief in the superiority of Roman society, administration, and militarism, as well as the base desire for riches, that justified the conquest of Gaul, Hispania, Britannia, and Germania (these including only the European conquests). The dialogue of the film even legitimizes wars of conquest for the purposes of imposing civilization, for the "Romanizing" of non–Romans. Marcus Aurelius, who is supposed to be the moral center of the film, the fatherly philosopher king, is responsible for twenty years of expansionist policies, and Maximus agrees with the philosophy that justifies the imposition of Roman rule: "Rome is the light. The rest of the world is brutal and dark."

One can trace the violence at the perimeter of the empire to the violence at its center. The games in the arena celebrate the brutality of the wars of conquest and continue the dehumanizing philosophy that justifies uncivil military action in the civilizing of the "brutes." The gladiatorial games are re-enactments of battles from Roman history, including the defeat of the Carthaginians by Scipio Africanus. Here the film may offer a subtle criticism of Roman militarism. When Maximus and his companions are first introduced to the Colosseum, they are named the "barbarian horde." Since the sympathies of the film audience are clearly supposed to lie with Maximus' group, there is a glimmer of hope that the film may be subtly interrogating the idea of militarism; yet, in all likelihood, it is instead redoubling the decadence of the Roman people by demonstrating that they do not honor their war heroes, thus not so subtly alluding to the mid–twentieth century counter culture. The condemnation of militarism is not very convincing because Gladiators do not fight like barbarians, but as a cohesive unit, following Maximus' lead. They are clearly the most civilized group within the arena. The civilized/barbarous dichotomy is defined through the exercise of violence. While both groups employ physical force, civility exercises its cruelty with order and ritual. The barbarians in the opening battle of the film do not honor the rules of war, decapitating the Roman Emissary, and do not maintain order within the fight. The violence in the Colosseum is reminiscent of the organized cruelty of the legions, violence executed according to rituals and expectations. However, when the film condemns the violence of the Colosseum, it is not also condemning the violence at the empire's margins. It is transporting the civilized violence of the legions to the center of power to vanquish the barbarians there. Although it recognizes a problem at the center of Roman power, the film, nevertheless, assumes that cultural superiority of Rome and continues to legitimize the forced subjugation of diverse populations for the purposes of uniformity.

Gladiator invokes most of the themes that are likely to appeal to a mainstream, middle class, American audience without consideration of their anachronistic relationship to the historical subject of the film. Moreover, the political semi-unconscious of the work is excessively conservative. The filmmakers—cognizant of the target audience of an action movie—have accepted the unspoken task of socializing young men to be good husbands and fathers, but they have done so at the expense of sexual diversity, seeking to define hegemonic masculinity through contrast, and all of those features that are traditionally defined as anathema to mainstream American manhood are also coded as homosexual traits. In the effort to create a villain out of Commodus, the screenwriters have invested in his character all those features that would make him utterly repugnant to a contemporary American audience. As we have already seen, these include a contempt for camaraderie, diversity, and democracy; but the idea that is developed with the least subtlety within the narrative is the politically charged issue of Family Values. *Gladiator* celebrates the twentieth century, bourgeois, American family in ancient Rome, and its inclusion invokes many of the same falsehoods, paradoxes, and inconsistencies that plague the Family Values and Promise Keeper campaigns in their contemporary context.

Maximus is coded as the well intended American family man who, because of his professional duties, has been an absentee father/husband for over two years. Maximus' heroic defeat of the Germanians at the outset of the film is exacted in order to expedite his imminent return to his home. His actions literalize the contemporary paternal cliché that he has gone out to conquer the world so that he can care and provide for his family. When Marcus Aurelius asks what can be done to reward the man who won the wars, Maximus asks only for the opportunity to return to his farm in Hispania. He repeatedly declines the invitation to participate in Roman politics, suggesting that he is a simple soldier and family man, too honest and forthright to enjoy the backstabbing machinations of the senatorial class. He prefers to look his enemy in the eye. He even balks at the offered throne. When Commodus kills his father, seizes the throne, and orders Maximus' execution, the General would, more than likely, have quietly acquiesced in his own death had the Emperor not also given orders for the murder of his family. As a last wish, Maximus requests that Quintus look after his family, only to be told that they will join him in the hereafter. What follows is a sequence of images intended to reveal Maximus' devotion to family through his desperate, self-destructive, and homicidal effort to reach Hispania before the Emperor's assassins, an effort that ultimately fails; his wife and child are crucified and immolated, hung up at the door to their home. The remainder of the film is a revenge narrative, dramatizing Maximus' effort to kill the murderer of his family. Although he has been charged by Marcus Aurelius with the restoration of democracy, he is motivated exclusively by concern for family — until the two tasks can be united, at which time he also undertakes the reformation of the state.

Commodus, in contrast to Maximus, violates the sanctity and integrity of the family in every conceivable way, but, most meaningfully, in not having one. Although he engages in no queer sex, nor reveals any queer desire (save the inordinate fascination with gladiators), Commodus is in every other way the cliché of the menacing homosexual who threatens to destroy Family Values. He is always alone and has no wife and children, no normative sexual desires, only an incestuous longing for his own sister. For an unmarried adult male, he spends too much time with the crown prince Lucius, his nephew. To the surprise and terror of the mother Lucilla, Commodus is discovered looming over the young boy's bed, admiring his innocence. The image of Commodus, Lucilla, and Lucius serves as a demonic parody of the bourgeois family tainted by incest and paedophilia. Insidiously, Commodus tries to win the boy's allegiance away from his mother, a thinly veiled metaphor for recruitment and the gay threat to children. Instead of bringing stability and love to the family, Commodus brings violence. He murders his own father. He orders the torture, rape, murder, and mutilation of Maximus' family. He forces his sister to become his lover by threatening to kill his own nephew, and also promises to kill Lucilla the first time she does anything to offend him. The representation of Commodus as an occulted homosexual is continued in the heavy-handed rage and bitterness he harbors toward his own father, thus invoking the cliché of the neurotic gay man acting out his resentment toward, while simultaneously seeking the approval of, his father. Commodus laments that he would have sacrificed all his power to attain his father's love and approval.

Indeed, the issue of fatherhood is central to the narrative, and, of course, Commodus is the primary representation of the corrupt and unsuccessful father, and not exclusively in his failure to procreate. Unlike Maximus, Commodus put his personal ambitions before his paternal duties. The recurring fatherhood thematic raises many of the vexed arguments associated with the Promise Keeper campaign, the primary promise being to spend more time with the children. There are many unsuccessful fathers in the film, including Marcus Aurelius. These fathers fail because they would not put their family obligations before their professional duties. Aurelius admits that he has neglected his family and offers this admission as a consolation to his disappointed son. He invites Lucilla to imagine that she is a "loving daughter" and he a "good father." She characterizes this fancy as a "pleasant fiction." Maximus, despite his devotion, has also disappointed his family; for his own faults "fell slaughter on their souls," and he was unavailable to protect them. The film offers an explicit program for the reformation of fatherhood, and one that goes beyond merely spending time with the children. The narrative offers a warning against both the neglect and the over-indulgence of sons. Aurelius' failings suggest that the neglect of sons may result in the creation of a perverse, narcissistic, disloyal, immoral, isolated, and violent adult male, all of the qualities with which hegemonic masculinity invests the demonized homosexual. Admitting that Commodus' faults are his own, Aurelius, nevertheless, refuses to enfranchise the wounded man, denying Commodus ascension to the throne. The politics of paternity reveal the hysterical fear that lies at the heart of the Family Values and the Promise Keeper movements, that the children may turn out to be gay. Paradoxically, in the ideology of both campaigns, such an eventuality is then sufficient justification for the rejection of the child in the name of family and religion. The vices of the child must not be indulged, even if those vices are the result of paternal neglect.

The paternal thematic has a social and political dimension as well. The leadership of the empire is repeatedly represented as fatherly, and Commodus is an overly indulgent father, who, unlike his own, will not deny his children the satisfaction of their basest desires, explicitly the longing for blood. Commodus claims that the people of Rome are the Emperor's children, and he maintains that his father Aurelius neglected his people through his preoccupations with war and philosophy. Commodus intends to avoid his father's mistake by indulging Romans' love of ghastly spectacle. The film is very clear in its condemnation of such an approach to paternal authority, suggesting that the father needs to teach the child temperance and humility. Desiring popularity over husbandry and good stewardship, Commodus allows the games to continue, squandering the national wealth for the immediate and base gratifications of violent entertainment. However, this pandering to the people's vulgar appetites ultimately destroys him since it brings Maximus to Rome and offers the war hero a venue within which to win the people's hearts. The image of Commodus as the corrupt father invokes a number of homophobic stereotypes. It suggests that feminized men are poor role models who corrupt the young through their irresponsibility and hedonism. The only mitigation of this all too obvious slur lies in the fact that Aurelius, too, is guilty of a more subtle form of pandering. Aurelius gave Rome blood and spectacle as well, through his constant warring and conquest. Indeed, the events in the Colosseum are a celebration of the wholesale slaughter and subjugation at the nation's frontier. Unlike Commodus, however, Aurelius recognizes, regrets, and attempts to rectify his mistake, confessing to Maximus that he has not brought civilization to the barbarians, but only the sword.

While Maximus is the paragon of the loving family man, Senator Graccus is the exemplar of the paternal politician who will bring his people justice and freedom but will not encourage their corruption. He admits that he is not a "man of the people," but "a man for the people." Graccus tries to direct the new Emperor's attentions to social problems of the city, explicitly plague in the Greek Quarter; however, Commodus will not receive counsel on the real issues of government. The Senator is concerned over the fiscal irresponsibility of Commodus' celebrations, complaining that the massive expense will soon leave the city starving. Graccus will not indulge the Roman's craven appetites; he is repulsed by the ghastly spectacle of the gladiatorial games. Unlike Maximus, who is too honest to be a politician, Graccus is politically savvy, retaining those skills requisite to competition among politicians: intrigue, subtlety, restraint, resolution, integrity, and courage. Like other Senators, he does not compromise his principles in order to curry favor with the Emperor, but he is sufficiently circumspect in his behavior to save his own life. Graccus is not so good and honest a man that he cannot and will not compete with the scheming politicians surrounding him. He is a pragmatist who takes those actions necessary to his political and literal survival. He is the man capable of restoring Rome's republic.

The moral and commercial barometer in the film is the child Lucius, who signifies the future of Rome, but who also represents the target audience of the film in which he plays. His fascination with the bloody spectacle in the sand of the Colosseum invokes the American preoccupation with the corruption of children through violent entertainment, so his excited response to the growing celebrity of the gladiator Maximus and his efforts to imitate the heroism on the floor of the arena is a disturbing sign that the decadence of Rome is corrupting its children, and particularly its future leaders. His gradual disillusionment with his uncle and his growing admiration for Maximus is intended to direct the sympathies of the adolescent audience toward the appropriate male role model, Maximus, thus reinforcing hegemonic masculinity. The isolated, effeminate male becomes an object of odium even for his own nephew. The casting of Lucius at first seems ill-considered, the young actor too soft, much like an American bourgeois child, the product of 19th century constructions of childhood — an ideal of innocence (Kincaid 72). His long blond hair seems out of place among the Mediterranean stock. However, the casting may be political, intentionally creating an exhibition of the American middle class child under duress, facing potential taint but recognizing the appropriate role models for male behavior, dispelling the threat and directing the sentiments of the target audience to the same conclusion. Imitating his hero Maximus, "the savior of Rome," Lucius points his wooden sword toward his uncle and feigns a thrust to his middle.

Gladiator both affirms and undermines the complaints of Family Values advocates about violence in American entertainment. Ostensibly, the film sermonizes about the potential corruption of young and old by violent entertainment and blames the proliferation of such diversions on poor political leadership, the vulgarity of our amusements a reflection of the corruption of our power structure. It would be difficult to imagine a more conservative conclusion if it were not for the fact that the film *Gladiator* itself can and should be counted when the cinematic spectacles are condemned for their brutality. The most enduring subject within the narrative is the sustained effort to shut down the very entertainment of which Ridley Scott's film is a contemporary example, and for which the director is notorious (*Alien, Black Rain, Blade Runner*). The image of the empty Colosseum in the final shot of the film signifies both the cessation of Roman games and the conclusion of Scott's narrative. The director is, of course, attempting to draw a parallel between American and Roman blood lust and to show that the violence in our entertainment is a reflection, not the cause, of violence in America: The games in the Colosseum are re-enactments of the contemporary military exploits. The director may also be suggesting that such entertainment can have redeeming social virtues by reinforcing normative American values regarding masculinity, democracy, fraternity, and paternity. With such thematics, the director counters one complaint of the Family Values censors by pandering to another. The film may be violent, but it also demonizes those who do not live up to normative gender codes, a tactful maneuver, since the family bigots are always more preoccupied with the corruptive potential of sex and gender than they are with violence. The hero is an ideal family man who longs to rejoin his wife and child and who only wishes to protect them from harm, and he is never comfortable with his violence, even in war; he simply performs his duty, first for the Empire and then for his family.

5

Twilight of the Golds: Jews, Gays, and Eugenics

Twilight of the Golds (1996), directed by Ross Marks, is a made-for-television movie that examines the ethical complexities surrounding the recently completed Human Genome project, which has as its objective the mapping of every gene in the human organism, or the identification of the nucleotide sequence of human DNA. This new understanding could allow scientists to diagnose and treat genetic abnormalities in living organisms and to eliminate genetic based diseases such as cystic fibrosis and Tay-Sachs Syndrome. However, many fear that gene based discrimination practices will ensue when the human genome is mapped and genetic screening of fetuses becomes commonplace. Such discrimination might be based upon the genetic predisposition of certain people to develop diseases or conditions, and could manifest itself in loss of employment or the denial of insurance benefits.

Twilight of the Golds creates a hypothetical scenario in which a Jewish family, the Golds, is faced with a dilemma resulting from the genetic screening of the daughter's unborn child. Suzanne finds that her fetus carries the gene that has been associated with homosexuality, and although her own brother, David, is gay, she nevertheless considers aborting the child. Her plans become the source of much debate and bitterness in the film as the various family members try to influence her decision. Of course, a decision to terminate the pregnancy is a personal slight against her brother, the talented and charismatic director of Wagner's *Ring Cycle*.

The film interrogates the assumption that the discovery of a medical basis for homosexuality would create more tolerance and acceptance for the gay community. Whereas there are those who may be more open to gays and lesbians if they were given proof that these inclinations were not merely poor moral choices but were dictated by biology, the medical determinism implicit in such discoveries is, nevertheless, anathema to many. Foucault has revealed that the history of gays and lesbians over the past two centuries has been defined by medical regulation, by efforts to pathologize homosexuality. In *The History of Sexuality: An Introduction*, Foucault observes the moment in history when the sodomite evolved from a momentary "aberration" to a new "species," the homosexual defined entirely by sexual predispositions (43, 101). One of the most notorious campaigns to eradicate homosexuality has come from the psychiatric community, who, for most of its brief history, maintained that gays and lesbians were mentally ill and could be cured by psychoanalysis. The cruelty and ineffectuality of such efforts is well documented in Martin Duberman's autobiographical *Cures*, which culminates with a psychiatrist's advice that the author never again speak to his mother, a directive evidently born from the Freudian observation that male homosexuality is the fault of domineering mothers. The rhetoric of Freudian psychoanalysis also held that gay men and women were emotionally infantile, arrested at an early stage in the process of psychosexual development and, therefore, prone to neurosis. Perhaps the most insidious example of America's effort to medicalize and subsequently demonize gays and lesbians has been the myth that AIDS is an explicitly gay disease resulting from unhealthy sodomitical practices. Of course, the proliferation of the disease among normative segments of the population has served to discredit this theory among thoughtful individuals; however, the wrath of God explanation for the evolution of the disease remains a viable alternative theory for Evangelical Christians and other naive and ill-educated segments of the population. Unexpectedly, some gay activists have sought a return to the characterization of AIDS as a "gay disease," suggesting that the effort to make the disease gender neutral, to win public support by revealing that all segments of the population are susceptible to infection, have been too successful and have distracted gay men from a healthy vigilance against infection. The theory that AIDS is not a gay disease has permitted the mainstream public to ignore the large concentration of cases among homosexuals, to direct prevention campaigns toward portions of the population who have a much lower risk of infection but who are much more valued members of society, and to develop the specious dichotomy between those who deserve to have the disease and those who do not (Vaid 74–78). The campaign to dissociate the gay community from the disease involved a necessary bow to the least important controversy arising from the pandemic, one that would have had to dissipate with time and reason, the ridiculous assumption that a medical condition had a metaphysical origin.

The more recent medical studies attempting to explain the origin of homosexuality have some unexpected detractors who believe that such information is merely another effort to pathologize alternative sexual identities. These include the study by Dr. Simon LeVay, who contends that the hypothalamus region of the brain is structured differently in gay men than in heterosexual males (Allen 242), and the discovery of the so called "gay gene" by Dr. Dean Hamer and his colleagues (Allen 252–253). On the surface, such observations seem to be advantageous to the gay community because they undermine the contentions of the most committed homophobes who argue that homosexuality is a conscious decision, a lifetime of poor choices. However, such studies may create more problems than they resolve. The belief that scientific discoveries will resolve the moral dilemmas surrounding homosexuality may be naive because it is based upon the fallacious assumption that homophobia results from a reasoned consideration of the facts about human sexuality rather than upon irrational motives such as religious hysteria, fear, social conditioning, or self-loathing. More medical theories may only contribute to the catalog of rationales for discrimination against the gay community.

It is upon the above complex consideration of prejudice that Marks' film is predicated. *Twilight of the Golds* recognizes the dangers inherent in the discovery of a gay gene, particularly because one purpose in identifying such genetic markers is to take action in the event that undesirable traits are identified. Rob (Joe Tenney), the geneticist in the film, explains that his work is offering people "more choices," the term "choice" alluding to the potential for terminating a pregnancy. However, we generally assume that the information offered by genetic testing and engineering will be related entirely to the fetus' medical outlook, and that decisions regarding the fate of a fetus will be rational ones. *Twilight of the Golds* examines the potential exercise of prejudice in the decisions surrounding genetic testing. By focusing on homosexuality within the context of a loving family, the writer and director demonstrate that even those who ostensibly support gays and lesbians, if given the choice, may take extraordinary precautions to guarantee that a loved one is straight.

The preoccupation of the Golds with the medicalization of homosexuality is evident in the first scene of the film when the family twice alludes to David's HIV status. David complains that he is tired of the overly aggressive concern for his health. He jokes that every time he sneezes, the family considers what they will wear at his funeral. In another incident, the mother rashly tries to pluck food from Suzanne's mouth because David has also eaten from it. Although the mother experiences guilt, her actions reveal that she is not entirely comfortable with her son's health. The fact that the film never explicitly determines David's HIV status may be relevant, intending to undermine the public assumption that to be gay is to experience a lifetime of hysteria over the potential for infection. David may be HIV+, but he is not preoccupied with the diagnosis. Without any firm evidence of his condition, the family's concern for his health is paranoia based upon the presumption that all gay men are infected and/or sick. The film does, however, offer alternatives to this point-of-view, particularly in the person of David's lover (Sean O'Bryan), who is a very masculine male, seen first boxing and then winning at tennis with David's father. These brief scenes remind the audience not only that there are many healthy and athletic gay men, but also that there is no reason to fear those infected with the virus if one takes reasonable precautions. Steven is, in all likelihood, sleeping with David regularly and is still healthy. Moreover, Steven teaches David's father, Walter, that all gay men do not have the same interests. Walter is surprised to discover that Steven hates the opera, despite David's enthusiasm for it. The scenes involving Steven serve to undermine the recurring image of the hysterical and overly passionate gay man. Steven is clearly the most reasonable individual in the film, the individual who is instrumental in bringing the family together after their falling out. Of course, it is easy to be reasonable when it is not your own family crisis.

The film also explores the historical and ethical significance of a Jewish family facing a decision reminiscent of Nazi eugenics and genocidal programs during the second world war. The unborn child's paternal grandfather is a holocaust survivor and is unhappy with his son's participation in the genome project. He refers to his son's work as "medical experiments," obviously alluding to the fiendish practices conducted within concentration camps. Rob's father reminds him that he should not try to "do God's work," that his medical experiments are "dangerous," and that, as a Jew, he (Rob) ought to know this. Rob contends that "knowledge is neutral," that the information is only dangerous in the hands of bad people. Unconvinced, his father reminds him that the good people are the ones who are most dangerous. This final comment is pivotal within the film, because those actions that are morally questionable are conducted entirely by those who have good intentions, who act from what they believe to be a position of compassion and consideration. The entire Golds family justify their desire to abort Suzanne's fetus on the most humane grounds. They have seen how their son/brother David has suffered for his orientation. The father remembers that he was unable to console David when the boy was hysterical after being dumped by a lover in college; the mother recalls how unhappy David has been at various times in his life; and Suzanne considers the stories she has heard of people dying of AIDS or being bashed.

The commonplace theme in all of the above considerations is the fetus' potential for a happy and healthy life. Suzanne wants to wait until she can bring a child into the world who has "no disadvantages." Such considerations remind the audience of the dangers of eugenics programs, particularly for Jews, who were subject to the most notorious eugenics campaign in historical memory. However, the Nazi's genocidal effort was not limited to Jews, but was extended to encompass the mentally retarded and homosexuals as well. The Jewish family's initial failure to recognize the destructive potential of their decision regarding Suzanne's pregnancy exposes the inherent threat of such considerations. Even a liberal Jewish family who has been conditioned to recognize the dangers of prejudice and discrimination can blunder into a decision that would under other conditions remain anathema to them. Rob, who is the most homophobic of the family members and who admits that the "idea of a gay child bothers [him]," leaves his position with the Human Genome Project, stating "I don't believe in this anymore. There's a difference between what we can do and what we should do." Rob's insight is a concession to his father's argument that people should not be having to make such decisions. Of course, by this time, the dilemma has already destroyed his marriage.

David considers Suzanne's dilemma to be a personal slight, a repudiation of his lifestyle and his person. The parents, who obviously dote on both children and who have a great deal of admiration for David, admit that they are so troubled by his homosexuality they cannot be certain they would not have aborted him had they been offered similar information. His father refers to David as "sick and diseased," and then tells his son, "maybe you would be here and maybe you wouldn't." The father's homophobic rhetoric, intended to suggest that homosexuality is a mental and/or medical defect, is reminiscent of Nazi propaganda campaigns calculated to demonize Jews and to win the support of the German people for aggressive reprisals against the Jewish community. Nazi propaganda sought to portray Jews as diseased and unclean, a threat to the health of the fascist state (I allude here to the infamous Nazi newsreel equating Jews to rodents). The allusions to Nazism reveal the slippery slope that people tread when they rashly categorize people as genetically inferior.

The above exchange between father and son, of course, creates much antagonism in an otherwise close family. A reparation of the relationship is accomplished, not through a direct reconciliation, but through the mediation of David's lover Steven, who has encouraged him to make things right with the Golds. One of the early signs that the parents are not entirely comfortable with David's lifestyle is their refusal to acknowledge the legitimacy of his relationship with Steven. They will not invite the gay couple to the house for Suzanne and Rob's anniversary. David inscribes the card on his anniversary gift "to my favorite legally recognized couple," and then explains, sarcastically, that "Steven would have come, but he wasn't invited." In an effort to reach their discontented son after their falling out, the Golds first befriend Steven, implicitly recognizing the authenticity of the relationship between the two men.

The film does not oversimplify the contentious issue of abortion by dividing the faithful into two clearly distinguished camps. Even David, who despises his sister's determination to abort her fetus, is firmly pro-choice in other circumstances. Perhaps his situation demonstrates his hypocrisy by undermining his convictions on the issue. After all, a scenario in which a woman has "the right to choose" only when her choice is agreeable to others is not actually "the right to choose." Steven defends Suzanne's authority to determine the fate of her unborn child by reminding David of his convictions on the issue and by suggesting that he ought to leave the decision to his sister. David's position problematizes the issue for him because he has discovered conditions under which the woman's choice should be invalidated. Suzanne does finally make a choice on her own, even ignoring her husband's suggestion that they "wait for the next one."

The continued association between brother and sister is only achieved by Suzanne's decision to keep her child. Curiously, it is not through consideration of her own brother that she decides to carry the pregnancy to term, but through a series of conversations with co-workers. In an exchange with her friend Jackie (Rosie O'Donnell), Suzanne realizes that she is being cavalier with her pregnancy. She learns Jackie cannot have children, and the discovery makes her more appreciative of her own condition. If she were unable to have children, she would not be so quick to toss away a child on the pretense that it may be gay when it grows up, a consideration that has some insidious implications, since it suggests that having a gay child is better than having no child at all. In an exchange with Brandon, a gay co-worker (Patrick Briston), Suzanne comes to terms with issues explicitly related to homosexuality. Suzanne learns that most of the problems faced by gays and lesbians are a result of prejudice and discrimination rather than any inherent inferiority or any specific sexual practice. When Suzanne asks Brandon if there is anything that his parents could have done to "make things easier" for him, he quips, "they could have not thrown me out of the house at sixteen." As the two converse in a pub, Brandon's flamboyance irritates an individual drinking at the bar. The man later accosts them on the street corner, calling Brandon a "faggot" and knocking Suzanne to the ground. This heavy-handed incident demonstrates that homophobia is a defect of the aggressor. Moreover,

Brandon's general demeanor serves as a foil to David's artistic brooding and demonstrates that gays can be happy in spite of adversity, and it is out of concern for her child's happiness that Suzanne considered aborting the pregnancy originally.

The title of the film, *Twilight of the Golds*, offers another clue to the nature of its message, particularly for a Jewish family. The title is partially derived from Nietzsche's 1888 book *Twilight of the Gods*, in which the philosopher concisely summarizes ten years of philosophical ruminations, some of which would later be adopted as a basis for Hitler's racial ideology and propaganda, the same that fueled his war machine and, in his fanatical mind, legitimized genocide. Nietzsche's theory of the "Superman" is particularly implicated in the film's commentary on the human genome project, which seems to affirm science's eugenic objective, the desire to eliminate randomness from human procreation and thus to create perfect people. Nietzsche's philosophy postulates the emergence of a race of extraordinary individuals who are not only physically superior but are also intellectually and morally advanced beyond the rest of humanity. The "superman" would not be bound by traditional morality, but only by the limits of his own volition, a philosophy easily perverted to justify Nazi racial theory and instrumental in the formulation of the "final solution."

In the context of Marks' film, the titular allusion to Nietzschean theory constitutes another warning of the slippery slope of genetic engineering. The "superman" is unfettered by any traditional moral and ethical systems that limit his desire to dominate his surroundings. This desire, the "Will to Power," Nietzsche defined as amoral, "beyond good and evil." The scientists of the film begin to resemble the Nietzschean superman, making decisions based on scientific objectivity without consideration for the moral consequences, which are viewed as beneath consideration. Rob's objectivity is ultimately compromised by the fact that the genetic tests are conducted on family members. His boss Adrian tries to encourage him to continue in his work, to avoid being dissuaded by ethical and emotional considerations. He scolds Rob for his weakness: "You are devoted to science and objectivity. Now you're making a value judgement and running scared. Every time we are on the verge of a positive change, we run into fear and prejudice. Then we end up taking two steps back." Adrian fails to understand the ways in which his own work perpetuates and facilitates fear of and prejudice toward diversity. Instead of being unfettered by traditional moral systems, this science empowers and validates moral agendas. If homosexuality can be traced to a particular gene, how does the scientific effort to identify and eradicate the gene associated with homosexuality differ from other genocidal programs? Nazi experiments often involved a fiendish logic, but they showed no concern for the physical integrity of the experimental subject; thus they are an extreme example of the effort to divorce scientific experimentation from moral considerations, the same philosophy that is espoused by Rob and Adrian. When the Nazis dropped a Jew into freezing water to determine how long it would take him to die, they were ostensibly trying to determine the life expectancy of German pilots who were forced to ditch their planes in the North Sea. While they may have had an objective that surpassed mere cruelty and sadism, the lack of consideration for the subject of the experiment reveals the ethical objectivity of science taken to its most inhumane conclusion. A more subtle allusion to Nazi eugenics may lie in the nature of the gay gene study itself.

The film also poses the following question: If homosexuality can be traced to a particular genetic make up, does not the eradication of those genes constitute the elimination of a type of humanity with its own unique characteristics that go beyond mere sexual practices? David responds to his sister's question regarding the sagacity of waiting to "bring a child into the world with no disadvantages" by explaining that "we [humanity] would lose too much," thus suggesting that gays and lesbians have unique talents and traits to offer civilization, and, as it turns out, that contribution is art and literature. He asks, "What if Michelangelo's mother felt the same way as you do, or Tennessee Williams', or Herman Melville's?" David suggests that the most compelling reason the group should escape annihilation is because it periodically produces a genius. Although his rationale may be overly simplistic and may suggest that people should be spared eradication only if they can justify their contribution to human culture, he must be correct in suggesting that eliminating a particular trait from the human gene pool is a dangerous practice.

The Wagnerian link to the film is still stronger than the allusion to Nietzsche's philosophy, although the two are obviously interrelated. The title of the film borrows from Richard Wagner's *Der Ring des Niebelungen*, a portion of which is subtitled *Götterdämmerung (Twilight of the Gods)*, the ostensible origin of Nietzsche's title as well. In the film, David is directing an abridged six hour production of Wagner's *Ring Cycle*, a work which, in full, is over twenty hours long. He explains that he wants to make Wagner relevant to a younger audience, and clearly he has taken the message of the opera to heart. A portion of Wagner's epic becomes a leitmotif within the film, a point which is driven home at the conclusion when the audience sees a portion of David's project, particularly the moment when the hero Siegfried rescues Brunhilde from the flames to claim her love. Narrating this portion of the opera, David explains that the man who has no fear is the only one who will be able to brave the magic flames and win Brnnhilde. Of course, Siegfried must also overcome the god Wotan who blocks his passage with his "Runespear," the symbol of his power and authority, the source of his thunder. Undaunted, Siegfried breaks Wotan's staff and robs the god of his power before proceeding through the magic fire. Siegfried's actions are parallel to the actions of David, and gays and lesbians in general, who must have the courage to overcome adversity in order to earn the right to love the individual of their choice. Moreover, the disarming of the God Wotan signifies the triumph of the human will over god-based systems of morality. In the context of the struggle for human rights, this moment is particularly relevant, as the overwhelming amount of hostility directed at gays and lesbians is fomented by the indefatigable bigotry of conservative Christians. Homosexuals must have the courage to love in spite of thunder. David comes to understand his predicament as a gay man in these terms. He argues with his sister, "You have to stop looking at this as some kind of curse. It's not. What it is is a challenge." His gift lies in the recognition that he "could not live the life ... [he] was programmed for," and he explains that his sister may find her own "greatness" in the struggle to raise a gay child. For David, meaning lies in life's challenges; the way in which one manages those struggles is what defines and creates character. He reminds his sister that all she loves about him is linked to that gay gene: "Every human being is a tapestry." The need to overcome adversity in order to love is also relevant to the position of David's parents, who have to learn to accept David's sexual predisposition, particularly by embracing his lover as a family member.

Perhaps the most important comment in Marks' film is Suzanne's off-handed observation, "No one has ever had to make this decision before," a statement which captures the central premise of the film — to generate alarm over the potential abuses of genetic engineering, to suggest that these scientific discoveries will create entirely new ethical considerations and may even serve to break up the current moral dichotomies surrounding issues such as abortion and homosexuality, the two most hotly contested social issues at the end of the twentieth century. David, a staunch pro-choice advocate, is not so sure of his position when the abolition of homosexuality and his own invalidation are put into play. The Gold family members are, on the other hand, forced to reevaluate their feelings toward David with these considerations. Despite the film's concentration on a family of liberal Jewish intellectuals dwelling in an urban setting, the target audience is Christian fundamentalists as well, a group whose two most detested moral issues are placed at odds with each other. *Twilight of the Golds* invites Christian fundamentalists to determine what they despise the most — homosexuality or abortion — to evaluate which impulse is strongest — to murder or create.

One of the more disturbing aspects of the film is the all too simplistic dismissal of the Human Genome Project because it may create dilemmas and previously unlooked for manifestations of discrimination against gays. *Twilight of the Golds* would seem to make a closet of the womb in order to avoid giving the bigots yet another means of perpetrating their crimes against gays and lesbians. But when further looked into, the silencing of the prenatal queer creates other ethical dilemmas. It implicitly advocates the closet suggesting that silence on the subject of sexual orientation will deter reprisals, but this is the same flawed philosophy that allowed lies and misconstructions to proliferate for so long. Silence coddles the heterosexist majority in their prejudices, making homophobia seem essential rather than socially conditioned. Instead of addressing the mis-characterizations and misunderstanding of gays and lesbians, it opts for safety. It does not interrogate the assumptions of homophobes; it allows them yet another opportunity to postpone a thoughtful consideration of the subject. The logic resembles the same employed to exclude gays from the military for their own good, because they cannot be adequately protected. Such assumptions accept the inevitability of homophobia, ignoring any effort to eliminate it through education. One might argue that *Twilight of the Golds* combats homophobia by dramatizing the moral dilemma of the family and their eventual decision to keep the child, but Rob's resolution to leave his work suggests that he never should have been faced with the uncertainty of the issue, leaving his homophobia unchallenged. Suzanne's decision to carry the child to term has little to do with the moral indefensibility of homophobia, but instead is based, at least partially, upon the fear that she might not have another child. She too feels that she is not prepared for the decision. The fact that the loving sister of a gay brother could have such difficulty with the potential sexuality of her fetus exposes the necessity of facing such issues in order to address the origins and the extent of hysterical hatred of gays and lesbians. After all, Suzanne so completely misjudges the quality of a queer life that she concludes it might be better for the child to have never lived at all than to have lived gay.

The discovery of the gay gene might actually be instrumental in the dismantling of homophobic assumptions since it would force consideration of the individual's fate while it is still mingled with assumptions, of the child's innocence, the same assumptions that are so potent in the mobilization of misdirected contempt for the gay community. It would break up the antithetical structure that characterizes gays and lesbians as the demonic foil to childhood. The film's heavy-handed condemnation of the genome project reveals the increased paranoia of the gay community regarding the indefatigable capacity of the straights to manufacture new justifications for persecution. However, the genome project may signal a shift in the attitude of science and medicine toward homosexuality. Aside from AIDS research, the discovery of the potential gay gene may be one of the few times in which science has served the gay community constructively. The recognition of a gay gene would bring less discrimination, not more. Although the religious right has already prepared themselves for the eventuality by maintaining that "biologically based traits or behaviors are not always socially sanctioned" (Vaid 136), the discovery would give many the requisite knowledge to reexamine their assumptions in light of reason and objective science. The gay gene would undermine the legitimacy of the argument from morality because it would expose once and for all that homosexuality is not a choice or a lifestyle. The one group that could most readily benefit the cause of civil liberties with such understanding, of course, would be the Supreme Court, whose decision to uphold sodomy laws was based on the long tradition of moral protest against homosexuality. The discovery of the gay gene would help to eradicate the assumption that gays and lesbians can be cured, the justification for the benevolent paternalism that offers discrimination and exclusion for "our own good." Such knowledge could release many gays and lesbians from guilt over their inability to conform to societal norms, and parents could finally be content that their children's sexual orientation is not the result of errors in upbringing.

Twilight of the Golds is one of several recent films addressing the dangers inherent in genetic manipulation, among them Gattaca and the recent television production of Brave New World. The former is a dystopic vision of a world in which genetic engineering has become the predominant instrument for discrimination. DNA testing has created a permanent underclass who have no hope of rising above limited expectations. Like Gattaca, Twilight of the Golds places genetic predispositions at variance with the human will and demonstrates the triumph of the latter.

However, Twilight's rejection of gene therapy is short-sighted and is a glaring example of the disparity between the concerns of the gay intelligensia and those of the mainstream gay community. The former have constructed complicated paranoid justifications for the repudiation of what could be of great comfort and benefit to the latter.

6

Forbidding Desire: Profanity, Protest Masculinity, and *The Usual Suspects*

In his cultural analysis of bodybuilding, appropriately entitled *Little Big Men*, Alan Klein defines masculinity as "the presence of an absence" (237). He thus invokes a common characterization of masculinity — the absence of any traits broadly construed to be feminine. Our culture constructs the masculine through negation; it is a "shrinkage of the self, a turning away from whole areas of life" (Horrocks 25), a fearful avoidance of the feminine. It is the hysterical fear of femininity in men that also accounts for the deep seated antipathy with which our culture regards male homosexuality. In her analysis of gender, *Slow Motion*, Lynn Segal identifies homophobia as "a powerful tool in the regulation of the entire spectrum of male relations ... the forced repression of the feminine in all men" (16). Relations between males, particularly within male cultures, such as the military and athletics, is founded upon the mutual repudiation of homosexual interests. This study of Bryan Singer's film *The Usual Suspects* will examine the way in which homophobia — particularly the hysterical fear of penetration — governs the interaction between men, and, in this case, between a group a criminals who have been unwittingly implicated in a nefarious plot.

When viewing *The Usual Suspects*, one is first struck by the vulgarity of the language, and if one is at all sensitive to gender issues, one next recognizes that most of the profanity in the film involves some type of homophobic slur. Most prevalent are references to the humiliation males associate with anal penetration. Western culture traditionally equates the humiliation of men with emasculation and subsequently with feminization. The heterosex act itself is viewed by many men and even by some women as a denigration of the passive (feminine) partner. Coitus is "the act in which power relations between men and women are embodied" (Pronger 137). The active role is "the position of superiority." "Fucking" is socially constructed as a sign of mastery, both in its literal and its figurative meanings; "the penis becomes the weapon that guarantees submission." The receptive partner, on the other hand, is regarded as subordinate and inferior (Pronger 138). In accordance with gender codes, the humiliation of passive penetration is intensified if the recipient is male. Indeed, the rhetoric of masculine performance in American culture prefers death before penetration. Thus obscenities suggesting that a particular male is the passive recipient of such intrusions are intended to articulate power relations, the struggle for dominance among competing males, and this is the role that such obscenities play in *The Usual Suspects*. The homophobia implicit in such insults mediates the relations between the characters. Men's fear of such insults and the resulting stigma is the negation of the feminine in the self. The film seems to suggest that narrowly defined notions of masculinity make the holder vulnerable to the machinations of those who are not afraid to compromise traditional masculinity. Unfettered by strict gender constructions, the feminized male can enjoy a wider range of behavioral options, and thus his actions are less predictable.

Thus far this account of masculinity may be somewhat reductionist. Recent sociological studies have identified multiple masculinities, each with its own behavioral expectations. The masculinity that I have defined thus far is related to the dominant, socially accepted concept of gender performance that has been traced to the self-definition of American men in the early nineteenth century, whereby they sought to negate the elitist, feminized, and cultivated manhood associated with European aristocracy (Kimmel 18–19). R.W. Connell identifies "hegemonic masculinity" as the

> configuration of gender practice which embodies the currently accepted answer to the problem of the legitimacy of patriarchy, which guarantees (or is taken to guarantee) the dominant position of men and the subordination of women [77].

Connell emphasizes the historical contingency of gender roles, suggesting that the currently dominant codes of masculine performance are not an extension of natural law, but are a temporary solution to power relations between the sexes. Connell also identifies configurations of "complicit masculinity" and among these "masculine protest ... an exaggeration of masculine conventions." Growing out of a sense of powerlessness, protest masculinity involves a hyperbolic "claim to the potency that European culture attaches to masculinity." It is a behavioral norm among young working class males and often involves hostility and sometimes even violence directed toward women and gay men (111). This violence is one of the principle means whereby gender roles are policed and regulated among men.

The machismo exhibited by most of the principle characters in *The Usual Suspects* suggests masculine protest. The film includes numerous "in your face" confrontations reminiscent of schoolyard posturing, intended to make an opponent capitulate without violence. These incidents are particularly commonplace between the characters McMannis (Stephen Baldwin) and Hockney (Kevin Pollack), who exchange insults and butt chests on numerous occasions. In one instance the two men argue over the appropriate procedure in collecting the rewards for a recently completed heist. Fearing that McMannis and his partner Fenster (Benicio Del Toro) will abscond with the money without compensating the others, Hockney conveys his distrust through a homophobic slur intended to shame them: "You and Fenster are off honeymooning in California, while the rest of us are left here holding our dicks." The encounter reaches a stalemate, with the two tough guys staring each other down — so close that their lips almost meet. McMannis even feigns a kiss. The tension is broken when Verbal Kind refers to the men as "ladies." The fear of being labeled feminine is sufficient to regulate the behavior of the renegade elements. McMannis laughs nervously in order to save face and then withdraws. Initially, the imagery of homoeroticism suggests homosocial bonding. The characters "left holding their dicks" are deprived of the implicit honeymoon dalliance of McMannis and Fenster. Rather than completely repudiating the compatibility of the homosexual and the homosocial, the imagery reveals an hysterical evasion of the receptive role in erotic activities. Such showdowns are not limited to the criminal element.

The police are as committed to this notion of masculinity as the people they arrest. Just as the values of gangland males activate homophobic sentiments in order to achieve behavioral modification, the police appropriate the language of sexual penetration in order to dominate and humiliate the suspects. While being interrogated about his potential involvement in a heist, Dean Keaton (Gabriel Byrne) assures the policemen that he no longer engages in criminal activities, that he is a businessman. His interrogator responds: "From now on, you're in the getting fucked by us business." The reply emphasizes the subordination of Keaton to the will of the police; the penetrator is in the position of power, and fearing the continual harassment implicit in the threat, Keaton is supposed to be cowed into confessing. In another interrogation, Hockney turns the tables on his captors, revealing that the police are also eager to assert their masculinity by avoiding any implication of homosexuality. When asked what "another turn in the joint" would include for him, Hockney quips: "Fuck your father in the shower...?" Later, after the five suspects are gathered in the holding cell, Fenster complains about having been strip searched for no apparent reason: "I had a guy's finger up my asshole tonight." The humiliation that Fenster reveals is not enough to win the sympathy of his fellow inmates who find the revelation amusing material for ridicule: "Is it Friday already?" In the course of interrogations, the police employ numerous techniques for intimidation, particularly physical and verbal abuse. Their effort to force Fenster's confession relies upon the humiliation of penetration. The violation is designed to break his will, but, ironically, his ability to endure the emasculating degradation becomes a measure of his manhood. Verbal Kind (a soft-spoken cripple played by Kevin Spacey) describes his own feelings during the incarceration: "I hadn't done anything they could do me for." Verbal's language equates arrest and conviction to sexual violation. "To do" is, of course, slang for the dominant role in sexual relations, and, particularly, the phrase expresses men's aggressive intentions toward women, thus perpetuating the notion that sex constitutes an imposition upon the passive partner.

Upon their release from jail, the criminals effectively reverse the power dynamics between themselves and the police. The five suspects, including the four aforementioned individuals and Verbal Kind, conspire to pull off a jewel heist, which involves exposing corruption in the NYPD. A group of policemen have a "taxi service" that provides protection and transportation for influential smugglers in exchange for a percentage of the sale. The suspects waylay a police car carrying a jewel smuggler, and, after appropriating the merchandise, they douse the car in gasoline and set it on fire, prompting an investigation that exposes the police's illegal operations. Verbal describes the decision to burn the car as Keaton's "fuck you" to the NYPD, and in providing an account of the disciplinary actions following the investigation, Verbal says, "Everybody got it right in the ass from the chief on down." The suspects' revenge against their former captors perpetuates the sexual terminology defining relations between men.

Homophobia is a variant form of misogyny; it is traditional sexism thinly veiled. The gay male is despised and/or abused for exhibiting feminine attributes, a manifestation particularly offensive to protest masculinity, which has a significant investment in displays of male difference and power. The contempt for feminine characteristics in males constitutes an implicit hatred of the subordinate condition of women. The male's fear of being penetrated like a woman reveals his unacknowledged contempt for the passive position in the sex act. Moreover, the systematic exclusion of queer sentiments maintained by the profane rhetoric of the film extends to women. The world of the film is a world without women, both in gangland and in the police precinct. Indeed, emotional attachment to women is represented as a betrayal of the masculine priorities of the two groups. None of the characters can believe that Keaton has exchanged his commitment to criminality for a monogamous relationship with Eady Finneran. During his incarceration Keaton faces the incredulity of the other suspects. McMannis, parodying the discourse of romantic betrayal, quips, "Say it ain't so." The imagery of the film seems to reinforce the mutually exclusive relation of monogamy to criminality. Upon his release from jail, Keaton is torn between his love for Eady and the shadowy figures of the other suspects, an idea reinforced by the juxtaposition of images of the couple and the waiting gang. As his fiancée tells him that she loves him, Keaton is distracted by the presence of the other men waiting on the far side of the street. Keaton's reluctant decision to join the other gangsters on one last job is an implicit betrayal of his fiancée, placing homosocial bonding before his relationship with Eady. Indeed, Keaton is hyper-sensitive to any suggestion that his love for Eady is not sincere. When Verbal encourages Keaton to participate in the raid on the NYPD "taxi service," he makes the mistake of questioning Keaton's domestic situation: "You look like you have a great little scam." The comment earns him a pummeling. Agent Kuian shares the same misogynistic assumptions as the criminals. Angrily questioning Verbal, he insists, "You expect me to believe he retired, for a woman? He was using her." The officer in the room further ridicules Verbal's emotional tale of Keaton's betrayal: "That's heart-warming. Really! I'm weepy." In the context of a single gender environment, the homophobic profanity becomes paradoxical, signaling the continued existence of male/female power relations in the absence of women, relations in which the less dominant are exploited and abused, and, at the same time, ensuring that none of the participants will mistake the intimacy for invitations to sexual dalliance. Keaton is, symbolically, crawling into bed with the other men when he leaves Eady for their company, and when more than one heterosexual man occupies a single bed, somebody is likely to be screwed, but nobody is going to be kissed.

The framing device of *The Usual Suspects* is the interrogation of Verbal Kind, who is under complete immunity and who relates events that transpired the night before when an Argentinean cargo ship exploded, killing twenty-seven men. The questioner, Agent Dave Kuian (Chazz Palminteri), refuses to believe that Keaton (the subject of his investigation for years) actually died in the explosion, and he hopes to get Verbal to confess to the ruse. Agent Kuian is aggressive and arrogant in his cross-examination of the surviving suspect. He reminds Verbal, "I'm smarter than you, and I want to know what you know, and I'm going to get it from you whether you like it or not," an oath intended to suggest the coercion of the spurned and aggressive male lover who will take what he wants in the event that his sexual advances are thwarted. His interrogation becomes physical at times as he attempts to intimidate Verbal into cooperating. The captive, on the other hand, feigns fear and stupidity to conform to the agent's inaccurate perception of him and composes a false tale of events leading up to the explosion in the harbor. He effectively dominates Kuian by feigning humility and cooperation. Kuian does not learn that Verbal has hoodwinked him until the criminal is already gone.

The dynamics of power represented in the interaction between Kuian and Kind reveal one of the more important issues of the film. I have already discussed the construction of protest masculinity and its reliance upon homophobia and misogyny to police the boundaries of acceptable behavior for males. Hegemonic and its complicit forms of masculinity include a hysterical fear of passivity, of any feminine attributes exhibited in a male, and the film suggests that such reductionist views of male behavior only serve to victimize those who share them. Although Verbal insists at the beginning of his narrative that his partners are not the type of men to "bend over for anyone," they, just like the NYPD, end up getting it "right in the ass," and it is Verbal who obliges them.

The profanity associated with male rape plays a previously unspecified role within the dialogue of the film, where the infinitive "to fuck" also means "to deceive," and here the weapons of domination are the tongue and the word. In this context, when one male is tricked by another, he has figuratively allowed himself to be penetrated by false words and deceptive thoughts. The integrity of the recipient's mind, rather than his body, has been compromised through this credulity. Thus the already precarious masculinity of the characters is made still more vulnerable by the inclusion of gullibility as a manifestation of emasculation. The criminal element relies for its livelihood upon the capacity to mislead others, particularly the police, and the police, perhaps not to the same degree, evaluate their own gender performance with their ability to recognize and neutralize deception, offering their own subterfuge to counter the felons'. The interrogation that frames the narrative, and the indeterminate nature of the speakers' veracity, is the quintessential manifestation of this sexualized struggle for intellectual dominance. It is valuable to note here that the use of language rather than physicality to achieve mastery is traditionally designated as feminine. One need only remember Hamlet's self-abuse, in which he genders his inaction, associating his use of words rather than deeds with feminine transgression: he "unpacks [his] heart with words" and "falls to cursing like a very drab" (II. ii. 586–7).

Verbal is the only one of the five suspects who does not participate in the macho posturing and the competition for dominance within the group. Instead, he "fawns like a spaniel" on Keaton, protecting him from the accusations of agent Kuian during the interrogation. Verbal is the soul of compliance. He feigns a club foot and patiently endures insults about his intelligence and his physical condition. When agent Kuian suggests that Verbal was being manipulated by Keaton, the former responds, weeping: "Why me? I'm stupid; I'm a cripple. Why me?" Kuian explains, "because you're stupid, because you're weaker than him." Here Kuian acknowledges the power dynamics that dictate relations between men, dynamics that stipulate the weaker party as the accepted subject of exploitation. However, Verbal's place within these power relations proves to be central. He turns out to be a legendary criminal mastermind, Keyser Soze, whose name is equated with violence and power, the mere mention of which is sufficient to make the other four suspects grow gray with fear. When Kobayashi first approaches the suspects with Soze's plan, the revelation of his employer's name startles the men and later inspires Fenster to run for his life. Even Hockney admits that he is not too proud to "run" after the four remaining suspects are told by Kobayashi where to find Fenster's body. Instead, the men play into Soze's hands by refusing to compromise their masculine honor, by rejecting humiliation. Rather than run, they commit themselves to revenge against Kobayashi, who has already anticipated their response.

Following the murder of Fenster, the suspects attempt to win back their safety and self-respect by entrapping Soze's agent and showing that they can "get to him" whenever they wish. The paradoxical aspect of the effort is that they attempt to bring Kobayashi under their power in order to break Soze's grip upon them, in order to manufacture the circumstances in which they can retreat in safety. Once they have captured Kobayashi, McMannis whispers in his ear like a lover: " I'm the guy that's gonna get you. I just want you to know that." In this context, dominance of a rival is couched in homoerotic terminology. The suspects believe that they have effectively emasculated Kobayashi, rendering him powerless; thus, in his boasting, McMannis uses the language of sexual penetration to suggest Kobayashi's symbolic castration. This effort is still another macho pose intended to frighten the opponent into competing no further and, ultimately, expected to create a situation in which the poseur can withdraw and avoid humiliation. However, Kobayashi refuses to capitulate, explaining that a loved one of each suspect will be the target of his revenge if the criminals do not agree to participate in the raid on the Argentinean ship. The threat is made even more insidious by the assurance that each of the victims will be subjected to a "most gruesome violation before they die." The first mentioned is Keaton's fiancée Eady. Other proposed victims are Hockney's father and Verbal's uncle Randall. However, the most potent threat is directed at McMannis: "I might only castrate Mr. McMannis' nephew Davy." In order to disempower McMannis, he will emasculate a family member. In all four cases, the criminal violation will take the form of a sexual domination. With this threat, the suspects submit to Kobayashi's and Soze's will, agreeing to raid the ship in the harbor.

Soze's criminal genius lies in his willingness to engage in those acts that are anathema to other men, particularly those portrayed in the film, men who will not submit to anyone. Because Verbal/Soze will yield, he enjoys a wider range of behavioral options. The other men's limited view of accepted gender roles makes them vulnerable to Soze's subtle machinations. However, Verbal's submissiveness is a ruse. Controlling the other characters with his passivity, he has discovered the power inherent in the role of a victim. In his masquerade, he recounts for Agent Kuian the actions that made Soze legendary. He was a small-time Turkish criminal. When the local Hungarian mob decided they wanted his territory, they abducted his wife and children. To demonstrate their determination, they raped his wife and waited for him to get home to cut his son's throat. Indicating that "he would rather see his family dead than live one day after this," he shot his wife and remaining children and then turned on the intruders, killing all of them except one, who was expected to relate the story of Soze's murderous resolution to the world. In the ensuing months he went on a rampage, killing everyone associated with the Hungarian underworld: "their kids, their wives, their parents, their parents' friends...." He burned their homes and the places they worked; he even killed "people who owed them money," and then "he disappears.... He becomes a myth, a spook story." The effectuality of Soze's villainy lies in his willingness to use his own vulnerability against his rivals, to wear weaknesses like a coat of arms. Unlike Soze, the suspects have allegiances to other people and an attendant concern for their well-being.

The fear of humiliation and the loss of honor is not sufficient to make Soze act rashly and "stick his head out." Instead, by posing as a cripple, Verbal Kind inspires others to take risks on his behalf. If the others believe that he is "stupid," they will not expect him to conspire against them. Thus Verbal/Soze executes his agenda while facing only minimal peril. The raid on the ship at the climax of the film is perhaps the primary example of Soze's passive manipulations. Through his agent Kobayashi, Verbal/Soze compels the unwitting suspects to assist him in eliminating the only man who can identify him, Arturro Marquez, a "stool pigeon for the Justice Department," who was on the ship because he was being sold to the Hungarian mob to identify Soze for their revenge. Soze manipulates the suspects into embarking on what they know is a very dangerous mission under the false pretense that there is 91 million dollars in cocaine to be acquired. However, to everyone's surprise, the ship is empty of its illicit cargo. After the four suspects have eliminated most of the Hungarians, Verbal slips onto the ship and kills Marquez, who is cowering in the hole. He also takes the opportunity to kill all of the remaining suspects who can identify him. The circumstance that has allowed Soze such easy access to his enemies is his pose as an ineffectual cripple, as someone too naive and submissive to dissemble. This refusal to embrace the restrictive behaviors common to hegemonic masculinity permits him to circumvent other experienced felons in safety.

Soze's willingness to allow others to take credit for his own criminal genius is still another manifestation of his unique brand of villainy. The other suspects derive self-satisfaction from their notoriety, at least among the criminal element. Success in cheating, deceiving, and, when necessary, killing others is the source of honor and pride within the group, a measure of their manhood. Soze explains to agent Kuian that, "the greatest trick the devil ever pulled was making the world believe that he doesn't exist," and Soze has achieved the same mystique. Keaton believes that the infamous criminal mastermind is just a "spook story": "There is no Keyser Soze." Incredulous and amused, Agent Kuian asks Verbal if he believes in Soze, to which the suspect responds mysteriously, "Keaton always said, 'I don't believe in God, but I'm afraid of Him.' Well, I believe in God, and the only thing that scares me is Keyser Soze." This, of course, can be taken as an affirmation, and one that perpetuates the mystery surrounding Soze. Verbal's project is to convince Agent Kuian that Keaton is Soze and that Verbal has been his victim; thus, to deflect suspicion he permits someone else to take credit for his notorious life. Moreover, like Shakespeare's Iago, instead of drawing suspicion on himself by accusing Keaton, Verbal subtly prompts Kuian to draw the desired conclusion and then feigns incredulity. When Kuian proudly announces to Verbal that Keaton is Soze, Verbal feigns denial, until, bursting into tears, he announces that the suspects had followed Keaton from the beginning.

Thus the camera becomes complicit with Verbal; his voice directs the eye of the camera to false conclusions. Verbal's narrative juxtaposes the cowering and complaining Marquez ("He is here.... I know he's here....

I'm telling you it's Keyser Soze") with images of Keaton searching the ship. Verbal's character becomes a meta-cinematic metaphor for the director/screenwriter. Eager to comply with his audiences' expectations (an audience both interior and exterior to the film), he spins a tale that conforms to the conventions of the action thriller, embracing the "usual suspects," the appropriate masculine gender performance for the genre, and one which initially appears to be a conventional plot, yet he eventually frustrates all of the expectations attendant upon these conventions. The theater audience occupies the same position in relationship to the story as Kuian; in fact, Kuian articulates the inevitable responses of the audience, and, consequently, the film audience is "screwed" along with Kuian, encouraged to conclude that Keaton is the supervillain and stunned by the revelation that Verbal is Soze. Kuian and the exterior audience discover Verbal's deception simultaneously. The eye of the camera is Kuian's eye as he searches the interrogation room and realizes that Verbal manufactured his story, deriving all of his ideas from words and phrases printed somewhere in the room. The film audience is left to question the veracity of all the events in the film. The camera becomes paradoxical, masquerading as a window on reality and simultaneously exposing the artifice of film. The inability of both audiences to discern truth from fiction, to identify that in the film which was real and that which was constructed, undermines the widely accepted objective of the movie and entertainment industry — to produce meaning. Ironically, at the conclusion of the film, as Verbal/Soze walks away from the precinct and the voice-over repeats the commentary about the unreality of Soze, the existence of the villain becomes the only element of the narrative that can be verified; the mystery is revealed while all that previously seemed real is obscured.

Verbal's machinations exploit the homophobic and misogynistic arrogance of protest masculinity. The villain manipulates other men's assumptions that effeminate males are ineffectual, unable to compete. Of course, one of the more blatant manifestations of this sentiment is uttered by McMannis, the same man who transforms the language and gestures of homoerotic romance into promises of violence between men. His role in the cocaine heist is to serve as a sniper, covering Keaton as he makes his way toward the ship. Celebrating his own marksmanship, he announces, "Oswald was a fag." The hyperbolic content of the statement is intended to equate "fags" with ineffectuality in the use of weapons and, more broadly, with incompetence in the affairs of men. Moreover, he figuratively associates the penetrating bullets with the penis, the instrument of domination; the inability to send bullets to the designated place is rhetorically associated with impotence and emasculation. Verbal very subtly exploits this particular sentiment among the suspects and the police by feigning an exaggerated sentimentality toward Keaton that can only be understood as a homoerotic fixation. He feigns admiration for Keaton, even quoting him at length, as though his words were the paragon of wisdom. Moreover, he appears to idealize Keaton's relationship with his fiancée, angrily defending him against Kuian's suggestion that Keaton was just using her. Verbal fervently insists, "He loved her," as though his own relationship with the man rested upon Keaton's fidelity toward his intended. Verbal recounts the intimate moment when Keaton asked him to hang back from the fray on the dock so that Verbal could take a share of the money to Eady and explain her fiancé's actions. Kuian's pronouncement of Eady's murder and Keaton's presumed involvement is the revelation that appears to break Verbal's impassioned attachment to the other suspect. The film suggests that Verbal was living a vicarious romance through Keaton's relationship with Eady. He behaves as though the betrayal were his own. Weeping, he incredulously insists that Keaton was his friend, only to turn on him like a scorned lover and acknowledge that he was the mastermind of the suspects' activities and, therefore, was probably Soze in disguise. Verbal's ruse finds the appropriate audience in agent Kuian, who interprets the passionate display as a sign of unmanly weakness and suggests that it was just this emotional vulnerability that inspired Keaton to exploit and manipulate him: "because you're stupid and because you're weaker than him." The failure of Kuian's interrogation is that he is trapped by his own presuppositions about the nature of manhood; he assumes that the emotionally castrated male could never manipulate more traditional men. He is gulled by his assumption that a supervillain would conform to the gender codes of protest masculinity. No honorable, self-respecting criminal would pose as a sniveling cripple with a latent homoerotic attachment to his partner.

Verbal's name is a clue to the construction of his character, and particularly to his passivity. Soze's father was German, and in German the word "kind" means "child." The narrator is thus named "verbal child," and Verbal's behavior is certainly appropriate to the appellation. He is soft-spoken and timid. He weeps and cringes and readily admits to his many fears. Agent Kuian regards him as naive and easily exploited. Certainly, Verbal's hero-worship of Keaton can be explained within this context. His recitation of Keaton's words of wisdom is reminiscent of the child taking direction from his father. The childlike susceptibility feigned by Verbal reinforces Kuian's belief in his naiveté and successfully deflects suspicion. A passive and naive man/child can hardly be the notorious head of an underworld empire. Most importantly, the male child is coded as feminine. The juxtaposition of Verbal's childlike passivity with the aggressive probing of both law enforcers and law breakers, in addition to the terminology of homosexual penetration, reinforces the idea that Verbal is a passive effeminate child, and his passive femininity is his disguise. He allows himself to be used by those determined to assert their masculinity, and this willingness to subvert gender codes gives him the upper hand.

Kuian's expectations regarding the behavior of the typical or "usual suspect" goes a long way toward recuperating the subversive energy of criminal activity. Contrary to the common perception of criminality as a fracturing of the social order, the film offers a deconstructive dissolution of the hierarchical binarism — law enforcer/ law breaker. The two groups are united in a broad set of shared values, ones that are supposed to make the actions of the opposing group predictable and comprehensible. Thus the subversive energy of the presumed renegade group is rehabilitated by the conformity of the criminal element to the socially constructed gender codes of hegemonic masculinity and its exaggerated manifestation, masculine protest. With the exception of Soze, the criminals in the film, despite their refusal to respect the law, police the norms of socially constructed gender roles, their arrogant aggression a fulfillment of masculine ideals. The refusal of passivity, which could be construed as an important contributor to criminal disregard for legal propriety, is actually a very potent tool in the regulation of the strict gender norms that organize society.

Verbal is remarkable among criminals because he refuses to conform to social codes policing male behavior. He then becomes the negation of the "usual suspect" because his behavior is governed by a set of values incomprehensible in light of social constructs coded as natural sexual differences. Thus, he is slippery and cannot be caught. Kobayashi's explanation of Soze's resistance to prolonged associations with other criminals seems to attain an allegorical significance in the context of gender: "One cannot be betrayed if one has no people." One might gloss the statement in the following way: One's behavior cannot be comprehended and thereby predicted if one refuses to appropriate shared gender and social codes. Verbal/Soze is the perfect subversive — having "kicked himself loose of the earth," he can be "appealed to in the name of nothing either high or low." In a sense, the film drives to the heart of hysterical homophobia, elucidating the sentiment behind the discriminatory and often murderous actions of hegemonic masculinity. The queer, or the feminized male, is coded as the ultimate subversive because his refusal of masculine pride and primitive honor permits him to employ his own passivity, vulnerability, and victimization in the struggle for power and dominance. In the profane discourse of the film, he "fucks" in the process of being "fucked."

While the film defines homosexual behavior as subversive, it also negates its role in the criminal underworld. While real men and religious bigots try to associate every villainous activity with homosexuality, *The Usual Suspect* constructs homosexuality as mutually exclusive of the criminal underworld. The homosocial bonding that composes and organizes exclusive male societies, particularly those associated with masculine protest, possess only one requisite condition — the total repudiation of homoerotic activity. Thus the only males who can be automatically excluded from criminal societies are gay men. Implicitly, the film recognizes the inherent contradiction in the construction of homosexual males in American society. At the same time that hegemonic masculinity associates homosexuals with "every sin that has a name," it also suggests that gay men are not physically or intellectually sufficient to compete with "real men." While gay men are the embodiment of all that is "excluded from hegemonic masculinity," they are adequate to put into action little of what they signify.

7

Will & Grace: The Politics of Inversion

In March of 2000, California voters passed the "Knight Initiative," a ballot measure that defines marriage in the state of California as a union of a man and a woman, exclusively. The measure was one of many efforts to invalidate the potential unions of same sex partners made possible by more permissive and progressive laws looming in other states. In the wake of Hawaii's legislative crisis regarding same sex unions, many states and the federal government passed laws defining marriage explicitly as a heterosexual bond. Some states have even gone further in the punitive action to stave off gay civil rights by enacting laws forbidding the adoption of children by gay couples. Such a law was passed in the resolutely hostile and backward state of Mississippi, where even "feminism" is controversial. The anti-gay marriage laws are intended to give states the right to refuse recognition of legal domestic partnerships enacted elsewhere, and whereas previously trembling state governments were reacting entirely to a potential threat to their marital proprieties, they now finally have something to worry about: Vermont voted to recognize same sex domestic partnerships.

In preparation for the contentious California vote, the cast of the popular television sitcom *Will & Grace*, which features a gay man and his straight female friend, agreed to make a public service announcement urging voters to oppose the restrictive definition of marriage included in the Knight Initiative. Network executives at NBC were reportedly furious over what they deemed to be the politicization of a mainstream program through the cast's entrance into a public debate. The network maintained that *Will & Grace* is not a political program and that the actors made the announcement without the permission or endorsement of NBC. Even without Fredrick Jameson's theory of the text's "political unconscious"

(Dowling 114–142), one would be challenged to view even the most benign episode of *Will & Grace* as apolitical, particularly since merely facilitating the visibility of gays and lesbians is in itself a political act intolerable to many. While it would be naive to think that NBC would support this or any other program if it were not lucrative and reasonably well received by the public, the very existence of a program such as *Will & Grace* necessitates a progressive political agenda, but in this case it is an agenda that is compromised in many subtle ways to make it palatable to a mainstream bourgeois audience.

The public life of any narrative depicting gays and lesbians is charged with political controversy. Even when the indefatigable detractors, always at the ready to offer their venomous and ludicrously inaccurate judgment of gay lives, are absent, their criticisms are, nevertheless, present. In the issues that are broached, gays and lesbians capitulate to the slanderous agenda of vitriolic homophobes. With every positive statement made about gays and lesbians, an objection is raised, either implicitly or explicitly. Either the narrative will include the opposition's voice to maintain a pretense to political neutrality, or it will resurrect and implicitly legitimize the homophobic agenda through the topics it raises. Queer friendly art is thus always arguing with shadowy opponents who control the debate's agenda with spoken and unspoken accusations that must be addressed but can never be resolved because they will seldom be heard by anyone save the already convinced. Any narrative is politically charged and poly-vocal, and a television program such as *Will & Grace* assumes a position on a public debate with virtually every line of dialogue.

One of the most common criticisms of the television series *Ellen*, after the titular character's coming out, was that it was too political, perhaps even too gay. Most of the shows following the notorious coming out episode were charged with political debate and were extremely didactic, veritable lessons in queer socio-politics, as Ellen's friends came to accept, understand, and support her orientation. When the show was canceled, it seemed unlikely that there would be another gay sitcom anytime soon. So the production of *Will & Grace* and its immediate success was somewhat surprising. The entirety of the main cast was nominated for best acting Emmys, and two were awarded. Moreover, the show itself received the Emmy for the best comedy and was moved to a coveted spot on NBC's *Must See TV* Thursday, the time slot previously held by *Seinfeld* and *Frasier*. Why did *Will & Grace* succeed (at least thus far) where *Ellen* failed? The answer might lie in the principal criticism of *Ellen*, that it was too gay and too political. While *Will & Grace* continues a socially charged dialogue rebutting our culture's objections to homosexuality, it does so

The cast of *Will & Grace*, from left to right, are Sean Hayes, Eric McCormack, Debra Messing, and Megan Mullally, all of whom were nominated for Emmys for the 1999/2000 season. In this publicity photograph, as in much of this gay situation comedy, the principal intimacy is between a man and a woman.

in a more subtle fashion than did *Ellen*. It compromises with the dominant culture in many important ways, and it tempers its political agenda with outrageous humor. The two gay men are frequently the butt of the jokes. While thus far there have been no televised homophobes within the show to call Will and Jack "fags," the gay characters have obliged their tremulous audience by making fag jokes about each other, a practice which characterizes camp humor, but which here serves the dual purpose of advocating and denigrating gay culture through a single practice. Camp is employed to appease homophobes by reinforcing negative stereotypes, but it simultaneously perpetuates gay culture through its articulation of gay sensibility (Babuscio 19–20), and it is an indispensable contribution to the success of the show's humor. Moreover, the sitcom also negotiates with the dominant culture by making the most important relationships in the lives of the two gay characters heterosocial and quasi-heterosexual.

The names of the characters are helpful in understanding the program's cultural politics. The two principle male characters, Will Truman (Eric McCormack) and Jack McFarland (Sean Hayes), are foils representing diversity within gay masculinity, a diversity which argues for and against gender stereotypes about gay men. The name "Will" signifies resolution and courage, which he maintains in spite of adversity in his personal life (the breakup with his longtime boyfriend and the zany escapades of his high maintenance friends) and his public life (a culture that disenfranchises gays and lesbians). The surname Truman suggests that Will is a "real man" despite popular presumptions that all gay men are ineffectual sissies or are emotionally immature, unable to occupy a respectable place within American society. Will is masculine without machismo and with only a hint of camp. He is a successful lawyer who longs for a permanent, monogamous relationship with another man. He is loyal to his friends, practical, and sometimes even mildly conservative in his attitudes. The surname Truman also invokes the respectability associated with a former president, thus subtly dispelling the myth that gay men and women are un–American. The popular appeal of Will's character results because he is safe, scarcely deviating from the stock television stereotype of the new sensitive male, i.e. Frazier and Niles (*Frazier*), Ross (*Friends*), Raymond (*Everybody Loves Raymond*), and Greg (*Greg and Dharma*). Each of these characters may be mildly neurotic and occasionally foolish, but they are respectful and patient toward women, honest, and well intentioned. Will departs from this character type only insofar as he has an occasional date with a man and makes constant declarations of his alternative sexual orientation (probably so that the audience will not forget, since he is coded as a straight male in so many ways). He is, nevertheless, primarily focused on women, his relationship with Grace the principle bond in his life.

Silly, irresponsible, immature, narcissistic, effeminate, insulting, and promiscuous, Jack McFarland is the embodiment of many negative stereotypes about gay men, but he is made lovable by humor and childlike unselfconsciousness. An unrepentant sissy, he is the embodiment of camp humor, the representation of gay sensibilities. However, he does retreat from some of the most trite assumptions about gay men, that they are all cross-dressers and gender-benders. Even Jack McFarland goes to the gym. The name "Jack" itself is a common appellation for a trickster or joker. While the name "Truman" invokes the common, the safe, and the respectable, "McFarland" suggests both literal and figurative outlandishness. Will's moderation is foiled by Jack's flamboyant behavior. They are the respective embodiments of the familiar and the unfamiliar, although, paradoxically, what is coded as familiar here is actually unfamiliar in the history of gay representation. The presentation of gay men as respectable, middle class citizens is an uncommon and recent popular culture phenomenon, but the presentation of gay men as dangerously and/or ridiculously unfamiliar has a lengthy history. Because gay men are expected by the dominant culture to be odd and outrageous, Jack's character collapses the familiar/unfamiliar binary. He is the expected representation of gay men, yet he is portrayed as unusual among gay men. There have been no other gay male characters as flamboyant as Jack on the show thus far. Will is offered as the norm, a representational strategy intended to redetermine the dominant culture's expectations for gay men. While Jack is the butt of much of the humor, he is, nevertheless, handled with love. Indeed, tolerance and acceptance of Jack is offered as a measure of homophobia in the straight characters. The program frequently emphasizes the enthusiastic acceptance of Jack by the straight male characters— i.e. Will's boss, Benjamin Dusett (played by Gregory Hines), and Will's father, George Truman — ostensibly to reveal that they are not threatened by his excessively gay histrionics; their responses constitute a lesson by example. The other characters' playful indulgence of and occasional exasperation with Jack may be patronizing, but it is not judgmental. The foil structure that governs the presentation of the two male characters is not intended to demonize either representation of gay men, but it is clearly intended to prioritize Will's masculinity over Jack's, to offer a preferable alternative to stereotype. However, because he is so much funnier and more stylish than Will, Jack could easily be the preferred image of gay masculinity to much of the audience. While Will ridicules Jack for being a sissy, Jack refers disparagingly to Will as a "repressed straight guy."

The title *Will & Grace* refers as much to human virtues as to people, revealing that one must possess both courage and style to flout social conventions as fundamental as those dictating sexual object choice. Of course, the style ostensibly belongs to the titular character Grace Addler (Debra Messing) who, appropriately, is a designer. And while her personal assistant Karen (Megan Mullally) subjects her to withering criticism about her

apparel, Grace is, nevertheless, tasteful and fashionable, generally enduring the satiric barbs in a predictably patient and gracious manner. However, as Grace's surname "Addler" indicates, she can become confused or
flustered (addled) occasionally as a result of the devious machinations of
her more callous companions. Thus her full name generates a clever oxy-
moron, revealing a duality in her character that encompasses contradiction: dignity and perplexity, decorum and confusion. "Grace," of course,
also suggests beauty and charity, features easily applicable to her character. Her close relationship with Will Truman makes his life ostensibly
quite conventional; she plays the wife in what Jack refers to as Will's "sexless marriage." Even the titular names Will and Grace imply masculine
and feminine virtues respectively, thus reinforcing traditional gender roles
in this non-romantic relationship between a gay man and his female
friend.

Grace's personal assistant, Karen Walker, is a callous, shallow socialite
who works in Grace's design firm only because she needs an activity to
structure her day. She is the foil to Grace's considerate and obliging nature.
Karen drinks heavily, spends much of her time trying to dodge her rich
husband Stan's sexual advances, and cannot even remember her own children's names. Her Salvadorean maid Rosario quips, "I did not sign on to
work for a decent human being; I signed on to work for Ms. Karen." While
Will and Grace are genuinely kind and loving people, Karen and Jack find
displays of human compassion laughable. Both Karen and Jack cynically
ridicule their same sex counterpart, and both are consumed by the love
of money and fashion. If one can rely on Susan Sontag's characterization
of "camp" as the performance of "snob taste" (qtd. in Bergman 8), then
Karen is the gayest character in the program, as she is the quintessential
snob. Karen is Jack's alter-ego: rich, imperious, fashion conscious, and
promiscuous. Karen's married name "Walker" implies the pride and superiority that attends money, status, and influence. She "walks all over"
friends and family. Paradoxically, her name also suggests "street walker."
While these traits may seem incongruous, they nevertheless define Karen's
personality. Her marriage to Stan and her luxurious lifestyle have not
affected her desire for other men. On several occasions she becomes infatuated with Jack, most memorably when they film a sexual harassment
video, during which Karen is devastated by Jack's kisses. In another episode
she becomes enamored of Will's boss Ben.

The subdivision of the cast into two male/female pairs is clearly a
compromise with the dominant culture, which is not comfortable with
same sex intimacy, particularly between two men. Thus the show is intellectually and philosophically gay and yet is visually straight. The subjects

that it broaches and the conclusions that it reaches are gay friendly, but the images of intimacy are universally heterosexual. Even the title of the series, *Will & Grace*, suggests a normative heterosexual relationship, one that bows to the traditional sexist priority of men. In the remainder of this chapter I will examine the ways in which the program engages contemporary politics, and then I will discuss the tempering of its conclusions to appeal to a mass audience, much of which is heterosexual.

Despite the network's insistence that *Will & Grace* is not a political program, virtually every episode addresses a social issue relevant to gays and lesbians, and the program's very existence challenges the position of religious/political conservatives who insist that issues of alternative sexual orientation be kept out of the public view, that there be no platform for the articulation of queer ideas. The mere visibility of gays and lesbians is politically subversive. However, the politics of *Will & Grace* are more overt than that visibility.

One of the darkest phases in the history of gays and lesbians over the past one hundred years was the effort to alter sexual orientation through psychoanalysis, the failure of which has been documented repeatedly in contemporary gay literature, i.e. Martin Duberman's *Cures* and Edmund White's *A Boy's Own Story*. While respectable psychoanalytic organizations have abandoned the effort to convert homosexuals, opting instead to encourage gays and lesbians to accept their orientation, there has, nevertheless, persisted among conservatives a presumption that homosexuality is a form of mental illness (Norton 22). While the psychiatrists have accepted the inevitability of homosexuality in certain personalities, some religious leaders (such as Pat Robertson) have continued to perpetuate the idea that homosexuality is psycho-pathology and can be cured with a heavy dose of Jesus, an alchemical conclusion mixing pseudo-science and mysticism. *Will & Grace* playfully inverts and lampoons the presumption of mental illness in at least two episodes. In the first of these, Will is having erotic dreams about Grace visiting him in the middle of the night and engaging him in sexual dalliance (episode 34, 2/8/2000). Instead of being encouraged by the sign of potential heterosexuality, he is troubled, and when he tells Jack, the latter is horrified and overwrought, exclaiming that Grace does not even have an album. Will decides to see a psychiatrist — not because he is encouraged by the heterosexual content of his dream, but because it frightens him. The episode parodies the traditional narrative in which the young male or female seeks professional help in order to eradicate what s/he perceives to be awakening homosexual desire. However, in Will's case, the objective of psychoanalysis is inverted, attempting to restore his natural inclination toward Stone Philips, who is the usual partner in his dreams. His analyst makes no effort to cure Will of his homosexuality. Instead, he develops a crush on Grace. As it turns out, Will is dreaming of Grace not because he has heterosexual potential, but because Grace dominates every aspect of his life and has finally even invaded his dreams. Of course, this revelation allows him to reintroduce Stone Philips to his fantasies.

Jack experiences a similar sexual identity crisis in a separate episode intended to reveal that his sexual inclinations are inalterable (episode 41, 4/18/2000). When Rob and Ellen announce their marriage plans, Will and Grace decide to throw bachelor and bachelorette parties. Will and Jack, in charge of the former, mistakenly hire a stripper, assuming that all straight men enjoy such performances. When the stripper arrives, only Jack will agree to a lap dance, and, after a few moments of the performance, he realizes, to his horror, that he is becoming aroused. Running from the room in a panic, he exclaims in a humorous inversion of normative sexuality, "I'm a freak; I'm an aberration; I'm a man that gets turned on by women." He explains his predicament to Will, who finds it more amusing than troubling, and suggests that he has become "so gay" that he has "looped around to straight again." Grace responds in a similar fashion: "Well, he couldn't be straight. So what, now he's a lesbian?" Of course, all of these remarks indicate the inevitability of Jack's homosexuality; he cannot be cured or converted. Even Karen tries to help by explaining that the phenomenon was merely friction, and she demonstrates by sitting on Jacks lap and churning, a practice that has no effect on him but arouses her. When he discovers that the stripper is actually a transsexual who has not yet had h/er operation, Jack triumphs, "I'm still gayer than Christmas." The final exclamation parodies the stereotype of the sullen homosexual who fervently desires to be straight, and the idea that Jack could, either intentionally or inadvertently, thank God for his orientation reveals his unwillingness to accept the idea that his life is retrograde to divine plan.

Will & Grace also parodies those religious organizations, such as Exodus, that endeavor to convert homosexuals to heterosexuality and Christianity; however, the potentially inflammatory satire of the episode is mitigated because the recipients of ridicule are converted homosexuals rather than religious leaders (episode 42, 5/9/2000). The organization called "Welcome Back Home" distributes flyers at gay bars inviting the patrons to attend their meetings and be cured. Jack becomes enamored of Bill, the organization's leader whose picture is copied on the flyer, and convinces Karen to accompany him to a meeting in spite of her objection that she does not want to spend her time with "a bunch of self-loathing closet cases." Of course, the objective of the episode is to demonstrate that homosexuality cannot be prayed away. At the meeting, Jack and Karen meet the organization's greatest success story, Kevin and Jody, a butch lesbian and an effeminate gay man, who query, "Can you believe we used to be gay" prompting Karen's confusion, "was that two men or two women?" Jack spends the session trying to seduce Bill, and, ironically, Jack is so gay that he succeeds in converting the entire group back to their former gay lifestyles. Provoked by Jack's persistent advances, Bill explains that "Welcome Back Home" is not a "pick-up service" and invites anyone who thinks it is to leave. As expected, everyone departs, including Bill, who, confounded, accepts Jack's last proposition that they shower together. The subversion of traditional values and politics in the episode is recuperated by Jack's questionable motivations. While he initially claims that the organization's objective is morally wrong, assuming a self-righteous pose, he eventually admits that he really just wants to "make out with Bill." Thus Jack is not allowed any potentially incendiary ideals, only lust. He is denigrated at the same time that he is elevated by a socially constructive project. So the portion of the audience who might find the satire of the episode offensive are palliated by the fact that Jack is ridiculous and easy to dismiss.

Another episode (25, 12/14/99) addresses the common complaint that gay adolescents are alienated and offered no emotional support in their struggle to understand their untraditional desires. In a hysterical effort to guard children against that phantom recruitment, American culture refuses to acknowledge that children develop their sexual predispositions in childhood and that the compulsory silence imposed upon the issue in our school system is, therefore, damaging to many children. The failure of the school system in this area is obviated by the high incidence of suicide among gay adolescents. Of course, conservative interests maintain that the suicide rate results from the psycho-pathology which they believe is inherent within homosexuality, while more progressive thinkers argue that the suicide rate results from the absence of proper counseling that urges self-acceptance rather than conformity. Despite his protests, Jack is compelled to accompany Karen to her children's grammar school for a parent-teacher conference. His initial reluctance results from his traumatic memories of being bullied on the playground: "This is my Nam." However, he recognizes his true embassy when he rescues an effeminate child from bullies and subsequently counsels him on deterring aggression. The scene reveals the genesis of another Jack, and despite the amusing irony that Jack should be any child's role model, he is offered as the appropriate counselor for a child so similar to himself. Moreover, the child seems bored rather than impressed by Jack's counsel. The potentially inflammatory nature of this subject matter is mitigated by several factors. While the child is obviously gay, there is no mention of sex or sexual orientation, thus discrediting the default assumption of homophobes that any meeting of homosexuals and children will result in a molestation or a conversion. The conflict from which Jack rescues John is waged over competing views of masculinity. The bullies are an instrument in the imposition of obligatory masculine behavior; their violence and taunts are weapons forcing conformity. John is a sensitive, passive, and creative child, while his tormentors are aggressive, physical, and callous. An even more compelling mitigation of the audience's expectations for the subject matter is the subtle commentary on absent and irresponsible parents. The potentially corruptive quality of Jack is diminished by the irresponsible behavior of parents, specifically Karen, who gets drunk before her parent-teacher conference and is irritated to discover that she has been summoned only to be told her child made the honor roll. She instructs the school to call only when one of her children "gives birth at the prom." Jack offers John constructive advice about coping with his difference, while Karen invites the boy to join them for Martinis. Moreover, Jack was invited to join Karen on the excursion to the school only because the father was too busy repairing his Mercedes to assume an interest in his child's education.

The contentious issue of gay marriage has been handled cautiously thus far. Neither Will nor Jack reveals an interest in same sex marriage; indeed, one is literally and the other figuratively married to a woman. The program's subtle commentary on gay marriage is offered through the comedic inversion of traditional values. While Will and Jack plan Rob's bachelor party, Jack offers an impromptu satire on heterosexual marriage intended to reverse moral standards, placing heterosexuality on the defensive: "You know why we're blocked — because heterosexual marriage is just wrong. If God had intended man and woman to be together, he would have given them both penises." The ridiculous assumptions made by Will and Jack in the planning of Rob's bachelor party invert and satirize the assumptions that straights make about gays. Will refers to the "straight world" as "backward world," and with the query, "What is the last thing you would want to see at a party," they decide to hire a female stripper, an obvious mistake based upon specious presumption about heterosexual men. The episode is an interesting reversal of the gay wedding episode of *Rosanne,* in which the titular character plans Leon's wedding around the most vulgar platitudes about gay men. While in *Will & Grace* the marriage tables are turned, the message is the same. Will and Jack are made ridiculous by their actions, but they are, nevertheless, indicative of comparable unexamined and ill-founded assumptions made about gays and lesbians by the heterosexual majority.

The demand of gays and lesbians to be protected in their jobs is an issue that has received very little sympathy within the political arena, at least partially because of a growing discontentment toward affirmative action in general. A handful of cities have enacted laws protecting gays and lesbians from employment discrimination, but federal legislation on the issue is not imminent, this despite the polls which indicate that more than 75 percent of the American public think that discrimination against gays and lesbian in employment is unacceptable. *Will & Grace* broaches the issue through positive example rather than reasoned discourse. Will, a lawyer, began working for a high profile legal firm after failing in his private practice because his most lucrative client pulled out. His boss, Benjamin Dusett, pursues Will as an employee with full knowledge that Will is gay and with the explicit intention of hiring someone who can practice law with compassion, reasoning that he (Ben) is sufficiently heartless himself and needs to balance his staff with someone who possesses greater sensitivity. Ben, who is somewhat eccentric himself, not only tolerates Will's alternative sexual identity but also encourages it by trying to set him up with a friend. The example of Will's successful employment confirms that openly gay men can function in a traditional work environment without incident.

Will & Grace predictably embraces the politics of coming out. The show itself is predicated upon the same rationale as that used to justify the individual declarations of sexual preference that constitute the openly gay subculture; and that rationale is the necessity of visibility, calculated to dispel negative myths as well as the public's irrational fears of gay men and lesbians. With the coming out episode of *Ellen*, the gay community emerged into prime time and mainstream media, and *Will & Grace* is a continuation of that process. Since there is no gay sex and little romance in the program, save the occasional date and declaration of romantic involvement, the principle indication of alternative sexuality lies in the proclamations of sexual preference. Even when the program's comedic situation is either heterosexual or non-sexual, the dialogue reminds the viewer that Will is gay. Of course, Jack's behavior speaks for itself, and, interestingly, the episode that directly addresses the necessity of coming out to family and friends involves Jack's relationship with his mother, who, as it turns out, does not know he is gay (episode 30, 11/25/99). Jack's friends are incredulous to discover that he has not told his mother, because he has been so insistent that others, including Will, come out, but even more so because she cannot see it for herself. Karen inquires sarcastically: "What is she, headless?" Will convinces Jack to come out by asking him the question that Jack broached when faced with the same dilemma:

"Aren't you tired?" The question reveals the pressures and complexities of leading a double life and suggests that self-respecting gay people deserve to unburden themselves. Will's coming out dilemma involves his father, George, who is conscious and supportive of his son's sexual identity but who has never been honest with his colleagues at work (episode 35, 11/15/2000). Thus the episode broadens the program of coming out to include parents who must be open about their children's sexuality in order to be fully supportive. The crisis of the episode occurs when Will and Grace, uninvited, attend an awards ceremony for George and discover that his colleagues do not know about Will's sexual identity. When the son shames the father for his reticence, the latter, determined to rectify the situation without delay, uses his acceptance speech to announce his pride in his son, of course, mortifying Will in the process by making him stand to be applauded for being gay. At a more subtle level, the episode teaches by example the importance of unconditional love, of accepting a child's sexual orientation without shame, recrimination, or ostracism.

The negotiation between moderately conservative and progressive political agendas within *Will & Grace* becomes the explicit subject of one episode: Jack becomes outraged when NBC refuses to televise a kiss between two men (episode 36, 2/22/2000). In a bow to *Seinfeld*'s self-reflective episodes, *Will & Grace* comments upon itself as a cultural artifact that is politically situated. When Jack urges Will and Grace to watch his favorite new sitcom, *Along Came You*, because it has promised to include the first prime time kiss between two men, the allusion is clearly to *Will & Grace* itself, which will fulfill the promise that the fictional program could not. Thus Jack encourages the audience to regard *Will & Grace* as its new favorite program. As expected, the kiss is disappointing: just before the lips meet, the camera pans to a fireplace, effectively erasing the image of gay romance. The disappointment arouses Will's cynical acquiescence and Jack's outrage. The resulting debate simultaneously advocates and ridicules queer politics. Jack wants to protest at the NBC corporate office, and Will is resigned to the idea that no one wants to see two men kiss on TV. He urges Jack to "leave the silly protests to Woody Harrelson and his hemp flip flops." In an effort to represent a diversity of opinion on political issues within the gay community, the program denigrates the process of political action that has made programs such as *Will & Grace* possible, that has demanded the fair and accurate representation of gays and lesbians in the media. Will, the level-headed gay man, is only compelled to join Jack's protest out of loyalty to his friend, not out of political fervor or personal fury. His moderation is intended to appease conservative viewers, demonstrating that not all gay men are radical activists. However, the effect of his reticence is to make political protests for gay civil rights seem ridiculous. Jack is represented as unrealistic and politically untutored. When he refers to his constitutional right to see "two hotties get it on," Will inquires, "Would that be the constitution that begins, 'Weeee … [claps] the people?'" Later Jack mistakes Supreme Court Justice Ruth Bader Ginsberg for a man.

While waiting in the NBC office to speak with a spokesperson from public relations, Jack is joined by a homeless woman who hears voices in her head and who wants the network to bring back Carson. The positioning of Jack next to the crazy woman associates his protest with madness, revealing that the network receives a variety of suggestions from the lunatic fringe. When Will and Jack are finally addressed by the public relations representative, he informs them that the network's official response to the protest is "no comment," and then he adds that the "network has a responsibility to its audience" and that, consequently, there will never be a kiss between two gay men on network television. Despite the network's unresponsive position on the complaint, the spokesperson reveals that he too is gay and disappointed, but is also resigned to accept the intransigence of the media. The complicity of the executive implies that the network would be willing to televise such intimacy if it were socially permissible.

Retreating from the NBC office building, Jack and Will see Al Roker interviewing people on the street for the *Today Show,* and Jack decides to make his complaints public by getting the weatherman's attention. Will, however, decides to take more decisive action in order to appease his still complaining friend. Just as the cameras are focused on Jack, Will kisses him, effectively and unexpectedly achieving the first network kiss between two gay men. Of course, the kiss is laden with meaning, none of which is related to gay romance. The kiss breaches the divide between fiction and reality. While it accomplishes a portion of its intention within the fictional lives of the characters, it achieves even more within the social context of *Will & Grace.* The kiss within the show is limited to morning television, which is not prime time, one of the stipulations first set up at the beginning of the program. However, the situation comedy *Will & Grace* is aired at 8:00 pm on Tuesday (at the time this episode was first aired), so for the television audience the kiss is prime time. Here the social context of the situation comedy is prioritized over the televised fiction; the program becomes aware of itself as a cultural artifact, announcing, celebrating, and exhibiting a television first.

Nevertheless, the kiss is a political compromise in many important ways. What offends the puritanical American television viewer is not the kiss itself but the sentiment behind it. Will and Jack are not intimate within the context of the show, so the kiss between them is no more substantial than the exaggerated smack that men give each other when they want to show and negate platonic affection simultaneously, usually for the purposes of embarrassing the recipient. The kisser holds the recipients face with both hands while planting his lips on those of the surprised, resisting, and playfully humiliated partner. This is exactly the nature of the kiss between Will and Jack. To emphasize the fact that the kiss was not sincere affection, the verbal exchange that follows reveals Jack's vain belief that Will has a repressed desire for him. Ironically, the more Jack insists that Will desires him, the more certain the audience becomes that there is no queer sentiment behind the televised lip action. The kiss is discredited at other levels as well. The spokesperson for NBC says that there will be no kiss between two gay men, which, in fact, does not happen. While actor Sean P. Hayes is gay, actor Eric McCormack is not; thus the kiss is, in fact, not between two gay men. Moreover, in the past the unspoken rule in Hollywood has been that straight male actors can kiss on screen, while gay male actors cannot. In the embrace between straight males, there is little threat of authentic intimacy. Since the straight actor in *Will & Grace* is the aggressor, and the gay actor resists the kiss, the audience is given no context in which to imagine an intimate attachment between the two actors and/or the two characters. Consequently, *Will & Grace* televises a literal kiss but not a real kiss.

While the program is gay in much of its dialogue, it develops heterosocial bonds exclusively. Very little time is spent portraying gay relationships in any of the episodes, and there is seldom any same sex intimacy (kissing, hugging, etc.); when there is a focus on homosexual relations, the episodes frequently involve Jack, the clown, the character who is easy to dismiss. For both men the boyfriends are an absent presence. They plan and attend dates, but their partners seldom play a significant role in the episode, save when Will's ex-boyfriend asked Grace to decorate his new apartment. Both of the gay men are more intimate with women than with men. Indeed, the cast includes two male/female pairs, matched according to disposition.

The dialogue and imagery associated with Will and Grace, the couple, reveals a platonic marriage. They are a recognizable couple, double dating with Rob and Ellen and entertaining the respective parents. They shared an apartment for the first and third seasons. They go to therapy together, are very attentive of each other's moods, and bicker like an old married couple. The dialogue of the series constantly lampoons their relationship as a dysfunctional, sexless marriage. When they argue at Jack's fake wedding, the guest behind them asks how long they have been married and advises them to divorce. When they decide to get separate apartments, the episode is coded as a marital separation where the partners have been together so long that they cannot function as individuals. And when they visit their favorite professor after his retirement is announced, they discover a bitter old couple, a gay man and his female friend, indistinguishable from aging heterosexual married couples who fight and harbor a lifetime of resentment. Will and Grace recognize their own future in the couple. While Will's dates with men are made peripheral to the program's focus, the heterosexual relations of Grace with her boyfriends are more fundamental to the plot. Moreover, Grace and her boyfriends are occasionally shown in bed together, an image that has yet to be duplicated with two gay men in this gay sitcom.

Jack's marriage of convenience to Rosario is a parody of Will and Grace's relationship. It teaches the audience how to read the heterocentric indicators in the latter bond. The connection between Jack and Rosario both parodies the normative heterosexual marriage and is a bow to its universality. The humor of the situation lies in the improbable match between a vain and effeminate gay man and a "post-menopausal Salvadoran maid," and the subsequent parody surrounds Jack's futile effort to play the husband. The conclusion of the 1998/99 season depicts Jack's wedding to Rosario; the wedding is a staple season finale of many television series. The closing of the 1999/2000 season depicts Jack and Rosario's divorce after he finds her in bed with Karen's gardener on the couple's anniversary. He subsequently mimics the histrionics of the betrayed spouse. While the relationship between Rosario and Jack capitulates to the audience's demand for heterosexual intimacy exclusively, it also exploits that directive to its own destruction by demonstrating preposterous and farcical involvement of a gay man in heterosexual marriage. (Jack brings a male date to his honeymoon, his anniversary, and his divorce hearing.) Thus the relationship lampoons the demand for uniformity of passion at the same time that it surrenders to it. Jack's flirtation with women is not limited to Rosario. His relationship with Karen is also a foil to Will and Grace's. However, the bond between Jack and Karen is more intimate. The two greet each other with phrases generally reserved for romantic couples: "poodle" and "Who's your daddy?" Karen and Jack's relationship is in many ways coded as that of the "kept boy." Karen is rich and generous, and Jack exploits her for her money, although he does reveal a curious fascination with kissing her. Generally, in the scenes of intimacy between them, Karen becomes aroused, and Jack remains indifferent. When they make a sexual harassment video together, the shoot is disrupted because Karen is so overcome by Jack's kisses that she fails to play the reluctant victim. Moreover, Karen tries to console Jack after he becomes aroused by a female stripper, explaining that the incident was the result of mere friction. She sits on his lap and churns in order to demonstrate her theory. While the experiment has no effect on Jack, Karen becomes so excited she refuses to stop. Here again the imagery of heterosexuality has the effect of making the gay more palatable. It is a negotiation with the popular culture. Jack is allowed to be gay so long as he only kisses women.

The "gayness" of *Will & Grace* pivots entirely upon the production of camp humor, the playful interrogation of normative gender roles. Camp is the "total body of the performative practices and strategies used to enact a queer identity with enactment defined as the production of social visibility" (Meyer 5). It is a heightened sensitivity to "exaggeration, artifice, and extremity" (Bergman 4–5), and it frequently includes the application of gender specific language, attributes, and predicaments to members of the opposite sex. Camp allows *Will & Grace* to speak with two voices. Even when the program approaches heterosexual subject matter, it specifically appropriates gay humor, reminding the audience of its political program, which involves the increased visibility of gays and lesbians within the dominant culture. Camp creates an absent presence within the series, allowing gay sensibilities to be insinuated into an environment that, in all likelihood, would be hostile to explicit demonstrations of queer politics. Camp plays the same role among gays as the blues have played in the African American community, "turning our tortures into horrid arms," channeling rage and grief into the formation of cultural productions rather than destruction, disguising and sweetening the political outrage of the socially disenfranchised.

8

Rehabilitating the Camera:
Loquacious Queens and
Male Autism in *Flawless*

In the penultimate episode of CBS' summer series *Survivor* (aired 8/16/00), the host asks surviving castaway Rudy how he thinks he is being perceived by the public. As a former Navy Seal, Rudy immediately mentions his colleagues in the Navy. He asserts with confidence that "the entire seventh fleet is behind him." Inveterate schemer Rich questions Rudy's certainty: "Even after you said you liked the homo?" In order to save face with his audience, Rudy attempts to distance himself from Rich (the cast member with whom he has been allied for weeks) by asserting that when the program concludes he will shake Rich's hand and hope he "never sees him again." Rudy's curiously guarded response is a survival instinct calculated to eliminate the stigma of association. He has deemed it acceptable to ally himself with a homosexual in the pursuit of a million dollars, a circumstance in which any association with the socially marginalized can be justified by necessity. However, any expectation of a continued connection between the two men following their sojourn on the island might arouse a suspicion of intimacy. Traditional masculinity is constructed within our culture through the repudiation of homosexual interests. Thus Rudy makes a public gesture signaling his disapproval of Rich in order to disavow any unconventional sympathy between the two men and to assert his own observance of the demands and codes of hegemonic masculinity. In the final episode of the program, when he is voted off the island, leaving only two castaways, he dutifully falls on his sword, voting for Rich to win the game, but explaining that he made a pact and he was only living up to the agreement. In the wrap up show with Bryant Gumble, Rudy is asked about his homophobic slurs during the series, and he explains that he was only using the word "queer" so that his buddies in the navy seals would "know what he was talking about." When Rich defends him, indicating that the two had become very close in the thirty eight days, Rudy responds guardedly, "Not that close." Here again he has to disavow any intimacy between himself and a homosexual in order to save face with other men.

While most heterosexual males would elect to distance themselves publicly from a gay man and would be particularly emphatic in the denial of erotic interests, Rudy belongs to that category of masculinity even more demanding and restrictive than that characterizing the average male. Sociologist Roger Horrocks has coined the phrase "male autism" to define this category of hyper-masculinity: "a state of being cut off from natural feelings and expressiveness and contact with others" (*Crisis* 107). Rudy seems isolated even in the midst of isolation. He does not engage in the machinations and occasional histrionics of the other castaways. He established a single alliance and then sought to maintain it through thinly veiled threats that he would punish anyone who betrayed him. The threats effectively removed him from the game even in the midst of it. Indeed, the refusal to play may be considered his strategy, although it seems that he is simply unable to participate because involvement would reveal emotional vulnerability and undermine his masculine self-image. Rudy is mute, sullen, inhibited, and excessively rational. He will not participate enthusiastically in the tasks that the group is expected to complete each week. When asked to balance on a plank over water with the other castaways to win immunity, he jumps and wades back to shore. When asked to answer questions about Malaysian mythology in another bid for immunity, Rudy will not even guess. He places his public persona as a real man above all other considerations, including winning the million dollars. Perhaps he has allied himself with a gay man because a gay man will be too frightened to betray an ex–Navy Seal in the event that the two are the remaining survivors. His approach to the game is predicated upon a basic, perhaps even unconscious, sense of superiority, an imperviousness that will not even allow him to demean himself by participating in the game he expects to win. Rudy's masculinity is a performance, one that recognizes an audience who will evaluate the seeming authenticity of his manhood, and even in the contestation over a million dollars the maintenance of masculinity is a priority.

Horrocks further describes those men who embody "male autism":

> ...he has learned to be emotionally reticent, to be over-rational, to leave feelings to women, to use logic in arguments instead of his own passions... [109]. He cannot be tender or loving; he cannot be angry.... He doesn't know how to be intimate. He is frozen, remote, and austere [110].

The purpose of this definition and many other aspects of men's studies is to demonstrate how men are often victimized by cultural expectations of masculinity, and not just gay and/or effeminate men, but macho men as well, who are obliged to restrict their appreciation of life, to cut themselves off from many joys, and to constantly prove their worthiness in order to maintain credibility as a "real man" (Beneke 43). Men's Studies reveal that masculinity and femininity are performative, not the inevitable byproducts of nature and anatomy (Butler 141). The single behavior that effectively interrogates the equation of gender with nature and exposes the theatricality of gender specific codes is, of course, cross-dressing. Gay male camp is not only an imitation and parody of femininity, but also a demonstration of the artificiality of gender practices, including masculinity. It ruptures the seemingly natural and inevitable equation between sex and gender. Thus Rudy's compulsive and restrictive masculinity is as counterfeit as the flamboyant theatricality of Ru Paul Charles.

Among the many films about cross-dressers that have been produced in the past decade, Joel Schumacher's *Flawless* seems to be particularly conscious of the connection between female and male impersonation. When I say "male impersonation," I do not refer to women's gender bending, but to the way in which men perform masculinity. *Flawless* features a drag queen and a hyper-masculine male, and, forcing them into close proximity and into an uneasy alliance, the film dramatizes the hostility between antithetical masculinities, revealing the vicissitudes of their acquaintance and literalizing the metaphor of the "autistic" male as defined by Horrocks. The juxtaposition of oppositional personalities is contrived to elicit sympathy and tolerance for the socially marginalized drag queens from both the film's characters and its audience.

Walter Koontz (Robert DeNiro) is a former policeman who was granted an early retirement for his heroism: He saved two additional police officers and fourteen civilians from a hostage situation. The camera establishes Walt as the center of the film from its earliest images, as it mixes shots of Walt and a group of friends playing handball with images of a theft and the resulting chase across the rooftops of the neighborhood. The camera follows Walt as he moves along the street, meeting and greeting his neighbors with familiarity and enthusiasm, and subsequently reveals the respect and influence he enjoys within the community. The fluid movement of the camera between Walt's activities and the pursuit of a local thief is designed to reveal the forced, uneasy, and volatile proximity of the respectable and the illicit within the neighborhood, thus collapsing the comfortable spatial divide between the lawless and the law-abiding (or even law-enforcing, in Koontz' case). The cinematic sequence of the opening credits ushers both the local hero and the thief into the same tenement house, thus initiating the conflicts of the principal narrative.

The eclectic mix of personalities living in close quarters is complicated further by the presence of a drag queen in an apartment adjoining Koontz'. Rusty is a talented female impersonator who is MC at a local club, who plays the piano, and who directs a cast of flamboyant drag queens. While he is feminine, he is not passive, but caustic, fearless, and defensive, with an abusive tongue and a legion of colorful expressions. When Walt hurls abuse through his apartment window at the practicing queens, Rusty responds in kind, "The gay community thanks you for your support, Fucker," and then sings even louder.

Following their initial exchange of hostilities, Rusty and Walt begin their respective preparations for a night out. The montage of images that follow are intended to create a parallel between two diametrically opposed personalities. Both men undertake their complicated beauty rituals in front of the mirror while the camera occasionally wanders to adjoining areas to reveal the mementos and keepsakes that define them. Walt shaves and grooms in front of the bathroom mirror, and the camera scans bowling trophies, a medal for bravery, a picture of Walt and his police buddies, and a framed newspaper headline that says "East Side Hero." Rusty applies his makeup in front of a lighted mirror surrounded by cosmetics and memorabilia: lipstick, nail polish, perfume bottles, and a picture of Elizabeth Taylor. While Walt puts on his jacket, Rusty wraps himself in a shawl, and, leaving their respective apartments, they confront each other on the elevator, inciting Walt to take the stairs. The parallels do not stop with the grooming. Each individual proceeds to his favorite night club where they are both the source of others' admiration. Rusty officiates at the evening's drag show, engaging in a witty repartee with an audience member, to the amusement of the other guests. Walt reveals his success with women, acquiring a partner without effort and dancing the Tango while the other club patrons show their appreciation by standing aside and watching. The beauty rituals and the club scenes are intended to suggest a parallel between the artificiality of the drag queen's feminine performance and the masculine posturing of a traditional male.

The structural techniques designed to demonstrate the similarities between Rusty and Walt are also intended to expose some key distinctions. Both men encounter their desperate neighbor Amber Garcia Sanchez in the lobby of the apartment building; however, Walt abruptly dismisses her as a prostitute, while Rusty obligingly distracts Mr. Wilcox at the front desk so that Amber can sneak her thieving boyfriend (the same in the opening credits sequence) up to her apartment. Later it is revealed that

Flawless dramatizes antithetical masculinities and demonstrates that men of differing backgrounds can find terms upon which they can be mutually supportive. Robert De Niro, *left,* plays Walter Koontz, a former police officer and homophobe, while Philip Seymour Hoffman, *right,* plays Rusty, a flamboyant drag queen.

both men pay for sex, yet Rusty acknowledges that there is no "romance without finance" and supplies his married lover with gambling money, while Walt convinces himself that his financial contributions to Karen's rent money are merely voluntary and charitable. The defining difference between the two men is that Rusty displays a compassion traditionally associated with the feminine, immersing himself in the lives and concerns of others, while Walt imperiously imagines himself to have risen above the vulgarities of his environment. Rusty is associated with the seedy and illegal underworld of the neighborhood, a representation of the social outsider. Koontz, on the other hand, embodies the law and white, heterosexual, male privilege at the same time that he is not at all affluent.

The complication within the narrative occurs when Mr. Z, the drug dealer, kills Amber and her boyfriend in order to retrieve his money. A compulsive hero, Walt attempts to rescue the victims but suffers a stroke on the stairs instead and becomes partially paralyzed on one side of his body, no longer able to articulate clearly or walk without laboring. His condition becomes a metaphor for his hostility and uncommunicative-ness, literalizing the condition that Horrocks defines as male autism. Walt was not gregarious and talkative before his injury. When confronted by people he found objectionable, his response was silence or a single dis-missive comment. When the drag queens tease him in front of the eleva-tor, he silently chooses to take the stairs. When Amber makes a gesture of friendship to him in front of the building, he tells her to save it for her "paying customers" and ignores her. Tia asks him why he never dances with her, and he explains, "because you're a whore." She denies the accu-sation, but he turns away from her with his sarcastic retort, "Oh, you're not?" Walt encounters Rusty in full drag on the elevator, and he cannot even bring himself to hurl abuse, once again silently taking the stairs.

When Walt does elect to speak with his neighbors, he is generally lim-ited to vituperation or monosyllabic utterances. He shouts at the drag queens across the courtyard, but he does not invite rebuttal or conversa-tion. Instead he tries to shut them out by closing the window after his ini-tial barrage of insults. The neighbor whose company he appears to enjoy is the only other white male resident, a lovelorn drug dealer and crooner. Even here he can only offer a few sentences, and his comments are not without judgment. He tells the neighbor that his girlfriend appears to be underage.

Walt is an embittered homophobe, although he is only verbally abu-sive toward gays. He has a collection of colorful insults with which to degrade Rusty: "Fucking Faggot," "cocksucker," and "girly man." How-ever, his contempt for gay men, particularly drag queens, is directly related to his contempt for women. Sociologist Lynn Segal has identified homo-phobia as another manifestation of traditional sexism, of men's hatred of women. It is the hysterical fear of discovering female attributes (especially feminine desire) in a man (158). Walt's behavior embodies the polarities of the whore/madonna complex in which women are dichotomized between saints or devils. He regards Karen as a refined lady, while he treats Tia contemptuously, and when he complains that Tia is a whore, his friend Tommy reminds him that all the women at the club are whores. Even when Tia tries to create an honest relationship with Walt, he assumes that she wants his money. He has very clear ideas of appropriate behavior of gender performance, and these rigorous expectations keep him from eval-uating others compassionately. Tia is not a lady because she does not appear to be, and Rusty is neither man nor woman. However, the progress of the narrative is didactic. Walt must be taught to see beneath superficial gender roles, to appreciate the person beneath the dress— male or female. Ironically, Walt learns how to treat a lady through his interaction with

Rusty. When he comes to accept Rusty as a person and as a woman, he also recognizes that he has been unfair to Tia and makes a romantic gesture toward her.

Male autism has a public element that influences personal relations (Horrocks 107). The traditional male is hyper-conscious of the necessity of disassociating himself from homosexuality, from any taint of femininity or vulnerability. Walt is embarrassed about his paralysis. In a brief time he degenerates from a very physical individual who commands the respect of others to an invalid who requires sympathy and assistance. His single adventure out of the building to see a physical therapist ends on the curb in front of his apartment, where he falls trying to hail a cab and creates a spectacle of pity. He is infuriated by the loss of his independence. When Rusty tries to assist him in the laundry room, Walt guards his little remaining self-respect with verbal abuse, driving Rusty away because he cannot abide the compassion of a person for whom he has developed so much contempt, and a contempt, moreover, predicated upon his unflagging sense of superiority. His decision to seek Rusty's assistance as a speech therapist is not a surrender of his public persona but an effort to maintain it. Since he has no respect for Rusty, he overcomes his fear of being vulnerable around him. In his view, Rusty is the only person who is more pathetic than himself. However, his association with the drag queens does become an embarrassment when one comes to visit while he is entertaining his police buddies.

The autistic male is also prone to compulsive displays of masculinity represented through heroic actions, and these actions are a portion of the individual's public performance. Manhood requires constant proof; one is "only as masculine as the last demonstration" (Beneke 43). The heroic action need not be motivated by concern for the distressed, but can be an act of self-promotion, an effort to prove once again one's worthiness as a man. Both times that Walt climbs the stairs of his apartment building to rescue a neighbor, he is driven less by solicitude than by duty and impulse. He has shown contempt for Amber the same evening she is killed, and he has had a falling out with Rusty and tries to ignore the sounds of Mr. Z's assault on him. Walt is incapable of ignoring distress even after he is no longer physically capable of offering effective assistance because he is compelled to reproduce the most profound affirmation of his masculinity — his rescue of his buddies and the fourteen hostages.

One of the most important projects of men's studies is to demonstrate that males themselves are the victims of culturally constructed and rigid notions of manhood, and not exclusively in the most ostentatious ways, such as the violent cultural prohibition against femininity in men.

Walt is a victim of compulsory masculinity as much as an agent of its imposition. Performing masculinity often involves shutting oneself off from entire aspects of life that are retrograde to hegemonic masculinity (Horrocks 25). Walt's behavior is restricted by the rigorous demands of proving his manhood. Following his accident, he cannot ask for or accept help from others because he is afraid to reveal vulnerability. He is too proud to allow his friends to see him in his debilitated state, so he will not return their phone calls or agree to meet them, nor will he leave the apartment to seek the assistance of a physical therapist because he is embarrassed to be seen in public. He is emotionally disengaged because he cannot express his grief or share his feelings with others. Rusty is not an acceptable agent for Walt's rehabilitation, although he is conveniently situated, since straight men are obliged to disassociate themselves from gay men in order to avoid the mere suspicion of sexual impropriety. Heterosexual masculinity is defined through its opposition to homosexual desire, and the separation is imperative to the maintenance of distinctive gender categories.

Walt's disability is the catalyst that draws together these otherwise repelling personality types. Rusty has one of the skills requisite to Walt's rehabilitation, and when they agree to work together, the power imbalance between the straight man and the gay man has been reversed. The social outcast whom hegemonic masculinity will not countenance is thrust into the position of power, and Walt has to subordinate himself to the individual with whom he previously could not even speak, save in curses. Ironically, Rusty's task is to teach Walt to speak clearly, but also to speak with respect to those different from himself. The process is a metaphor for the rehabilitation of the straight male in his relationship to gay males. Rusty teaches the language of social tolerance, which is, interestingly, music or singing, a traditional representation of lightheartedness, a point emphasized more clearly by their repeated rehearsal of the ridiculous "Banana-fana." As they begin their lessons, the single exception to Walt's inability to express himself is verbal abuse; the initial lesson degenerates into name calling, a verbal exchange in which Walt can be plainly understood. The continued lessons not only bring about improvements in speech clarity but also an increased tolerance and personal openness. Walt learns to appreciate Rusty's feelings and to share his own. He listens sympathetically as Rusty tells of his dead mother's disappointments and of his intentions to undergo a sex change operation, and Walt offers an account of the loss of his wife and the betrayal by a work buddy. Increasingly, Walt is able to relate to the drag queens as women rather than as failed and misguided men, gender subversives unable or unwilling to abide with culturally imposed gender roles. Along with his increased personal tolerance is a growing acceptance of a public association with gay men. By the time the drag queens throw him a graduation party, he has overcome any embarrassment over his association with them. The final disagreement between the two men reveals the extent of Walt's acceptance, and this despite the homophobic curses that ensue. Walt recognizes that he was Rusty's cover for the stolen money. Rusty would draw the suspicion of the drug dealers if he showed signs of any new affluence, so he agreed to help Walt in order to appear to need money desperately. Walt is offended by the revelation, and his disappointment exposes his victimization. He accuses Rusty of having "used" him, an expression commonly associated with romantic betrayal. The ability to admit that a drag queen could exploit him also signals a reversal in his former masculine bravado. Prior to his transformation, male pride would have deterred him from any admission of susceptibility or injury, particularly at the hands of an effeminate and passive gay man. The reversal can be accounted for in his growing acceptance of gay men's humanity.

The film does not concentrate exclusively on the victimization of heterosexual men by the restrictions and limitation of rigorous gender codes, although such an angle may constitute the novelty within the character development. *Flawless* also visits the common theme of the victimization of gay men by an unsympathetic culture where even the drug dealers and murderers can enjoy a greater level of social acceptance. Jack Babuscio, in "Camp and Gay Sensibility," suggests that camp humor transforms rage and bitterness into laughter, the rage and bitterness that results from social stigma and discrimination (28). Thus camp plays the same role that the blues have played in African American culture. Both are vehicles for the conversion of anger and potential violence into creativity and art rather than destructive action, and both are an exclusive language for the conveyance of social protest by disempowered people, those who have no voice and few advocates within the dominant culture. The most prominent manifestation of camp is gay drag, one of the strategies whereby gay men "declare the conventions of masculinity oppressive" (Segal 146). Much has been said about the potential parody of women within male transvestitism, but the behavior is actually a rejection of more traditional males. Just as Walt defines his masculinity in opposition to "faggots," Rusty revolts against the high drama of machismo, which is every bit as much a performance as queer drag. Donning women's vestments is a repudiation of men, not women. Rusty's humor is often self-deprecating, but it is also defensive; it involves an acknowledgment that his power lies in language, in satire and irony, not in brawn. During his drag show, he derides a more masculine male:

> Don't come any closer. Guys like you beat my ass as soon as I leave
> the club. You love me when I'm here, but as soon as I leave, you beat
> the shit out of me. I want you to bend over now. I want you to kiss
> my ass.

The playful insults concede to an absence of the physical prowess and self-reliance that most men cultivate and rely exclusively on wit, wisdom, and humor. The film suggests that Rusty has cultivated verbal and intellectual power in the absence of physicality, while Walt has substituted the physical for the intellect. Rusty has a clever rebuttal and/or wise aphorism for each emergent occasion; Walt, on the other hand, is confined to the verbal equivalent of grunt and clicks, punctuated by violent physical rage. His disability creates an ideal circumstance for the domination of Rusty's personal virtues, and, subsequently, Rusty is able to transform a devoted homophobe.

The capacity of transvestites to revolutionize their environment and to rehabilitate those around them is well documented in popular cinema. The flamboyant queens of Beeban Kidron's *To Wong Fu* awaken a small Midwestern farming community from its dull stupor, making the local denizens more stylish, more romantic, and more fabulous. They liberate a housewife from an abusive relationship, reform violent gay bashers, and facilitate romance all over town. Chi Chi, the Latino transvestite played by John Leguizamo, even teaches an awkward and inexperienced young man, Bobby Ray, how to woo a lady. Their residence in the sleepy town is partially motivated by their desperate effort to hide from officer Dollard, the representation of patriarchy and the single unredeemable and unrepentant homophobe in the film. He hopes to prosecute the drag queen Vita for her assault upon him, perpetrated when he tried to molest her following a routine traffic stop. Officer Dollard, whose name is repeatedly mispronounced as "dullard," constitutes the antithesis of the transvestite's style and flare. Similarly, the Australian film *The Adventures of Priscilla, Queen of the Desert* depicts the transformation of the Australian outback by three drag queens from Sydney journeying to the remote town of Alice Springs. Their passage through the desert is incongruous with the stark and lifeless surroundings. Yet they enliven an aboriginal village and a rural tavern, repel violent homophobes in a degraded mining town, and even manage to find romance. In Mike Nichols' film *The Birdcage*, a gay man and his transvestite partner promote a heterosexual union between their son and the daughter of a conservative Senator. The clash of the traditional and non-traditional families results in the transformation of both. The non-traditional family must appear more conservative, altering its behavior and its surroundings in order to advance the marriage arrangements, and the right-wing Senator must disguise himself in women's clothing in order to escape the gaze and pursuit of curious reporters. Here again the representation of the unyielding and unsympathetic law is forced to recognize and appreciate the power of gender bending.

In *Flawless* Walt is forced into a similar recognition. The process whereby he comes to accept Rusty as a person and even as a woman also includes a compromise of his machismo. Just as Rusty escaped his enraged boyfriend by hiding behind the steel reinforced doorway of his bedroom, Walt will later escape the violent drug dealers whom, prior to his accident, he might have succeeded in confronting directly. Rusty has had to employ subterfuge, masquerade, and cunning his entire life in order to escape the violence of heterosexual men; thus he has developed skills of survival that circumvent direct physical encounters. Walt has previously been able to compete with desperate and violent men on their own terms, yet his disability has altered the circumstances of this interaction. Walt must learn to employ the tactics of the socially marginalized and the physically unfit. He escapes from Mr. Z by employing the same tactic Rusty used to escape his boyfriend, a relationship that acknowledged the physical superiority of a dominant male. Moreover, Walt only escapes Mr. Z through Rusty's own act of heroism and courage. While Rusty cannot effectively fire a gun to rescue the imperiled Walt, he does manage to brave the precarious catwalks of the apartment's exterior in order to bring a gun to his friend trapped in the bedroom. Thus each man borrows from the other's repertoire of survival skills in a constructive compromise of antithetical masculinities. Rusty becomes a flawed hero for the first time, and Walt is force to recognize, even in the midst of heroism, that he no longer is one.

Walt also accepts Rusty's advice in the pursuit of romance. Disheartened because he believes that women will no longer want to sleep with him, Walt accepts Rusty's advice that he pursue those women who still find him attractive. Walt is subsequently able to distinguish between true affection and insincere and superficial displays of romance. The same circumstances that force him to see beneath the superficial vulgarities of Rusty and to obey the pretenses of a false and rigorous propriety also inspire him to reevaluate Tia, whom he had previously condemned as a whore. Rusty's encouragement leads to what in all likelihood is the most fulfilling romantic involvement since the breakup of Walt's marriage. Walt and Tia actually talk about their feelings after having sex. In his previous involvement with Karen, the only post-coital chatter addressed the exchange of money. His association with Rusty has reconstituted and reformed Walt on multiple levels. His new loquaciousness creates a Shakespearean paradox: He could not speak until he was mute.

The transformation of Walt has a social dimension. The subject of this book is the examination of gay and lesbian film as social action, and few of the enclosed films are as direct in pursuit of this project as *Flawless*. The incongruous mixing of filmic genres to include action, romance, comedy, and drama is clearly an effort to generate a crossover film that will appeal to a broad audience and an audience that is not generally gay friendly. Such an objective may be partially achieved through the inclusion of Robert De Niro, who is frequently cast in large budget Hollywood action films and who appeals to young, working class, heterosexual males, the single group most hostile to gay men. De Niro's work includes frequent portrayals of cops and mafia kingpins, as well as other violent and illiberal souls. Moreover, as the Joe Pesci Show parody on Saturday Night Live reveals, De Niro is perceived as simple and monosyllabic. Thus it would appear in *Flawless* that De Niro was cast to play and reconstitute himself, or at least his most common public image, and Walt's progressive reformation is to be replicated by his audience.

The techniques used to film the show reiterate the political agenda of the narrative. At the beginning of the film the camera shares Walt's squeamishness toward gay men and drag queens. It identifies so completely with Walt's point-of-view that it limits the access of the audience to the noisy queens who are the objects of its hostile gaze. While it follows Walt home from the park, it only glimpses the collection of queens moving toward the apartment building. The first annoying outburst of raucous singing emanating from Rusty's apartment is received only through Walt's window. Even the source of the disturbance is obscured by distance and window shades. The movement and placement of the camera embodies Walt's narrow-mindedness, his tunnel vision. When he shuts out the noise, he deprives the camera and the audience of a more complete knowledge of the disturbance. The cinematic metaphor generated here recreates America's demeanor toward gay men. The mainstream American populace regards the gay community as a disturbance that violates the peace and comfort of their insulated lives, and instead of desiring to learn more about this disturbance, America, like Walt, tries to shut it out without first gaining any understanding. Rusty's sarcastic response to Walt's curses are particularly appropriate to the broad cultural understanding of their interaction at this moment in the film: "The gay community thanks you for your support, Fucker."

The metaphor of exclusion represented by the camera is continued until Walt is forced to seek speech therapy from Rusty. With the exception of the brief glimpses of his make up rituals, the camera only encounters Rusty in public places, such as the hallway, the elevator, the subway, and the communal laundry room. It only follows the heterosexual male into Rusty's apartment and, by extension, into his personal life. So there is always an element of judgment involved even when his apartment is invaded by desperate drug dealers. The camera peeps out of cracked door-ways into the hallway occupied by a parade of eccentric characters, and it looks through open windows. It follows Walt rapidly through the apartment lobby, avoiding sustained contact with others and revealing their troubled lives only peripherally. Even when it concentrates on Rusty's act, it only divulges his public persona. Perhaps the most meaningful example of the camera's heterocentric myopia is the fact that Rusty is not named until late in the film. The only indication of Rusty's identity is a show bill emblazoned with the name "Busty Rusty," and even that name is merely his stage name and his public role. The audience does not know what he calls himself in an informal situation because the audience is not allowed a familiarity with him until Walt establishes it.

When he becomes desperate enough to retain a speech therapist, Walt knocks on Rusty's door, and eventually the camera follows Walt into the drag queen's apartment, revealing a room elaborately decorated with the gaudy trappings of Rusty's profession. Decked in veils and beads, the room itself is in drag. While Walt's apartment exposed the spartan simplicity of his minimalist life, Rusty's room signifies the colorful insulation of his imaginative existence. The sensory overload of the environment, Rusty's flamboyant mannerisms, and Walt's aggravated contempt bring the first lesson to an abrupt and histrionic conclusion. The camera retreats from the room with Walt, hesitating in the doorway, gazing inward as the two hurl insults at each other. Gradually, as Walt acclimates himself to Rusty and his environment, the camera becomes more comfortable, even venturing into Rusty's abode unaccompanied by Walt. In effect, the camera becomes more open to Rusty and all that he signifies. This interaction between Walt, the camera, and Rusty reenacts Hollywood's growing acceptance of gays and lesbians on film. *Flawless* includes two actors from opposing generations, one (Robert De Niro) who has had a long and successful career appealing to the mainstream audience, and another (Philip Seymour Hoffman), a relative newcomer, who has played smaller roles and who is a more versatile actor. De Niro signifies Hollywood's preoccupation with promoting hegemonic masculinity and gender conformity, while Hoffman can, and frequently does, portray weak males (i.e. his role in *Boogie Nights*). The camera's acceptance of Rusty, both through its movements within the film and through the existence of the film itself as a cultural artifact, dramatizes the emergence of a new gay friendly Hollywood cinema. However, at the same time that the mainstream film industry embarks upon more daring artistic enterprises, namely those positively depicting the socially marginalized, it also appropriates traditional star power to ensure economic success, hoping to coax the audience into a more progressive and compassionate view of the social outcasts by offering a model for reformation, a traditional male point-of-view rehabilitated.

However, the camera is coaxed into Rusty's apartment because that is where the stolen money is hidden. Rusty has agreed to the lessons only because he hopes to create a diversion for desperate drug dealers searching for their money. If he is trying to take in extra money through additional employment, then he is less likely to reveal his new financial independence. Thus the camera follows the money into Rusty's life, a potentially over-determined metaphor for Hollywood's understandable preoccupation with profit margins. Films such as *Flawless* only get made when they promise a return on investments. Hiding the money in Rusty's female body suit signifies the marketability of transvestites, as *To Wong Fu, The Birdcage,* and *Priscilla, Queen of the Desert* revealed previously. Drag queens sell because they are amusing and because they confirm stereotypes. The mainstream Hollywood audience is not nearly so comfortable with sentimental portraits of the average gay man.

Hollywood's singular fascination with transvestites when it decides to make films about gay men may be interpreted as regressive and even homophobic because it suggests that all gay men are drag queens or are frivolous and effeminate; yet, the representation of drag queens constitutes a "strategy of inclusion" (Dollimore 51). The narrative negotiates with the dominant culture to generate an art form that promises a mainstream audience for a narrative of social protest. The dominant culture is uncomfortable with the conformity of gay men because it erases the clear gay/straight dichotomy of masculinity and obviates the possibility of sexual deviation in all men. Transvestites are actually less transgressive because they dramatize the predicted femininity of gay men and can be conveniently stigmatized and dismissed. However, *Flawless* does demonstrate that the femininity of gay men is not uniform. The inclusion of gay republicans, depicted as masculine and traditional, dressed in business suits, reveals the effort of some members of the gay community to obtain social respectability through exaggerated conformity. The gay republicans are constructed as the visible opposition to the transvestites, their masculine performance as much a manifestation of drag and camp as the queens' sartorial choices. The republicans want to eliminate drag from the upcoming gay pride parade in order to depict the gay community as safe, obedient, and conventional. However, Rusty quickly points out that sartorial conformity does not guarantee acceptance by the mainstream. He reminds the gay republicans that Bob Dole returned their campaign contribution in order to appease religious conservatives and adds that their fantasy of inclusion is a political ruse; they are invisible and every bit as marginalized as transvestites so long as they continue to engage in queer sex. Moreover, the success of films such as *To Wong Fu* and *The Birdcage* argues that gay republicans are wrong in their assumption that visual gender will win civil rights faster. It is drag queens that the public love (even as they simultaneously disapprove), and thus drag queens are the vehicle for representation and inclusion in popular culture.

The inclusion of images of gay masculinity are useful insofar as they demonstrate diversity and the potential for conformity within the gay community, and it is indeed true that the resolution of the film involves a rehabilitation and convergence of antithetical masculinities. However, Rusty's own conformity is not so great that he must become a republican and dress in conventional men's clothing. His capitulation necessitates he embrace biological masculinity and platonic male bonds. His decision to use his sex change money to pay for Walt's emergency care is an affirmation of masculinity. When Walt acknowledges the selfless act, "Good thing you didn't cut your balls off yet," his commentary has dual significations. It is first a recognition of the availability of the money which would have been spent had Rusty gone through with the operation, but it is also a recognition of Rusty's bravery, employing the vulgar association between masculine performance and "balls." The implication is that Rusty would not have been able to assist in Walt's rescue within the apartment building had he completed the sex change process. Walt's own capitulation is represented in his assertion that Rusty is a family member and thereby entitled to an ambulance ride, as well as a place within American society. Rusty does not claim to be a brother, but a sister. Thus Walt's assent is an acceptance of Rusty's feminine gender performance. Walt is forced to broaden his conception of both masculinity and femininity and to find a place for gay men in his world view.

The film is more misogynistic than it is homophobic, and not because transvestitism is occasionally interpreted as a parody and degradation of women, but because the representations of women in the film are limited to prostitutes and female impersonators, and Walt's newfound respect for Tia does little to alter the preponderance of degrading images of women in the film. In addition, the statement "Good thing you didn't cut your balls off yet" suggests that women are ineffectual and incapable of bravery and physical exertion. However, the misogyny of the film may be partially rehabilitated in the same way that transvestitism is. The debate between the drag queens and the gay republicans indicates that gay men should be accepted on their own terms, even when those terms reveal no effort to assimilate with the dominant culture, and to accept inclusion on any other terms is to participate with and perpetuate homophobia. The representation of women in *Flawless* may be attempting to interrogate obligatory gender conformity by suggesting that a woman can be a prostitute and a lady, which is an accurate, if paradoxical, evaluation of Tia's character, just as it is accurate to accept Rusty as a man and a woman simultaneously. Tia may take money for sex, but she is nevertheless a decent and dignified woman, capable of experiencing intense passion, unlike her counterpart Karen, who conducts herself in a dignified fashion but is incapable of emotional commitment and vulnerability.

As Walt learns to speak again, he simultaneously learns respect for others, both women and gays. *Flawless* is thus an exemplum, progressively luring its audience into an acceptance of the humanity of gay men by offering a paradigm for the sympathetic transformation of the most close-minded and intransigent male bigot. The example literalizes the metaphor of "male autism," demonstrating how the emotionally unavailable and hyper-masculine male is redeemed. The juxtaposition of antithetical masculinities is not intended to prioritize one over the other, but to urge an effective compromise that borrows the virtues of each gender performance to create males better equipped to cope with the vicissitudes of their lives. The rehabilitation of Walt is also metaphorical for the increased acceptance of gay men and women in Hollywood cinema, as the camera's perspective broadens, evolving from a myopic identification with Walt's point-of-view to an enthusiastic embrace of the socially and sexually marginalized.

9

Queering the American Family

In 1999 the state legislature of Mississippi passed a bill banning adoption of children by gay couples or individuals. It was a curious decision, particularly for the most intransigently atavistic state in the union where no one would have endured the adoption of a child by a gay couple, male or female, even before the decision. The new law must, therefore, have an exclusively performative significance, publicly conveying the continued hostility of the state to what religious hysterics have characterized as the "gay agenda." The bill constitutes a continued effort to avert the formation of gay familial units, which are regarded by many as a destructive parody of the traditional nuclear family. The law banning adoptions is the second such decision, the first being the defense of marriage legislation outlawing gay unions, a bill signed by a governor who had been publicly separated from his wife for most of his term and who had been seriously injured in an accident driving home from an extra-marital affair with a woman in Memphis. Indeed, marriage needs a defense, but mostly from its principal participants. The gratuitous adoption legislation in Mississippi is grounded in a widespread, fallacious assumption that gays and lesbians are a danger to children, that children are more likely to become gay themselves or to become confused about gender difference if they have gay parents (Raymond 117). Of course, the recruitment myth that fuels so much hostility toward the gay community wrongfully assumes that gay parents will be more likely to molest their children than heterosexual parents. Such assumptions persist despite evidence to the contrary, and they can even continue to inspire official action by legislative bodies untouched by the contemporary world.

The damage to the child predicted by the detractors of gay parenting has consistently been contradicted by research into the subject. Instead of creating confused and emotionally disabled adults, gay parents have instilled in their children a highly developed appreciation for diversity and a recognition that the important factor in a relationship is not the gender of one's partner but the sincerity and endurance of one's love (Raymond 114–118). Even the incendiary assumption that the children of gay parents will be more likely to become gay because they are more tolerant does not seem to be true, although, admittedly, it is difficult for gays and lesbians to perceive more gay people as a negative eventuality. Children reared in gay households are not more likely to develop alternative sexual identities than those raised in traditional families (Lehr, 139), nor is there substantial evidence that gays have had distinctly different childhood experiences than their heterosexual counterparts (Beneke 160). Indeed when one considers that virtually all gay people were reared in households that were extremely hostile toward homosexuality, it becomes difficult to recognize an inevitable connection between the values disseminated within the nurturing environment and the sexual identity of the child (Lehr 139). Indeed the only conclusion that would be reasonable, based on a casual observation of the phenomenon of gay origins, is that heterosexual households are veritable factories for the production of queer identities.

The irrational fears for the safety and well being of children with gay parents have become the subject of much attention within popular culture, and particularly within the film industry. In the past ten years no fewer than three mainstream Hollywood movies have directly addressed the issue of gay parenting: *The Birdcage, The Object of My Affection,* and *The Next Best Thing.* While all three films adopt a progressive point of view, revealing the benign influence of gays and lesbians on children, they, like all queer cinema, also offer an alternative discourse on the subject that consistently interrogates the wisdom of gay parenting. The four films (all of which focus on gay males) indicate that the androgyny which the straight community finds so intolerable within gay men may be indicative of a nurturing quality that could make gay men more effective parents than are many heterosexual men. After all, our culture consistently values maternity over paternity in custodial disputes. The gay males in the above films are shown to be loving, nurturing, stable, and responsible parental figures. However, each of the films also offers a subtle critique of such domestic arrangements. From the child's perspective, the disadvantages could include a social stigmatization that inhibits his or her ability to gain full social acceptance because he or she was brought up in a non-traditional family, as is the case in Mike Nichols' *The Birdcage.* These examinations of non-traditional child rearing also offer warnings to the gay parents who may become emotionally bound to the child only to have their parental rights stripped by a disappointed and vindictive partner, a subject emphasized in both *The Object of My Affection* and *The Next Best Thing*. Thus, while all three films offer gay parenting as a viable and valuable alternative, they are not utopian in their progressive agenda. They examine the domestic arrangement with an appropriate level of cynicism, perhaps even enough to discourage a potential gay parent.

The Birdcage

Mike Nichols' *The Birdcage* (1996), an adaptation of Jean Poinet's play and film *La Cage aux Folles*, focuses on the social stigmatization of an adult child who comes from a nontraditional home. Val Goldman (Dan Futterman) is the child of two gay men who own a drag bar on Miami's South Beach. His biological father, Armand Goldman (Robin Williams), has had a long-term domestic partnership with Albert (Nathan Lane), the star of his drag show. The couple raised Val from infancy and are his only familial influence. The complication comes when Val decides to marry his college sweetheart, who is the daughter of a right-wing politician, Kevin Keeley (Gene Hackman), the co-founder of the "Coalition for Moral Order." While the film is very clear in its assertion that Val has had a loving and effective upbringing, it also reveals the potential damage to a child's prospects by such alternative arrangements, and while those who object to Val's home life are characterized as narrow-minded and hypocritical, the film, nevertheless, dramatizes at length the potentially harmful social impact of nontraditional familial arrangements.

In the opening scenes of *The Birdcage* the audience's expectations are consistently frustrated, revealing the unreliability of mainstream assumptions about gay relationships and gay narratives. The film viewers are first introduced to the histrionic gay couple, Armand and Albert, who quarrel like any long-married heterosexual couple. Albert fears that Armand is having an affair while the former is performing in the club downstairs. The audience is initially encouraged to accept Albert's view of Armand's preparations, all of which seem to suggest an impending romantic encounter. Armand prepares the room, adjusting furniture, pouring wine, and fidgeting nervously. When a young man enters and the two kiss and embrace, the accusations of infidelity appear even more credible until the audience learns that the scene which has been coded as a romantic encounter is in actuality a reunion of father and son. This revelation does not, however, bring an end to the audience's apprehensions. The visual connection that the scene makes between the romantic and the paternal invokes the most virulent fears of the heterosexual majority regarding gay parenting: the potential for inter-generational sex and incest. This fear, too, is quickly dispelled by the son's announcement of his decision to marry a "girl," but now the audience, who has been prepared for the potential hysterical reaction of the father by the son's warning, "I don't want you to get how you get," assumes that Armand will react negatively to the announcement of the potential partner's gender, a presumption based upon the heterosexual community's concern that gay parenting is an opportunity for the socialization of more gay youths. A portion of the tension is broken when Armand voices the common paternal concern, "but you're only twenty." To this point, the father has not voiced a clear opinion about the idea of his son pursuing a traditional heterosexual marital union. Thus the audience's concern that the father may desire the son to emulate his own lifestyle choices is not entirely dispelled and is even reinforced when he informs Val that he can expect no support if he follows through with the wedding. This final expectation is burst when the father reveals that he is bluffing and indicates that the potential wedding is the culmination of all his hopes for the boy: "I always dreamed you'd do this, just not so soon."

The technique that the director uses in the above scene reveals the necessary connection between the positive gay friendly discourse and the objections of the heterosexual majority. In his effort to reveal that Armand Goldman is a good parent, Nichols must allude to all the fears of the counter-discourse that constructs gay men and lesbians as a threat to children. Thus, in the initial scene Armand Goldman navigates all the most damaging presumptions about gay parenting to emerge as a loving father who has very conventional hopes for his child. The remainder of the narrative becomes a gloss upon the desire of the father to achieve a conventional life for his son through very unorthodox means.

The Goldmans are a parody of the bourgeois family, revealing the irrelevance of biological sex to gender performance. While both Albert and Armand are male, they, nevertheless, represent positions within the traditional gender hierarchy of marriage. Armand is the rational husband, constantly attempting to calm his emotional wife and mitigate the effects of her outrageous actions. Albert feels neglected by both husband and son and worries about losing her youthful attractiveness. Val recognizes that he has both a mother and a father, and he interacts with them in a fashion that reveals this gender difference. He confronts his father first about the emotionally charged topic of his marriage, assuming that Albert will become hysterical as soon as he hears the news, and, like most adolescent males, Val responds toward Albert's effusive affection with embarrassment. While Armand's role is stern and even occasionally forbidding,

Albert is extremely maternal. When she learns that Val has returned home, Albert goes out shopping for groceries to ensure that he is well fed, insists upon a welcoming kiss, offers motherly advice about marriage ("If you throw yourself away on some dormitory slut, you'll be sorry the rest of your life"), and laments the loss of her child: "Oh Armand, our baby is going to leave us and we won't have any others."

Albert's maternal nature addresses one of the most important concerns of gay male parenting, the fear that the child will not have any motherly influence. Albert is so feminine that he, despite his acting skills, is not even capable of impersonating a man convincingly. In conversation with Val's biological mother, Katherine (Christine Baranski), Armand explains that Albert is so maternal that he is "practically a breast," and he admits that he, too, is "very maternal." Moreover, the lifelong indifference of Val's biological mother further reveals that the relationship between sex and conventional gender roles is not inevitable. Val, at twenty, has never even met his biological mother, although she lives in the same city. The most compelling affirmation of Albert's feminine and maternal nature is voiced by Kevin Keeley, the radically conservative father of Val's fiancée, Barbara. When the families finally meet, Senator Keeley is convinced not

In *The Birdcage* Nathan Lane (*left*) and Robin Williams play longtime companions whose lifestyle is a parody of the traditional American family.

only that Albert is a woman, but also that he is the kind of woman that Keeley admires most, a conservative housewife. Defending her against his wife's doubts, he declares, "This girl is a lady..." and, "They don't make women like that anymore." When Val's biological mother arrives at the party unexpectedly, the Keeleys, confused by the sudden proliferation of mothers, ask Armand, "Exactly how many mothers does your son have?" The answer to the question is actually more complex than is at first apparent. The film suggests that the child of gay parents is, in some ways, at an advantage because each parent is a synthesis of both genders. The most masculine gay man may be more maternal than many heterosexual males, restricted by traditional gender conditioning, because a gay man does not accept the necessity of compliance with the dictates of rigid gender codes. The film suggests that Val has two fathers and three mothers, all represented by the varied attributes of only three people.

The most important issue associated with gay parenting is, of course, the welfare of the child, and *The Birdcage* is very careful to suggest that Val has turned out well — and not necessarily because he pursues a normative sex life, but because he is a person of integrity and tolerance. Most of the commentary on Val's maturity is designed to compliment his upbringing. When he is trying to convince his father to condone the wedding, Val cites his own good qualities and then offers his father credit for nurturing them:

> I have an incredible role model.... You've always said I was a very levelheaded guy. I'm the only guy in my fraternity who doesn't come from a broken home.

The comment specifically invalidates the common accusation that gay people are poor role models for children and that the children from such homes will have emotional problems and difficulty adjusting to the outside world, and this in a film where virtually every eccentricity would seem to reinforce the interrogation of gay guardianship. The discrepancy is resolved by the alternative interpretation of what it means to be a "good role model." While the expression itself is often employed to refer specifically to the parents' capacity to condition their children in traditional gender codes, *The Birdcage* emphasizes other important aspects of parenting, such as building the child's character and cultivating love and tolerance. Indeed, Val is not offered a commendation on his good character by another person until he is willing to acknowledge openly the sexual orientation of his parents and the true gender of his mother. When he finally informs the Keeleys that Albert is a man and is his mother, Katherine, his biological mother, offers her compliments to the boy and to Armand: "Very nice, you have done a nice job." This is a particularly important pronouncement because the biological mother is the single person who would have a legal right to interrogate the quality of Val's parenting. Moreover, the single act that earns her admiration involves courage and tolerance.

Initially, one might not associate the term "tolerance" with Val, who spends most of the film showing his disapproval of his eccentric parents, particularly for their gay qualities. When he discovers that his fiancée's conservative parents will be visiting, he embarks upon a panicked effort to change everything about his father and to eject Albert from the meeting altogether. He demands changes in the decor of a household that usually includes a phallic motif, and he reveals his disapproval of his father's mannerisms — walking and gesturing — both of which he believes are distinctly gay. His disapproval clearly serves as a counter-discourse to the gay friendly atmosphere of the home, offering the point-of-view of the straight conservatives in the film's audience; but, paradoxically, his displeasure also serves to highlight the camp humor in the film by accentuating those aspects of his parents lives that are the most queer. Camp humor is most funny when it is directed at a straight audience, when it involves the flaunting of gay identity in the face of a disapproving world. Just as the blues in African American culture constitutes a rebellion against racism, camp, in the gay community, is a coded revolt against the oppressive nature of gender norms. Val's efforts to clean up his parents only serves to demonstrate the depth of their gay identity. When Albert dresses in a suit in order to pass as a straight man, he recognizes that his sexuality is even more apparent than when he dresses as a woman. Val's insulting disapproval of his parents offers an opportunity for the father to demonstrate the extent of his love and indulgence. Armand goes to great lengths to accommodate his son's wishes, even after expressing his unwillingness to apologize for his lifestyle. He redecorates his entire house, alienates his longtime companion, and even enlists the assistance of Val's biological mother, whom he has not seen in twenty years. The single feature that most clearly redeems Val's behavior is his youth. His disapproval of his parents is coded as the expected adolescent rebellion. An adolescent can be embarrassed by even the most conventional parents, and the male child is particularly distressed by his mother's effusive affections. Thus the film reveals the normality of his life even in the midst of extreme eccentricity.

The quality of the Goldmans home is also developed through contrast to the Keeleys'. While the Goldmans are indulgent and self-sacrificing, Kevin and Louise Keeley are self-centered, viewing Barbara's wedding only as a political opportunity to repair Senator Keeley's damaged public image. This is particularly true of the father, who does not approve of the match until he recognizes its political utility. The Keeleys reveal that the extreme right wing of the political spectrum is every bit as eccentric as the left wing, and they demonstrate that conservatism does not guarantee good parenting. Unlike the Goldmans, the Keeleys are not willing to sacrifice their self-image or reconstruct their pubic image in order to accommodate their daughter's happiness. Senator Keeley complains, "I realize you want to get married, but how many lives do you have to ruin to do it." Only when the eccentric skills of the Goldman household are appropriated to aid Kevin Keeley's political ambitions is he able to condone the wedding. By dressing the Keeleys in drag, the Goldmans help them to escape *The Birdcage* undetected by reporters surrounding the building.

It is not only their sexual orientation that the Goldmans must hide from the Keeleys, but also their ethnicity and religion: they are Jewish. The family's religion is invoked to create a parallel to the persecution of gays and lesbians. *The Birdcage* dramatizes the practice of "passing," "a performance in which one presents oneself as what one is not, a performance commonly imagined along an axis of race, class, gender, and sexuality" (Rohy 219). "Passing" generally denotes the necessity of concealment arising from the impulse for self-preservation, the marginalized individual attempting to pass as heterosexual, Caucasian, or Christian in order to escape violence or discrimination. Of course, the experience of Jews in predominantly Christian Europe has been a history of periodic persecutions which necessitated that the religious minority conform to the faith of the majority in order to avoid discrimination, violence, or death. The organized efforts to force Jews to convert necessitated that they practice Christianity in public while remaining faithful to Judaism in private. The encounter between the Goldmans and the Keeleys invokes the tradition of Jewish passing. The visitation of the Keeleys is coded as a scrutinizing by the inquisition. It includes a panicked effort to conceal all ostensibly gay and Jewish artifacts within the Goldmans' apartment, which includes removing almost everything. The apartment is redecorated with a distinctly medieval, Christian, monastic motif, with a gigantic crucifix mounted in the sitting room, denoting the family's effort to feign Christian piety. The decor in the room shifts from flamboyantly gay to Christian camp, revealing that the gay Jewish family are not capable of impersonating Christian heterosexuals convincingly; they have no clearer an understanding of their visitors than their visitors have of them. The allusions to the forced conversion of the Jews creates an ignoble historical context for the persecution of gays implicit in the film, and specifically for the necessity that gays pass as straight in order to be fully enfranchised members of society. The scene reveals the Goldmans' devotion to their child through their willingness to renounce their religion to facilitate his happiness.

The film is constructed upon the juxtaposition of two families that occupy polarities within the political spectrum, the Goldmans representing the far left and the Keeleys the extreme right. The political allegory implicit in the resulting confrontation demonstrates that these seemingly antithetical positions are less remote from each other than a cursory glance might reveal. The film implies that the right and the left need to come together for the sake of the young, the country's future represented through the union of two rival households. Thus the marital negotiations of the film are reminiscent of the antiquated practice of arranging marriages for the purposes of political alliance. The complicity of the two families at the conclusion of the film is politically advantageous to each. The Goldmans help the Keeleys to escape the public stigma of being discovered in a drag bar, and the Keeleys bestow a level of social legitimacy on the Goldmans by allowing Val to marry into their family and by staging a public wedding that includes Val's eccentric relatives.

The Object of My Affection

While *The Birdcage* depicts a child who is an adult, Nichola Hytner's *The Object of My Affection* (1998) concerns a child that is still gestating. The film dramatizes the mother's search for an idealized mate with whom to raise the child and concludes that neither the biological father, Vince (John Pankow), nor the gay friend, George (Paul Rudd), constitutes an adequate mate for Nina (Jennifer Aniston) or appropriate father for her child. The screenplay of *The Object of My Affection*, written by Wendy Wasserstein, deviates substantially from Stephen McCauley's novel of the same name (1987). The alterations that were made in preparing the text for the screen offer some compelling insights into the subject of gay parenting and marketability of gay subjects in mainstream films.

Hytner's work deviates from other recent films on gay parenting insofar as it offers a less idealistic outlook on the practice. While George is certainly nurturing and loving enough to discharge his duties as a parent, there is some question as to his ability to offer the long-term commitment to the child that is requisite to parenting responsibilities. The portrait comes dangerously close to reinforcing the traditional homophobic view that gays and lesbians are too unstable and hedonistic to act

This image captures the dilemma that Nina (Jennifer Anniston) face in *The Object of My Affection.* She must choose between a supportive but disinterested gay man, George (Paul Rudd, *left*), and a boorish controlling straight man, Vince (John Pankow), for the father of her unborn child.

as responsible parents. George is rejected by Nina because he decides to add a boyfriend to the equation rather than commit himself entirely to a sexless union with a woman and a child that is not his own. The screenplay deviates meaningfully from the novel on this issue. In McCauley's novel, George's choice between Nina and Paul (played by Amo Gulinello in the film) does not involve a decision regarding parenting, since Paul has an adoptive Salvadoran child, Gabrielle. George's choice is not then between family and no family, between responsibility and personal fulfillment, but between the traditional family and the nontraditional family.

The contrast between the familial options have not disappeared from the film, but have shifted to register the alternatives open to Nina. While George's choices are central to McCauley's novel, Nina's are the moral compass of the film. The shift in emphasis probably capitulates to the predictable heterocentric bias of the movie audience who would not find the parental yearnings of a gay man very sympathetic. Nina's unconventional choices regarding her domestic arrangements, such as her decision to raise her child with a gay man, are contrasted with those of her sister who enjoys a more conventional familial arrangement, involving a child and the two biological parents. Nina's well-meaning yet meddlesome sister, Constance Miller (Allison Jannie), is determined to match her sister with some eligible bachelor who is capable of giving her both sex and companionship. When Constance complains about her pregnant sister being in love with a gay man, Nina argues that all marriage eventually turns into friendship and that hers will simply start out that way. The Millers are entirely the fabrication of the screenwriter, and their function is to offer a foil to Nina's decisions; however, their behavior is intended to suggest how unconventional the nuclear family can be and, by contrast, how conventional the nontraditional often is. The audience is forced to conclude that the Millers are scarcely an enviable domestic unit — narcissistic, self-absorbed, and constantly in a state of riotous upheaval. The peacefulness of Nina and George's flat seems an ideal environment for a child when compared to the boorish egoism of the Miller home, and the final images of the film reinforce this interrogation of the inevitable effectiveness of the normative family unit. A glimpse of the Millers' daughter, Sally, in the final scene of the film reveals her to be a demanding and discontented adolescent with unnaturally colored hair and multiple face piercings. The audience is forced to conclude that Nina's child, Molly, has a much better chance of being a well-adjusted adult despite the uncommon circumstances of her upbringing. Nina does, however, decide to break off her alliance with George, not because he would be a poor father, but because he cannot be Nina's lover. She replaces him with the African American policeman who helped her home when she had her purse stolen. Her final choice is a negotiation with her sister's view of normalcy. Nina has a partner with whom she can have sex and raise her child, but who nevertheless constitutes a less common choice, creating an interracial union.

While George's domestic dilemmas were evidently not sufficiently marketable for mainstream film, the screenwriter does take pains to reveal that George has the potential to be a very good father. On this subject the deviations from the novel actually serve to ennoblize George at the same time that they remove him as the center of interest. Filmic George is a very resourceful and professional grammar school teacher who has the respect, admiration, and trust of the parents. He confidently commands his environment, transforming mere children into talented performers in the school production of *The Little Mermaid* and demonstrating a sincere, platonic affection for his students that undermines negative stereotypes about gay men and children. Indeed, the male grammar school teacher is one of the stereotypical surrogate parenting roles commonly associated with gay men who wish to have children in their lives but who cannot or will not become biological parents (Bozett, "Gay Fathers" 3). George confesses that he envies the fathers who come and pick up their children every afternoon and wishes that one of the children was his own to raise, and it is this recognition that compels George to accept Nina's proposition that they raise her child together. When Nina rejects George as her companion and as her child's father, there is no suggestion that George might be an unfit parent or an inappropriate role model. Even Vince, angry because he has been rejected in favor of George, does not invoke arguments against gay parenting, but only interrogates George's ability to offer Nina romantic companionship.

The refusal to impugn George's parental skills is important in a mainstream film that does not wish to reinforce damaging platitudes about gay men through its characterizations; however, a novel that has overwhelmingly gay and gay friendly readers can afford to be more frank. McCauley's George is not nearly so responsible and professional as his filmic counterpart. The novelistic George is something of a spiritual drifter who wanders into the kindergarten job by accident when he overhears two schoolmates talking about the difficulty the principal has in finding male teachers. The decision is not at all motivated by a love of children, and there is little indication that he is particularly well suited to the job. Indeed, his capacity to act as an effective guardian is called into question when he is fired from his job for allowing a child to be picked up by his mother who does not have custodial rights and who proceeds to abduct the child. Paul impugns George's capacity to appreciate the emotional vulnerability of children. While George tries to decide between the traditional and the non-traditional family, his abandonment of Paul and Gabrielle has an emotional impact upon the child, who has grown to love him. However, George's eventual decision to embrace a gay lover rather than a platonic heterosexual bond does not constitute a repudiation of parental responsibility, as in the film, and the implication of the novel's conclusion is that George will make a loving and nurturing father to Gabrielle. Nina is given all of George's prerogatives in the film. She gets to decide between sex and shared parenting, or just shared parenting; this is George's dilemma in the novel.

The potential negative criticism that could be leveled against George (and, by extension, to gay men) for his decision to embrace romantic rather than paternal love in Hytner's film is mitigated by the actions and dispositions of the movie's other males, including heterosexuals such as George's brother Frank. McCauley's Frank is transformed for the movie into an amusing womanizer whose wedding at the end of the film results because he was trapped by his fiancée's pregnancy. He is the structural equivalent to Constance Miller, both committed to finding a permanent mate for their respective siblings and both inept in judging the appropriate partner. Both, however, want to match the sibling with a professional in order to encourage traditional bourgeois ambitions and values, and both have such dysfunctional relationships themselves that their roles as advocates for normative romantic relations (both heterosexual and homosexual) are rendered ridiculous. Neither has an enviable domestic life. Ironically, it is at Frank's wedding that Nina decides she cannot settle for the arrangement that she and George have created because she wants a domestic union that includes sex, romance, and ceremonial affirmation. The irony lies in the fact that Frank, except in a purely economic sense (as he is an MD), cannot be construed as an exemplary husband, nor is there much hope for a happy union resulting from a surprise pregnancy or a commitment to fidelity from a womanizer who was forced to marry, and yet Nina's desire for a romantic wedding is inspired by the occasion. George's decision to embrace sensuality rather than a sexless marriage and parental responsibility is foiled by the brother who, although he marries, cannot be said to have made a mature decision to suspend his hedonism, but is instead trapped by his own sensuality. George's decision to pursue Paul is only a repudiation of responsibility by default; any gay union, no matter how exclusive, is coded as promiscuous, since our culture refuses to recognize the legitimacy of such commitments. Nevertheless, George is committing himself to one person whom he loves.

Vince, the biological father of Nina's child, is developed as a foil to George. Indeed, Nina elects to raise her child with George because he retains none of the qualities associated with the boorish and controlling heterosexual male represented by Vince, who wants to make all of the decisions regarding the pregnancy and the child. Nina revolts against his arrogant domination, turning to George because he is supportive of her decisions; she believes that any man who does not force his opinions on her must be gay. Vince's character has been so completely altered from the novel's portrait that the screenwriter felt compelled to change his name from Howard. While Howard does try to micro-manage the pregnancy, he also dotes on Nina and has much more self-knowledge than Vince. Howard knows he is obnoxious, but he has none of the anger that Vince displays in the film, anger which results in confrontations, including hysterical accusations that George is sleeping with Nina. Unlike Vince, Howard never abandons his interest in the child because he is angry at the mother. George harbors a sincere affection for Howard and even facilitates the reunion of the biological parents at the conclusion of the novel, ending experimentation and restoring the traditional family unit to prominence.

The creation of a very unsympathetic biological father serves an important function in the gender ideology of the film. Initially, it allows for the alternative, gay unfriendly discourse to have a voice within the film. While, in principle, Vince is not a bigot, he nevertheless assumes that gays are immanently convertible; he patronizes George in the same way he does women, even attempting to bully him physically; and he offers some biting criticism of the way in which gay men mess up their female friends' relationships. Howard's character has been exaggerated in the creation of Vince so that the film will have a villain, and Vince's aggressiveness toward George generates an opportunity for the audience to repudiate irrational suspicion and hostility toward gays via their disapproval of Vince. However, the inclusion of such portraits can reinforce gay bashing by suggesting that a hysterical reaction toward gay men is a natural response of straight men, and by reinforcing the idea that homosexual and heterosexual men are diametrically opposed to each other. The novel includes none of the film's criticism of gay men. Vince's character becomes a capitulation to the popular opinion that all gay friendly discourses must include an alternative disapproving voice, and while Vince is not the traditional hysterical homophobe, he certainly retains many of the obligatory assumptions of such people; the inclusion of an angry and suspicious character who is a well-educated civil rights attorney may be even more damaging than the inclusion of a narrow-minded religious hysteric because it suggests that homophobia is inevitable even in trained minds.

Vince's rage signifies the mythical marginalization of straight white guys within mainstream culture, a movement presumably resulting from the increased social acceptance and prominence of gendered minorities, including the movement to empower and multiply women's choices in domestic arrangements. The polarization of George and Vince is calculated to alter *The Object of My Affection* from a gay political text to a feminist text, moving the focus of the narrative and the audience's sympathies to Nina's choices. In such a context, Vince and George's animosity initiates a masculine dialectic that includes Louis the African American cop as its synthesis and as the appropriate choice for Nina's domestic partner. As a heterosexual man he is mainstream, and as an African American man he is marginalized, retaining some of the revolutionary potential that was included in Nina and George's relationship. Like Vince, Louis is capable of offering romantic fulfillment, but, like George, he understands the necessity of allowing Nina to run her own life. The construction of masculine types in the novel implies that both homosexual and traditional heterosexual men are inadequate partners and fathers. Neither can fulfill the mother's needs.

Ironically, in the film *The Object of My Affection*, gay men are marginalized and displaced within their own narrative. The character Louis, who constitutes an improvement upon Nina's choice of George, is not included in the novel. Of course, the alterations are a compromise with popular culture, making the narrative more palatable to a crossover audience who would regard feminism and interracial romance as more acceptable than gay rights. While such capitulations are necessary to create an audience for a relatively gay friendly discourse, they nevertheless perpetuate the marginalized condition of gay men and reinforce the stereotype of gays as victims. The narrative does include a positive image of gay men as parents, since the rejection of George is exclusively over his inability to offer Nina sex and romance. However, the film broadens the focus of the gay parenting motif to address the broader value of alternative families. At the conclusion of the film, George directs a second play; this one includes Molly, Nina's child, approximately six years old, who is the star of the show and who is doted on by George, Vince, and Louis. The scene suggests that Molly has more than her share of fatherly attention; she has three fathers, all of whom are still in her life. She observes that more people came to see her performance than anyone else in the play, a remark which signals the beginning of a healthy self-image.

The Next Best Thing

While the split between George and Nina in *The Object of My Affection* is completely amicable, John Schlesinger's *The Next Best Thing* (2000) dramatizes a dispute between a gay man and a straight woman that deteriorates into litigation. The film is a cautionary tale revealing the pitfalls that gays and lesbians face when they elect to become parents, including the dangers of emotional involvement without the security of law. Schlesinger's film is overly sentimental and generally less effective than *Object*, yet it specifically improves upon the sexual politics of the earlier film. In *The Next Best Thing* the gay character is central to a narrative that focuses on his choices and is primarily sympathetic toward his emotional needs. Both films concentrate on the dissolution of a progressive domestic arrangement in which a homosexual male and a heterosexual female agree to keep house and raise a child in an atmosphere devoid of mutual sexual attraction and involvement, and both films offer a romantic entanglement as the complication that results in the disintegration of the previously blissful arrangement. However, contrary to *Object*, Schlesinger's film offers the straight parent's extra-domestic romance as the problem that dismantles the familial bond.

The argument of the film is similar to that of *The Object of My Affection*. An openly gay and well-adjusted man, Robert (Rupert Everett), decides to create an alternative domestic arrangement and raise a child with his best friend Abbey (Madonna). Like Nina, Abbey believes that a gay man will make a more nurturing and attentive father than will a straight man, and they both mistakenly believe that bonds of friendship will be sufficient to guarantee a lifetime of devotion. These agreements between friends work quite well until romantic partners complicate matters and jealousy begins to erode the alternative family. The significant difference between the two situations lies in the parental responsibility. The bond between George and Nina involves a conscious agreement to share parenting responsibilities, despite the fact that George has no paternal obligation to the child. Abbey and Robert, on the other hand, engaged in sexual intercourse during a drunken evening together, and for a time they both believed that the child Sam (Malcolm Stumpf) was conceived on that night, a belief that turns out to be false. Robert's decision to be the child's parent is at least partially motivated by the belief that he has a biological interest in the child, and he turns out to be an extremely devoted father. While in *The Object of My Affection* the child has not yet been born at the time most of the action takes place, *The Next Best Thing* concentrates upon the parent-child relationship, systematically raising and rejecting most of the objections to gay parenting.

As a work of art, the film is overly didactic in its methodical effort to demonstrate that Robert is a good father, so much so that one can easily believe the work was specifically conceived to counter misinformation on the topic of gay parenting. The film contains repeated testimonials to Robert's effective fatherhood. When Abbey's future husband, Ben Cooper (Benjamin Bratt), asks if Robert is a good father, Abbey responds, "the best," and after observing the relationship over an extended period of time, Ben agrees with the assessment and tries to reassure Robert that he does not intend to break up the family: "I'm not here to usurp your position. I think you're a great dad." Robert's own father, who was opposed to his son's paternity on the grounds that he (Robert) would not make a good role model for the child, changes his mind and offers money to fight for custody of his grandchild. Even the judge in the custody battle at the crisis of the film reaffirms the complimentary evaluation: "I know how deeply attached you are to this child and that you have been an exemplary parent...."

The cinematic imagery reinforces the testimonials regarding the close bond between father and child. Research into alternative parenting indicates that gay fathers are extremely solicitous toward their children

(Bozett, "Children" 45) and that they are often "more endorsing of paternal nurturance" than are heterosexual fathers (Bozett, "Parents" 15). Robert is frequently depicted hovering over his child in a maternal fashion. The imagery depicting the close proximity of father and son reveals not only the doting father's devotion, but also the son's comfortable attachment and security. The child is repeatedly depicted sitting on the father's lap. The relative absence of similar imagery involving the mother/child bond highlights the paternal relationship and reinforces the reversal of gender roles that is evident in the household. Robert's domestic role is by traditional standards androgynous. He cooks the family dinner, tucks the boy in at night, and offers him comfort and advice. The mother is shown working outside of the home after the child is born while the father keeps the house. The father is more emotional than the mother regarding the child's welfare. When Sam finds Ben in Abbey's bedroom, Robert becomes hysterical over the breach of propriety, while Abbey is confident the boy will not be harmed. by the experience. Although both parents have affairs outside of the home, Abbey's is clearly depicted as more disruptive of the familial union. Robert is content to place his domestic obligations before his romantic ones, but Abbey allows her involvement with Ben to alter her familial arrangement.

The film is not merely content to depict Robert functioning as a father; it must also address and discharge the common arguments against gay parenting. Among these is the suggestion that the child of a homosexual parent would be stigmatized among other children (Rivera 213). *The Next Best Thing* reveals how easily such problems can be discharged. When Sam is questioned by his friends regarding the sleeping arrangements of his mother and father, Robert tells the boy that they do not sleep together because his mother snores. The comments of Sam's friends also include answers to the questions that they raise. One child indicates that the father is "supposed to sleep in the same room of another house." Thus the film acknowledges the various ways that children can be stigmatized by the behavior of their parents; such matters are not the exclusive problems of homosexual parents. The comment also reveals that the traditional household containing two biological parents and their children is no longer the norm (Bozett, "Fathers" 17): over half of all marriages end in divorce. The prevalence of nontraditional households reduces the shame of such arrangements. When one child says that his father calls Robert a "fag," another corrects him, "You're supposed to say 'same sex partner.'" While the political correctness of a child is intended to be amusing, it nevertheless reveals the important point that bigotry is learned. Children can just as easily be taught to treat diversity with respect. Sam's questioning of Robert does not extend to his father's sexual orientation, and Robert does not broach the topic. Research into gay parenting indicates that it is preferable to tell the child of his parent's alternative sexual orientation as early as possible (Bozett, "Fathers" 14). The child is more accepting and has time to adjust to the news and bond with the parent before s/he is subject to the negative bias of a homophobic culture.

According to scholarship on the subject, Robert may be making a mistake in avoiding the early opportunity to talk about his sexual orientation with his son, but popular wisdom would condemn such a decision, assuming that early revelation could influence the child's own sexual development. Despite evidence that the sexual background of the parent does not influence that of the child, most people still fear that the child of gay parents will be gay, particularly if same sex practices were not adequately condemned in the child's formative years. The film is dismissive of these concerns. When one of Abbey's friend asks if Sam will be gay, Abbey insults her intelligence: "Will your children be stupid?" While the rebuttal may not be tactful, it does concisely indicate that thoughtful people ought to know better. Popular concerns over the supposed taint of gay parenting often reveal a fear that the child may be subjected to overt displays of sexual practices; the concern is related to the stereotype that gays flaunt their sexual behavior. Thus Schlesinger's film is careful to demonstrate that Robert is a responsible parent who will not allow his son to witness any sexual behavior in the home, hence Robert's hysterical response to Sam's discovery of Ben in his mother's bedroom. During the child custody suit, Abbey's attorney invokes many of the negative stereotypes about gay parenting, and Robert's denials demonstrate an obligation to protect his son. When the lawyer asks him if he has discussed his sexual orientation with his son, Robert dismisses the idea, arguing that Sam is only six years old, and when the lawyer asks Robert if Sam has ever seen him having oral sex with another man, Robert is incredulous; even Abbey objects to the suggestion.

As Abby's lawyer impugns Robert's parenting skills in order to prove him unfit, the questioning only serves to demonstrate that the homophobic bias against gay child-rearing is a hysterical fear unrelated to fact. Each of the lawyer's accusations have been so completely discredited by events prior to the custody battle that the charges are rendered ridiculous and unfair without even requiring a verbal contradiction. The lawyer explains that the "trial is about his character and whether he has the kind of character that would lead anyone to trust him with a young boy." Robert has already been entrusted with the responsibility for six years by the child's mother and has only been stripped of the responsibility because the mother wants to marry another man. The injustice of the accusation is intensified by the mother's own words who, when she first told Robert he was not the biological father, consoled him by saying that he was Sam's father in every way that counts. Yet her lawyer argues that Robert does not even have the right to use the word "father" when referring to himself in court, insisting that Robert call himself "caregiver." The scene thus reveals that a custody battle is frequently unrelated to the real capacity of the parent to raise a child well; instead, they involve accusations of poor parenting that even the opposing council knows are false. Robert's advocate tells him that there is a case pending in which a parent's custody is being challenged because s/he smokes. She advises him to settle out of court.

The female African American judge, a minority herself, proves to be more sympathetic toward Robert's case than even Robert's lawyer expects. Her decision is compassionate and includes a recognition that the law should provide for cases such as Robert's, but she also explains that she has no choice but to "award sole custody to Sam's mother." She acknowledges that Robert has been an "exemplary parent," thus refusing to accept the character assassination practiced by Abbey's lawyer and recognizing that the only hindrance to a compassionate and reasonable decision are the rigorous and draconian laws of the most progressive state in the union. The judge's commentary is directed toward the camera, rendered as though it were a plea to the audience for legal and social change, for flexibility in the laws that institutionalize bigotry, victimizing gay parents as well as their children. She refers specifically to the limitations in the law, explaining that she is obligated "to adjudicate the laws of the state of California, and at this time … [she] has no choice…." The time qualification invites and even encourages a reconsideration of the legal rights of gay parents.

Screenwriter Thomas Ropelewski's decision to make Robert's paternity situational rather than biological is a curiosity. The courtroom drama might have been much more compelling had it not been characterized by a hopelessness that becomes maudlin. The plea for the rights of gay male parents becomes overly sentimentalized, reinforcing the idea that gay men are victims and that the desire to parent is an idealistic dream easily dismissed by those who believe that sexual orientation is a choice. From such a perspective, gay men decide not to parent when they decide to be homosexual. Robert's situation belies the reality that most gay parents are biological parents, having conceived children in previous marriages or relationships (Bozett, "Fathers" 4), the situation represented in *The Birdcage*. Perhaps the screenwriter has decided not to make Robert the biological parent in order to maintain that successful parenting is unrelated to DNA. The biological father, Kevin, is shown to be disinterested and selfish. When he learns that he has a six-year-old child, his first assumption is that he is going to be subjected to a paternity suit. Even after he meets Sam and decides that he wants to explore his relationship with the child, his interest is spent after one visit. The injustice of the laws regarding paternity are further interrogated by Kevin's ineptitude. He is clearly unworthy of inclusion in the boy's life, yet he has a legal claim to the child while the man who raised and nurtured the child from infancy does not. The thematic is extended to include Ben, who has rights to the child through marriage to the boy's mother. Ben's competence as a parent is not impugned by the narrative, but he is shown to be rather distant and noncommittal. His fatherly disposition toward the child is clearly not as intimate as Robert's. Even Ben is convinced that Robert is the appropriate father to the boy. When he finds Robert outside of Sam's school, he explains that it is too soon for a reconciliation between Robert and Abbey. His comment acknowledges that a reunion with mother and child is a possibility. Ben's character is rather refreshing because he is a straight man who avoids hysterical homophobia and the related assumption that gay men cannot be good parents. Ben is very apologetic regarding the mess his inclusion in the familial equation created, and it is clear that he was instrumental in working the reconciliation that eventually reunites Robert with his son.

Both *The Next Best Thing* and *The Object of My Affection,* despite their queer friendly theses, serve as cautionary examples of the dangers of gay parenting. Even the gay men and lesbians who are the biological parents of a child run the risk of losing custody simply because of their sexual orientation. In many states, homosexuality is still sufficient cause to deprive a parent of unsupervised visitation rights (Rivera 203), and these laws are based on stereotype and fear that are unsupported by scientific data gathered on the subject. The hostility toward gay parenting is so virulent that it is difficult to understand why gay men and women would subject themselves to such maltreatment and injustice, and, while the above films are clearly calculated to intervene in the public debate on the subject and are intended to win sympathy for gay parents, they, nevertheless, act as a powerful deterrent to such involvement.

In defending the parental rights of gay men, the films become subtly sexist. They avoid the controversy surrounding the film *Tootsie,* which suggests that men make better women than women do; however, each film includes some unflattering images of women and/or implies that the androgyny of gay men compensates for female failings. *Object* and *Best Thing* suggest that women are too inconstant to be trusted when entering into a parenting agreement with a gay man; and in each case the complication involves a romantic entanglement, a bow to platitudes about women's emotional and romantic susceptibilities. Nina becomes enamored of her platonic gay roommate, and Abbey finds love outside of the home. These films also align gay men with straight men insofar as they invoke the priority that the courts award to maternity over paternity in custody cases. In *The Birdcage*, women are characterized as either daft and emotionally unstable (Mrs. Keeley) or overly rational, ambitious, and indifferent (Katherine).

The thesis of all three above films is that the desire to raise a child is unrelated to sexual orientation and that consideration should be shown to those who desire to raise a child but are unable to get one through sexual intercourse. Such arguments are reinforced by the knowledge that heterosexual couples who are unable to conceive a child are allowed to adopt and that there are too many orphaned children who need homes to be accommodated by the heterosexual couples looking to adopt. However, in most states the desire and the capacity to parent are not sufficient to win a gay man or woman legal consideration. The reason that the progressive film industry would try to intervene in this social debate is obvious, yet the impact that the above films should have on a gay audience are problematical. The films reveal that prejudice toward gays is so deep that the public refuses to acknowledge overwhelming evidence that contradicts popular assumptions about the inability of gays to parent well. The latter two films even suggest that the people who are most accepting of gay men cannot be trusted to eschew cultural stereotypes and defend the rights of the gay men whom they have elected to help raise their children. Thus the films urge social acceptance but offer such a bleak picture of gay parental rights that they do little to encourage people to embark upon a course that could end in such profound disappointment and emotional injury to everyone involved.

The three above films are universal in their agreement that heterosexual males do not necessarily make the best fathers. In all three cases the gay male parent is shown to be more suitable to fatherhood than at least one male who has a legal right to paternal authority. Indeed, the commentary is a subtle indictment of our culture's socializing of heterosexual men. In each of the films, the androgynous quality of the gay male is indicative of a capacity for nurturing that is not typical of hegemonic masculinity. Kevin Keeley's selfishness in *The Birdcage* is a sharp contrast with Armand Goldman's frantic efforts to change his life to please his son. George is chosen by Nina to be the father to her child because he is less domineering and arrogant than Vince is in *The Object of My Affection;*

and Kevin, in *The Next Best Thing,* is not even interested in his biological child, the same whom Robert is willing to humiliate himself in court to defend. In the above cases the heterosexual male is represented as too self-centered and arrogant to be an effective father, while gay males are characterized by humility. While such portraits are indeed flattering to gay men, since they negate the traditional efforts to demonize femininity in men and suggest that such men may have qualities that are socially beneficial, they are also reductive, tending to reinforce the stereotype that gays are essentially different from heterosexuals in ways other than sexual object choice, and difference activates the pretense to superiority on both sides of the debate.

10

Scared Straight: Rehabilitating Homophobia and the Dread of Proximity

In her theory of abjection, Julia Kristeva argues that self-definition involves the rejection and sublimation of those characteristics that the subject views as the "not self," those qualities that contradict and undermine the identity formation that the subject performs for the world. Thus, those attributes that have the potential to deconstruct subjectivity are integral to its original construction. Danger, therefore, lies in the potential and intermittent return of the abjected to consciousness, haunting and destabilizing the self. The return of these qualities produces horror and revulsion in the subject as well as a hysterical effort to repress the loathsome manifestation (1–13). Kristeva's theory is beneficial in understanding the hysteria generated by homophobia, particularly that which is frequently manifest between men. The intensity of heterosexual men's hostility toward gay men is disproportionate to the potential threat represented by the latter group (Plummer 10). The violent repression of homosexuals is incongruous with the very same gender stereotypes that code them as weak, effeminate, and ineffectual.

In the 1980s, heterosexual men who committed acts of violence against gay men frequently offered as a mitigating circumstance the "homosexual panic defense," which alleged that the perpetrator was momentarily overcome by rage and fear initiated by the revelation of his victim's sexual orientation (Plummer 21–22). Often the defense included the accusation that the victim deserved his injury or death because he was reckless enough to proposition a straight man. Such a claim was made by the father of Matthew Shepherd's murderer, who defended his son with the accusation that Shepherd had propositioned the two who tied him to a fence post and pistol whipped him. Such a defense would have to be grounded in the assumption that homosexuality is too horrible to countenance and that an invitation to sexual dalliance by a gay man is a violation worthy of a death sentence. The claim effectively renders the victim guilty of his own injury or death, and reveals the spurious vulnerability of heterosexual men who can be so completely disoriented by alternative sexual object choices that they experience temporary insanity. The $25 million court decision against the *Jenny Jones Show* for a murder perpetrated by one of its guests upon another is an example of the continued viability of "homosexual panic defense." Here the argument, however, was not used to the advantage of the violent perpetrator, but by the victim's family, who claimed that the *Jenny Jones Show* created the circumstances in which violence was predictable and perhaps even expected. The program that was the impetus for murder included the revelation that a gay man, Scott Amedure, had a secret crush on a straight man, Jonathan Schmitz. The latter had been invited to the show under the pretense that a secret admirer would be revealed, and he was told that the person could be either male or female. Although he handled the experience rationally during the taping of the show, two weeks afterward he murdered Amedure. The jury decision against the *Jenny Jones Show* was heralded by many gay rights activists as an effort to mitigate Schmitz's guilt, suggesting that the revelation of a queer sentiment is so humiliating for a straight man that it is a reasonable prediction of murder. Those who defend Jones indicate that she was trying to remove the stigma of homosexuality by talking about it publicly and by behaving in a fashion that suggests there is no shame in being gay or in being perceived as gay. However, Jones' detractors indicate that it is the secretive element of the show that created the problem. Schmitz was emotionally ill-equipped for the public manifestation that he is the focus of gay desire.

Aside from the debate over the relative guilt of the *Jenny Jones Show*, the fact remains that a straight man regarded the public revelation that he is the object of gay sentiment as an insult and a horror worthy of deadly violence. When it was first coined by George Weinberg in *Society and the Healthy Homosexual* (1972), the term "homophobia" referred to the "dread of being close to a homosexual" (Plummer 4). The current broader use of the term constitutes an extrapolation on the original description. The contemporary homophobe fears the symbolic proximity of homosexuality. Homophobia involves the dread of pollution (both literal and symbolic) through association. The homophobe fears the homosexual because he signifies the return of all that the heterosexual male has suppressed in the process of forming a normative sexual identity.

The homosexual has been abjected. In his book *Sexual Dissidence,* Jonathan Dollimore, reading Freud, argues that all people have already made a "homosexual object choice" and that some have acknowledged this aspect of themselves while others have forced the information into the unconscious (178). In the process of sexual identity formation, the young boy reduces the scope of his sexual options (the polymorphous perverse) in accordance with those restrictions imposed by social institutions, rejecting those qualities that are stigmatized as "not masculine" and associating the same with "disgust, horror, and shame" (180). The instrument for the imposition of normative sexual desires is homophobia, which is deployed to police the boundaries of sex, distinguishing clearly between male and female to maintain a simple, regimented, and, subsequently, coherent gender distinction. Dollimore characterizes homophobia as the "mechanism for regulating the behavior of the many by the specific oppression of a few" (245). The male homosexual deconstructs the male/female and masculine/feminine binaries; thus he becomes the repository of that which is excluded from traditional manhood (Connell, *Masculinities* 78). In sum, the heterosexual male defines his sexual orientation as "not gay" and "not woman." Through the above rationale, Dollimore concludes that homosexuality, which our culture takes great pains to reject and stigmatize, is actually central to the process of sexual identity formation for all members of our culture (182). That which is abjected is integral to the identity of the "abjector." The existence of the reviled desires within the normative subject are a potential source of psychic disruption. Thus, when the stigmatized and sublimated, desires become embodied in the homosexual, and the aspersions of association are cast upon the heterosexual male subject, the predictable response is the subject's hysterical and often violent effort to disassociate himself from the shameful subject.

In *One of the Boys: Masculinity, Homophobia, and Modern Manhood,* David Plummer examines the role that homophobia plays in the male heterosexual identity by observing the point at which boys begin to police gender roles by stigmatizing the less masculine of their peers. Interestingly, Plummer concludes that children begin to impose gender conformity through coercive and alienating practices even before they have developed a consciousness of sexual object choice. Young boys will begin to stigmatize their mates with slurs such as "poof" or "fag" before those terms include for them an assumption of sexuality (40–43). This insight reveals that the cultural project of homophobia has an objective that goes beyond the mere punishing of a portion of the population for their refusal to pursue normative sexual practices. Homophobia regulates the sexual socialization of young boys. The stereotype of a sissy boy becomes the representation of all that a "growing boy should not be": a baby, a loner, a coward, an academic, a girl, or a sexual deviant (78). The revelation that the stigmatization of homosexuality occurs at an early age and that homophobia is central to masculine identity formation, is disturbing because, by implication of this model, hatred of homosexuals is very deeply rooted in the male psyche, and its eradication could necessitate the destabilization of gender certainties:

> Clearly, if true equality were to be obtained, then homosexuality would no longer be available to symbolize otherness. As a result, the masculine identities based on these differences would be challenged by the possibility that the boundary between Self and other might dissolve and otherness could infiltrate notions of self [Plummer 88].

Plummer is not suggesting that equality for homosexuals is not a desirable objective, but simply revealing that the end of homophobia could constitute the end of what Foucault characterized as an era of sexuality.

The vexed relationship between gay and straight men is certainly one of the clearest stumbling blocks in the pursuit of full social equality for all gay people. Even some of those states (specifically Georgia) that have taken the progressive step of decriminalizing sodomitical acts between men continue to police and prosecute the propositioning of straight men by gay men. This residual law reveals that the antipathy toward homosexuals is the dread of becoming the object of queer desire, or of being thought queer by the sexual aggressor, or, even worse, by a third party. Perhaps more importantly, the propositioned straight man questions his own masculine gender performance when he recognizes that he has become the subject of a gay man's admiration and longing. Most gay men can attest that when propositioned, unwilling straight men react more to what they perceive as the insult in being thought gay than to any other discomfort generated by the invitation. They frequently need to be reassured that they do not appear to be homosexual. The invitation becomes the re-emergence of abjected desires requisite to gendered identity. The hysterical need to disassociate oneself from gay men in order to avoid the stigma of proximity, or the potential for a destabilizing confrontation with the constructedness of one's own sexual identity, or a lesson in the permeability of sexual binaries maintains a distance (both physical and intellectual) between gay and straight men. This distance is of incalculable importance in the struggle for gay rights because it is a space filled up with suspicion and misinformation, and because it is the space between those who retain all of the cultural power and those who are disenfranchised.

In her groundbreaking study *Between Men*, Eve Kosofsky Sedgwick recognizes that there is a breach within the continuum of male relations, a distinct division between the practices of men loving men and men helping men, while among women the two relationships seem to be more mutually beneficial. In order to be admitted to exclusive male cultures or to form male bonds, one must first disavow any homoerotic interest; one must disavow the love of men. Many suggest that Sedgwick's insight created queer theory and the explosion of queer friendly academic studies, which frequently retain her ideas as a foundational assumption. The multiplicity of gay representations within the popular media seem bent on repairing the breach between gay and straight men, specifically the harmful assumption that gay and straight men cannot be friends, cannot interact without suspicion and fear. Both the film and television industries have initiated a veritable blitzkrieg of gay friendly images directed at straight men, demonstrating that there is nothing to fear in forming bonds with gay men, nor any disgrace in being thought gay.

Many popular television programs now include gay characters who interact with the rest of the male cast without incident. In a recent episode of *Ed*, the titular character (played by Tom Cavanaugh) is asked to write a will for a friend's dying grandfather whom he discovers has had a secretive relationship with another man for many years, but who dies before he can reveal the fact to his family. Compassionate yet heterosexual, Ed facilitates the revelation of this information to the dead man's relatives and helps to form a bond between the secret lover and his "in-laws." *Spin City* includes the gay character Carter Heywood (Michael Boatman), who is the close friend and co-worker of Michael Flahrety (Michael J. Fox). Carter is notable for his normalcy and levelheadedness among a collection of eccentrics. The other characters interact with him without fear of association. In one episode, the womanizing and desperate Stuart Bondeck (Alan Ruck) recognizes the value of pretending to be gay when he discovers that women trust gay men and that he can form close bonds with them without drawing their suspicions. He also learns that women who try to convert gay men by offering the sexual opportunities will understand when he breaks off the relationship after the first time. The audience of NBC's *Veronica's Closet* waited with great anticipation, through marriage plans and other smokescreens, for the character Josh (Wallace Langham) to finally admit that he is gay. When he does, his well-meaning yet bungling co-workers, the stridently heterosexual Perry (Dan Cortese) and Leo (Daryl Mitchell), send an office memo announcing with pride and acceptance that Josh is gay. Of course, the action mortifies Josh, thus making Perry and Leo even more desperate to demonstrate their approbation, so they send a second memo, this one stating that he is not gay. The episode is intended to reveal that straight men can be supportive of gay men without feeling threatened. However, amusingly, at the same time they are trying to prove their loving acceptance of their friend, Perry and Leo only succeed in proving that they are not entirely comfortable with Josh's new sexuality; they do not know how to behave appropriately toward him. Their confusion is a safeguard against the stain of association; they prove their masculinity and heterosexuality through their awkward demeanor toward a gay man, even one who has been a longtime acquaintance. The effort to repair the contentious relationship between gay and straight men was the project of ABC's short-lived sitcom *Oh Grow Up*, in which a gay man, Ford (John Ducey), and a stridently heterosexual playboy, Hunter (Stephen Dunham), are roommates. Hunter is accepting of his friend's sexuality. He is secure enough to share a house with Ford without fear of molestation or stigma. The pairing of a gay man with a playboy reveals a specific gay friendly project, clearly intended to counter negative stereotypes about gay men's indiscriminate sexual practices. The presumption of gay promiscuity is undermined by the presence of the male slut Hunter, who has spread his seed so widely he is surprised to learn he has an adult daughter. Moreover, traditionally, those men who are the most obstreperous about their heterosexual inclinations are also the most frightened of being thought queer. Hunter reveals that keeping the company or even sharing a house with a gay man does not limit one's sexual opportunities or predict that one is also gay.

American Beauty

Alan Ball, the creator and head writer of *Oh Grow Up*, is also the Academy Award–winning author of the screenplay *American Beauty* (1999), a black comedy about alienation from one's family, one's neighbors, and one's self. *American Beauty* suggests that where there is the most vitriolic hostility toward gay men, there is likely to be repressed homosexual sentiments, an idea which is somewhat dangerous since it suggests that gays are to blame for the violence against them (Plummer 10). However, the continued symbolic presence of homosexuality, even among characters who are not gay, reveals the centrality of queer sentiments within the construction of gender identity. Marine Colonel Fitts sees "faggots" everywhere, even where there are none, but he will not accept the queer in himself, and when he is forced to recognize his own deviant desires, he lashes out at the symbol of that longing. *American Beauty* suggests that same sex desires within the homophobe himself are the primary subject of violent suppression and the obstacle to homosocial bonds between gay and straight men. The attack upon gay men is the symbolic effort to punish the perpetrator's own queer longings.

Although ostensibly the principal action of *American Beauty* is the mid-life crisis of Lester Burnham (Kevin Spacey), a crisis that leads him to quit his job, smoke pot, and start working out, all to seduce the friend of his adolescent daughter. He adopts as his role model a teenage drug dealer, Ricky Fitts (Wes Bentley), the son of an abusive marine colonel (Chris Cooper). The triangulation of suspicion and desire formed by these three men is the catalyst for the violence at the conclusion of the film. Colonel Fitts mistakenly believes that Lester and Ricky are engaged in a homosexual affair. The knowledge first awakens his violence toward his son, then his own repressed desire for Lester Burnham, and finally his desperate endeavor to punish the queer desire in himself through the murder of Lester.

Fitts continues to introduce himself as "Colonel Frank Fitts, U.S. Marine Corps," although it is clear that he is retired from the military. Military discipline has shaped his consciousness, and he attempts to impose that same rigor on others. He runs his house like a barracks. Ricky experiences constant intrusions into his privacy, random drug testing, and corporal punishment, and his room is subject to spot checks and searches. After beating his son for an intrusion into the father's private study, Colonel Fitts explains that the abuse is for the boy's "own good"; Ricky needs to learn respect for authority, as well as structure and discipline, and the boy has been trained to respond with military precision in order to placate his father: "Yes, sir. Thank you for trying to teach me. Don't give up on me, Dad." The artificiality and formality of the response would alert other parents to his insincerity, but the Colonel expects such humility from his family. The mother, Barbara Fitts (Allison Janey), has been subdued by a lifetime of her husband's abuse. She seldom speaks, staring blankly into space, and she cannot acknowledge the events transpiring in her own home when her son is thrown out.

Colonel Fitts is troubled by his inability to control people outside of his family as well, and the principle manifestation of this rage for order is his homophobia. The first indication of his exaggerated hatred of gay men is revealed when the neighbors Jim and Jim decide to welcome the Fitts family to their new home. Colonel Fitts is incredulous when the two Jims introduce themselves as "partners." He assumes that they are speaking of a professional bond and inquires into their work. Only after they name two separate jobs will he process the reality of their domestic arrangement. Colonel Fitts complains about the incident to his son: "How come these faggots always have to rub it in your face? How can they be so shameless?" Interestingly, Fitts' principal concern is the visibility of gay men. In his view, they should at least hide their perversion. When his son responds less than enthusiastically, the Colonel demands from the boy a complete affirmation of the validity of his homophobic slur. Recognizing the necessity of placating his father and the need to demonstrate his own heterosexuality through his renunciation, Ricky responds with artificial fierceness: "Forgive me, sir, for speaking so bluntly, but those fags make me want to puke my fucking guts out." As before, the exaggerated hatred and formality of the comment should have alerted the father to the son's insincerity, but the Colonel expects total humility, and his own sexual identity is predicated upon the vitriolic repudiation of homosexual interests, so the son's response seems appropriate to him.

The Colonel tries to punish his own abjected desire in his son. Interestingly, both of the principal adult male characters are preoccupied with fantasies about the pollution of an adolescent. Lester mistakenly believes that his daughter's friend is a teenage slut, and Fitts believes that Ricky is performing sexual favors for money. Just as Lester longs to possess Angela, Colonel Fitts desires his own son. The intensity of the periodic beating that the Colonel administers to his son suggests erotic passion, even a rape. The father intrudes into the boy's bedroom twice, beating him savagely only to conclude weeping and embracing after he has forced the boy to submit. The fight even includes an insult against the boy's masculinity: "Fight back you little pussy." The first time, the violence comes to an abrupt end when the boy reveals that he has a girlfriend; the father is noticeably stricken and repentant. His mortification is increased when he realizes that the girlfriend has witnessed the very private beating. The Colonel then tries to make the incident seem reasonable by offering a lesson on the necessity of respect. Despite this incident, Fitts begins to suspect that his son might be gay when he views a voyeuristic video that Ricky made of Lester Burnham working out naked in his garage. The father's fears are reinforced when he mistakenly interprets a drug sale between Ricky and Lester as oral copulation. The father once again attacks the son, explaining that he would rather see the boy "dead" than a "fucking faggot." Ricky recognizes his opportunity to escape his abusive father's control when the Colonel tells him, "I will throw you out of this house and never look at you again." Ricky lies about his sex life, stating that he offers men oral service for money. The father's threat is symbolic of the process whereby he constructed his own fragile sexual identity. Just as he will kick the boy out of the house and never look at him again, the father repudiates his own homosexual potential, refusing to acknowledge it in himself, only recognizing it in others, particularly his son.

The association of queer desire and violence is manifest in the crisis of the film as well. The son's false admission has so shaken the father that for a brief time he is ready to acknowledge his own repressed longings. He tries to embrace and kiss Lester, mistakenly believing that his neighbor is not only gay but also Ricky's lover. The incident has the quality of an attempted vicarious reconciliation with his son. The father embraces the man who enjoys the relationship with his son that he longs to have. The sex act with Lester would signify a vicarious erotic union with the son. When the Colonel is rejected, he murders Lester to hide his homosexual longings from himself and the world. Lester signifies the return of abjected desire that must be violently repressed.

American Beauty attempts to discredit homophobes by revealing that their hyperbolic hatred of gay men is indicative of their own pathological need to deny perverse longings. The danger in such a thesis is that it absolves the heterosexual community of responsibility for the violent repression of gays and lesbians. Moreover, it pathologizes gays as self-destructive. The idea that all people have repressed homosexual longings en route to heterosexuality does deconstruct human sexuality sufficiently to undermine the association between queer desire and symbolic self-anni-hilating violence, since only a portion of the population would be so guarded of their sexual choice that they would need to police its boundaries with aggression. In addition, the boundaries are exposed as constructs rather than hard and fast biological imperatives. In this context, the sexual subject is only the socio-sexual category that they will acknowledge. *American Beauty* is then a powerful revelation of the tensions that under-line human sexuality. The fact that Colonel Fitts attempts, through violence, to subdue and repudiate queer passion in others, even where no such passion is in play, reveals that the true struggle is internal. The Colonel is projecting his desire onto those who surround him and is subsequently exposing the binary mechanisms involved in the formation of sexual identity. Thus it is the internal struggle of the homophobe that interferes with the efforts to establish homosocial bonds between gay and straight men.

Urbania

Director Jon Shear's *Urbania* (2000) portrays the grief stricken gay man Charlie (Dan Futterman) on a surrealistic revenge odyssey through the streets of New York. He is determined to punish the hate crime murderer of his lover Chris (Matt Keesler). Portions of the non-linear story are the manifestation of the principal character's subconscious, and it is often difficult to distinguish between fiction and reality. The audience has been invited into the mad world of the protagonist's revenge fantasy, and the veracity of his experiences are further called into question by the film's urban legend thematic. The narrative dramatizes many of the most well known legends, mostly ones in which the characters are victimized by sex. Indeed, the story is an exploration of the violence of sexual domination and particularly the quasi-erotic violence of homophobia.

The openly gay couple Charlie and Chris were accosted on the street by a gang of thugs led by the Dean (Samuel Ball), who made Charlie watch while he forced Chris to perform sexual favors and then murdered him. The episode reveals the way in which the perpetrator's homoerotic longings are repressed through the projection of violence onto the objective manifestation of his desire, embodied in gay men. Dean is obsessed with his hatred of gays and is even willing to pursue it into their most private sexual enclaves, where he seduces and then slashes them. His strident tales of the sexual conquest and victimization of women are contradicted by his continual haunting of gay cruising areas. His determined effort to disassociate himself with the queer desires necessitates (for him) that he spend much time in their presence proving his difference through reprisal. As with Colonel Fitts, Dean's efforts to victimize gay men are initiated by abortive sexual dalliance, suggesting that he desires to punish his potential sexual partners for their attractiveness to him, because they represent that which he has abjected in the production of his own sexual self-image. His actions allow him to embrace through hatred those whom his conscious mind will not countenance. The fetishizing of Dean's violence against gays is revealed most clearly in the revenge sequence when Charlie forces the drunken homophobe to take off his pants and realizes that Dean has become aroused by his own potential murder.

The damaging notion that violence against gay people is perpetrated by other (closeted) gay people is mitigated by the point of view of the film. The events are filtered through Charlie's consciousness. This perspective opens up the possibility that the eroticizing of Dean's violence is Charlie's own invention, perhaps an effort to humiliate the perpetrator with aspersions of that which he reviles, or perhaps an endeavor to make understandable an act that in reality was random. The film is clearly intended to be cathartic for the gay community, revealing that the victim can strike back at his victimizer, but the issue is problematized when Charlie does not actually kill Dean after he has him in his power. If the abortive revenge actually took place, then the episode reveals that gay men are not sufficiently bloodthirsty to revenge even the most heinous crimes against them (weakness masquerading as civility), and if the attempted retribution is merely a figment, then gay men are not even capable of imagining effective retaliation. While the tragic division between Dean and Charlie suggests that a peaceful co-existence between gay and straight men is impossible because of the binary conditioning of their sexual socialization, the brief acquaintance between Charlie and the straight bartender reveals that positive relations can be forged if there is a mutual respect for human needs.

Oz

The association between gay desire and violence is a recurring theme in the HBO series *Oz*, which is set in an experimental prison. Here the struggle to survive and to meet basic human needs is dramatized in the most audacious fashion. The setting is virtually naturalistic, with even the strongest inmates periodically victimized. The program frequently kills off principal characters through some vicissitude of prison violence. The prison rape, which is ironically one of the principal deterrents to a life of crime for terrified straight men, is commonplace within Oz, but consensual sex is common as well, yet within Oz even the consensual sex is fraught with violence.

The prison sex motif is associated with the inmate Tobias Beecher (Lee Tergesen), who is a married father of two and a lawyer who killed a little girl in a drunk driving incident and was sentenced to a lengthy term in Oz. He is the program's cautionary example to well meaning straight men who may inadvertently go wrong; he is the "scared straight" story, and although he suffers the consequences of his actions in a legion of horrific ways (the loss of freedom, the breaking of all his limbs, the suicide of his wife, the kidnap and murder of one of his children), the most humiliating—and the one that initially defined his life is prison—is his sexual battery at the hands of Vern Schillinger (J. K. Simmons), a white supremacist who was Beecher's first cellmate. Schillinger forced Beecher to be his partner, subjecting him to rape and battery. The relationship between the two men was characterized by humiliation and violence rather than affection. By making Beecher into a woman sexually, Schillinger was able to maintain his masculine and heterosexual self-image despite queer sex. He assumed the role of the wife-beating husband, burning a swastika into Beecher's ass with cigarettes and forcing him to perform in drag at a prison variety show. Eventually, Beecher, in desperation, tries to kill

Schillinger, beating and defecating on him. These events initiated the show's most prolonged antagonism, one sustained thus far for the entire series, a struggle between good and evil to determine who can injure and humiliate the other most profoundly.

The relationship that develops between Chris Keller (Chris Meloni) and Beecher is fraught with violence, although it is the only arrangement that bears any resemblance to a gay union. Keller, originally in league with Schillinger, seduces Beecher, attempting to make the cellmate fall in love with him so that he can betray and destroy him for Schillinger's revenge. Incredibly, after the subterfuge works beyond their expectations and Beecher's limbs have been broken, the injured man is compelled to forgive Keller and to continue their relationship; this, of course, only happens after Beecher gets revenge by stabbing his violent lover in the store room and after Keller makes amends by confessing his guilt to prison authorities and subsequently alienating Schillinger. Despite their reconciliation, the lovers' relationship is not free of violence. In another of Schillinger's subterfuges, Beecher is led to believe that Keller is responsible for the kidnapping and murder of one of his children, so Beecher once again tries to kill him, this time splitting the two men up.

The violence that is a constant portion of sex in Oz is calculated to salvage the masculinity of the characters engaged in queer sex. The traditional heterosexist aspersions of weakness associated with gay desire are mitigated if the characters continue to behave aggressively toward each other. The implication is that they are not comfortable with their sexual practices and must constantly distance themselves from intimations of effeminacy with acts of gratuitous violence against love objects. The program carefully segregates sex from powerful emotions. While the entire cellblock is cognizant of the relationship between Keller and Beecher, they are only subject to ridicule when they begin to develop strong sentiment, such as when Beecher is lovesick over Keller's betrayal. Thus, in Oz sex is acceptable, but love between men is still dangerous and taboo. This separation of the act from its emotion recuperates the humiliation of prison sex for straight men, offering an opportunity for the fulfillment of human sexual needs as well as a mitigation of the social consequences of the subsequent actions. After all, the hyper-masculine males who compose most of the prison population also belong to the same gender profile (masculine protest) that most abhors and stigmatizes queer behavior, yet find themselves in a gender segregated environment where gay sex is the only outlet. The prohibition against feeling strongly toward one's partner and the abjection of homosexuality in the midst of its free play are a response to the paradoxical predicament of the incarcerated heterosexual male. He can have sex and guard his gender performance if he punishes and stig-matizes the object of his sexual gratification.

One of the visual images of this paradoxical predicament within the prison is the marginalizing of the gay characters. None of the show's prin-cipal personas are self-identified as gay. Indeed, while there is a group of obviously homosexual characters on the cellblock, they are generally given neither names nor dialogue. They are flamboyantly queer, wearing makeup and women's clothes, and they are only ever seen on the margin of the shot. The most central role that they have been given is to act as a foil to Beecher's victimization by Schillinger; they represented the descent of Beecher into an underworld that he was reluctant to join. When gay characters are given a more important role in the narrative, it is invari-ably a prelude to their murder or release. Thus even in the plot structure, homosexual orientation is repudiated, banished to the margins of the prison, leaving an all heterosexual male world for the traditional males to bustle in without aspersions against their masculinity.

The character who represents the abjection of homosexual desire most clearly is the same most often engaged in queer sex, Chris Keller. In the 2000 season the audience learns the nature of Keller's crimes, the same that landed him in Oz. He is a serial killer who seduces gay men and, after having sex, murders them. The revelation renders coherent the charac-ter's sadistic demeanor toward the man with whom he has a relationship. Keller's initial victimization of Beecher after seducing him is consistent with the crimes that he has previously committed; it is a desperate effort to salvage his masculine image by punishing the same desire in his sex-ual partner. When Beecher and Keller split up over the kidnapping accu-sations, the latter feigns indifference toward Beecher's subsequent sexual activities, yet Beecher's partners are mysteriously found murdered. Keller has been seducing and murdering Beecher's lovers out of jealousy, a strong sentiment that he will not own. In the 2001 season Keller admits that his violence is the repudiation of his own desire. Just before he murders a sexual partner in the act, he ruminates: "Sometimes I think I killed all those guys because I wanted to kill the part of me that I despise."

One of my colleagues has referred to *Oz* as the "queerest show on television," and there is an element of truth to the characterization. Who would be the target audience for a drama series that portrays grown men living in close quarters and meeting their sexual needs with the weaker members of their population, usually following their erotic dalliance with a violent repudiation of the sex object. While at one level the program is gay male fantasy of domination and submission, a subject frequently addressed in gay pornography, it must have a broader audience than the gay community, given the success of the series. It is hard to imagine that women are overly fond of the program depicting an all male prison population, a program laden with testosterone induced rage and subterfuge. The program's extreme violence and the universality of the straight male point of view within the series seems calculated to appeal to the heterosexual male population. The series is the straight male's heart of darkness, where he can witness the free play of forbidden desire yet also see the desire negated and punished. The show's trope of chaos within a controlled environment is then a metaphor for the mind of its audience, who act out vicariously the abjected longings and then banish them to death or solitary confinement.

The above narratives reveal the disruptive relationship between straight men and queer desire. This incongruity between homosocial and homosexual relations accounts for the impasse in the effort to forge a bond of mutual respect. There antithetical camps within the spectrum of male relations are separated by the entire apparatus of socio-sexual conditioning. In order to be heterosexual, the male must renounce homosexuals and homosexual desire, and this can be done symbolically through contempt or disregard or literally through acts of violence and discrimination. In an effort to circumvent this impasse in male relations and to promote more acceptance and social tolerance toward gay men, Hollywood has embarked upon a virtual propaganda blitz in order to reveal that gay and straight men can peacefully co-exist and can even on occasion be mutually supportive. The negotiation of this stalemate must be accomplished by removing the stigma of association and proximity. The straight male must be willing to be perceived as queer.

Kiss Me, Guido

Tony Vitale's *Kiss Me, Guido* (1997) is an unambiguous effort to negotiate a truce between gay and straight men. The film traces the vicissitudes of an initial acquaintance and an evolving platonic relationship from revulsion, to suspicion, to reconciliation, to cooperation, to accommodation, to trust, and to identification. Warren (Anthony Barrile), a gay actor, places an ad in the personals soliciting a roommate because he cannot afford his rent; Frankie Zito (Nick Scotti), a straight Italian male who also aspires to be an actor and wants to move to Manhattan, mistakes the abbreviation "GWM" for "guy with money" and responds to the advertisement. The panic and confusion that results from the meeting of two men with socially antithetical backgrounds is the source of much amusement.

Both men must overcome prejudice and stereotype in order to create a mutually supportive friendship, but, particularly, Frankie must overcome fear and suspicion as well as his preoccupation with his own attractiveness and superiority. His process of refusing homophobia includes his gradual acceptance that someone might think he is gay through his association with Warren.

The disparity between the two men is both cultural and geographical. Frankie is a stereotype of the Italian male who has close familial ties, living at home with his extended family and remaining hyper-sensitive to his mother's approval. He works in a pizzeria, engaging in the predictable macho banter of young Italian males, including homophobic slurs, and he idealizes Italian actors such as Pacino and DeNiro, impersonating their more memorable roles for the entertainment of his friends and co-workers. In contrast, the gay man Warren has only friends and ex-lovers, his relatives conspicuously absent from the film. To some extent, the absence of family is a sign of his maturity. The contrast between the two males includes a difference in age and experience. Warren is more

The intimacy between Warren (Anthony Barrile, *left*) and Frankie (Nick Scotti), a gay and a straight man, is achieved only after a lengthy period of fear and suspicion. The photograph suggests that gay and straight men should be able to interact without apprehension.

independent and worldly, more cosmopolitan, having left his familial obligations behind to pursue his personal growth. Frankie, on the other hand, is just beginning the same process. In Warren, Frankie encounters a man who has already seen some success in acting and who is in a position to educate and promote him in the profession. His gradual acceptance of Warren's greater life experience helps to facilitate the reconciliation and friendship between the two men.

The encounter between Frankie and Warren also has a spatial component which is emphasized during the film's opening credits. The Zito family's visit to Manhattan constitutes the meeting of two distinct cultures, both uncomfortable with the other. The camera follows Frankie's womanizing brother from a back alley purchase of a fake engagement ring, through the streets of Manhattan, and back into the familiarity of his Bronx neighborhood. Pino, Frankie's brother, registers disgust as he observes gay couples strolling down the street of their Manhattan neighborhood. His demeanor is aggressive and hostile until he almost runs over a bodybuilder in the crosswalk, a man who slams the hood of Pino's car, curses him, and then strolls over to a sidewalk café where he greets another man with a kiss. The motorist is clearly shaken and subdued by the incident, proceeding to his own neighborhood where he smiles, reassured by the familiarity of heterosexual couples holding hands on the streets.

Frankie has a similar experience when he ventures into Manhattan, a region occupied by unfamiliar and exotic people. He is initially so naive that he does not suspect Warren is gay, despite clear indications of the fact, including coffee at a sidewalk café with Warren's ex-lover Dakota and the pretentiously gay and affected director of Dakota's new play about gay men, *Fire in the Hole*. Frankie asks incredulously, "You got a bunch of faggots in this play?" When Warren reveals his own orientation, a moral panic ensues, with Frankie storming out of the apartment to find a place of his own. His anger and alarm are intensified as he encounters more openly affectionate gay people on the street. He only chooses to return to Warren's apartment when it becomes apparent that he cannot afford to live anywhere else. Warren's own reluctance over the arrangement is trumped by the landlord's insistence that he allow anyone to live there who has money for the rent.

Frankie's moral panic includes a fear that association with Warren will blacken his reputation, that others will think he, too, is gay. Even after Frankie is forced to concede that he needs to live with Warren, he is extremely uncomfortable with the arrangement. His apprehension results from a lack of experience with gay people and an assumption that all gay men will desire him. On the first night of double occupancy in Warren's apartment, Frankie is uncomfortable showering. He keeps his eye on the bathroom door, apparently expecting Warren to join him. Equally uncomfortable when he has to venture into the living room in a towel to retrieve clean clothes, he is puzzled by Warren's indifference.

Warren advises Frankie that if he wants to be an actor, he is going to have to become comfortable around gay people, and while he does eventually interact with Warren and his friends, he, nevertheless, continues to be fearful of developing a reputation for sexual deviancy. While helping Warren practice his lines for Dakota's queer play, some hostile straight males overhear and begin to harass them. Frankie, in defense of his masculinity, initiates a brawl and has to be rescued by Warren, who is injured in the process and is subsequently unable to fulfill his part in the play. Frankie, who is the obvious replacement, having learned all of the lines, is apprehensive about playing a gay man in public, and his fear is intensified on the night of his first performance when his family and friends unexpectedly show up. He is particularly fearful of having to kiss a man on stage. He does, however, follow through and has to spend the rest of the night explaining to his distraught mother that he is not queer. Having faced his fear — the compromising of his manhood — and found acceptance, he is able to openly embrace his friendship with Warren, free of the dread of association. This breakthrough experience suggests that the rupture between gay and straight men cannot be repaired until the stigma of being perceived as gay is eliminated.

The lessons to be learned in the film are not all for the straight men. Warren and his friends are clearly prejudiced toward heterosexual men, particularly those from Frankie's background. Warren refuses to live with a "guido," an ethnic slur that carries with it a number of stereotypical characterizations. He argues facetiously that if the "gay police" discover he is living with a guido, they will "take away [his] tutu and ban [him] from the club." Dakota complains that Frankie is too straight for a part in the play and later accuses Warren of adopting Frankie's vulgarities. The gay characters have to overcome their negative expectations of straight men and recognize that men like Frankie can be sensitive and considerate and, most importantly, can act. This reversal of traditional prejudice is no doubt calculated to empower the formerly denigrated; a mutual antipathy frustrates the effort to perceive gay men as victims, a position from which they never act but are acted upon.

Kiss Me, Guido includes a self-reflective trope addressing gender roles and the demands of acting. Because the cultural bias against gay male relations is so strong, there is a considerable amount of incredulity and suspicion on the part of the audience whenever a presumed heterosexual male is compelled to play a homosexual. The association between the fictional roles and the actors' own sexual orientation has in the past been so strong that many actors were deterred from playing gay parts because they were afraid it would ruin their careers. This perception has changed dramatically in the past decade, and now more straight actors are willing and even eager to play such roles. *Kiss Me Guido* illustrates the trepidation of actors having to perform queer roles. Indeed, the film itself becomes an illustration of its own subject matter. No doubt many of the unknown straight actors playing gay roles in the film have, like Frankie, been forced to accept the awkward necessity of being publicly perceived as gay in order to advance their careers. Similarly, Frankie, who reveres acting because of his macho idols Pacino and DeNiro, must kiss a man, compromise his masculinity in order to earn the opportunity to work in the profession that constructs our culture's most powerful images of traditional masculinity. Warren and Frankie forge a friendship out of a mutual love of acting, and, appropriately, each must adopt characteristics of the other in order to improve his art. Dakota tells Warren that he is starting to sound like his Italian roommate, and Frankie must face the fact that his mother thinks he is gay. In the final image of the film the two protagonists exit with their arms around each other, negotiating the conditions of their permanent platonic cohabitation.

Chuck & Buck

Director Miguel Arteta's low budget film *Chuck & Buck* (2000) literalizes the hysterical fear of exposure that heterosexual males experience when they become involved with gay men. Chuck (Chris Weitz) and Buck (Michael White) were childhood friends who experimented with gay sex at the age of eleven, an experience which meant nothing to the now heterosexual Chuck but which shaped Buck's sexual self-image and orientation. Chuck's family eventually moved away, and he matured conventionally, becoming a serious professional man. Buck, on the other hand, grew physically but became emotionally and intellectually arrested in childhood. When Chuck, along with his fiancée, returns to his hometown for the funeral of Buck's mother, the two men are reunited. Naively, Buck assumes Chuck is sincere when he offers to entertain him in California, so Buck sells his property, moves to Los Angeles, and begins stalking the now reluctant and incredulous Chuck.

On the surface, the film seems to suggest that gay men are emotionally immature and socially irresponsible. Buck lives like a child in a room full of toys and candy, and he seems incapable of comprehending complex social situations. He has not developed the sense of propriety that adults share in hiding their past indiscretions and their socially unacceptable emotions. He has no sense of embarrassment or shame, humiliating Chuck at a professional dinner party when he starts to reveal their childhood sexual relationship, only deterred by Chuck's abrupt departure. He shows up at Chuck's house late in the evening unannounced and makes obscene propositions, which get him expelled from the premises. He calls Chuck at work so frequently that the secretary knows him by name, and he produces a play that illustrates in metaphor the depth of his attachment and his smoldering resentment toward his boyhood partner, thus mortifying the unsuspecting Chuck and his fiancée, whom he invites to the first and only performance. The play includes heavy-handed allusions to their former relationship, such as the equation of cookies with sex and the alteration of the names Chuck and Buck to the similarly harmonious Hank and Frank. The play was supposed to provoke a reconciliation; instead, Chuck leaves embarrassed and furious.

The above portrait of Buck exaggerates the frequent unkind characterizations made of gay men, characterizations that suggest gays are irresponsible and sexually and socially under-developed. The uncomfortable predicament of Chuck captures and reduces to absurdity many of the fears that heterosexual men have of gay men, particularly heterosexual men who have engaged in sexual indiscretions with gay men. While our culture recognizes that sexual experimentation between same sex children is a common part of psychological development, social decorum, nevertheless, requires that men conceal the experience. *Chuck & Buck* reveals a person who is either unwilling or unable to participate in the cultural sublimation of adolescent desire and experimentation. There is always a fear that the homosexual male is likely to reveal the secret liaison and that he is even likely to do so in an environment where any person with a sense of propriety would remain silent. Buck exposes Chuck's childhood homosexual experimentation in every venue that could possibly cause embarrassment: work, party, home, and even the public theater.

Chuck's hyperbolic predicament is clearly intended to make the fear of gay men's indiscretion ridiculous, but also to encourage a greater openness about human sexuality and particularly the permeable boundary between gay and straight and the integral part that homosexuality plays in normative sexual development. Only after Chuck agrees to speak frankly with Buck about their past and to acknowledge that past by having sex with him one last time is he able to get any relief from the constant torture that Buck represents for him. The lesson that is so difficult for Chuck to learn is illustrated in the relationship between Buck and the principal actor in his play. The man is shocked when Buck makes a pass at him, but he is able to address the issue openly and can avoid the panic that Chuck experiences. Buck and the actor set down the conditions in which they can remain friends. The film concludes with the potential reconciliation of Chuck and Buck as well. Buck, having agreed to leave Chuck alone, receives a wedding invitation. His inclusion in the ceremony constitutes a confirmation of Chuck's adult heterosexuality, but also, by implication, an acknowledgment and acceptance of his childhood desires. The childlike Buck becomes the literalization of an early phase in Chuck's psychosexual transformations and one which he no longer has to refuse. In general terms, if American culture can openly acknowledge the centrality of homosexuality in normative sexual development, then there would be little motivation to punish alternative sexual identities in a false pageant of repudiated desires (the same that every child experiences) and the way would be cleared for a new understanding and even the potential fraternity between gay and straight men.

Billy Elliot

In the introduction to his screenplay *Billy Elliot*, Lee Hall endeavors to contextualize the narrative by placing it within the British class struggles of the mid-eighties, and particularly within the debate between the respective relevance of "high" and "low" art forms: high art was regarded by the masses as "pretentious" and "irrelevant," while low art was considered vulgar, maudlin, and simplistic. Hall recognized that there was only a vaguely discernable boundary between these two aesthetic provinces. The low earned the appellation not because there was anything inherently unworthy about its content or execution, but merely because it was enjoyed by the working classes. The high, on the other hand, was, in Hall's view, "ram-jam full of all the excesses of sentiment and manipulation that made the low stuff so great" (vii). In his screenplay *Billy Elliot*, he sought to dramatize the unity that he perceives between the elitist and populist, and this juxtaposition of antithetical qualities is embodied in the person of Billy, in the social context of his story, and in the film itself as a cultural artifact. For the purposes of this discussion, I will focus primarily on the issues of sexuality and the gendering of art forms as they are developed in the film.

In his book *The Wilde Century*, Alan Sinfield identifies the trial and conviction of Oscar Wilde as the seminal event in which high art became —

in the minds of the British public — associated with homosexuality and effeminacy (26–27). British working class masculinity developed as a negation of the pomp and frivolity of the aristocratic traditions represented as Wilde's sphere of interests. The principal conflict within the titular character, Billy Elliot, captures this contrast between masculinities, the first of these represented by the epic struggle of his father, his brother, and their co-workers against the establishment, depicted in the labor strike at the mining corporation. The male working class culture represented by the laborers is characterized by hardiness, brutality, courage, loyalty, solidarity, resourcefulness, and self-sacrifice. The miners embody the mass of commoners facing the omnipresent, invulnerable, and immovable inhumanity of the establishment, signified by the wall of armed and shielded policemen guarding the work site and erecting barriers throughout the town. While Billy's dad and brother are immersed in the heroic struggle for self-respect and a dignified living, they are oblivious to the needs of the sensitive boy who is maturing within the same household; moreover, they are not cognizant of the impact that their own preoccupations are having upon the boy's evolution.

Billy's father tries to cultivate the boy's appreciation for masculine pursuits, such as boxing; however, the boy has no propensity for the sport and is easily knocked down by much smaller boys. In frustration and defeat, he joins a ballet class practicing on the opposite end of the gym, where he quickly discovers that he has a natural gift for dance. The conflict arises when his father discovers that Billy has forsaken boxing for high art, and particularly one that is so closely associated in the minds of the working classes with effeminacy and male homosexuality. Even Billy has to be reassured that ballet does not make him a "poof." In the strict working class household characterized by rigid gender roles, he has been conditioned to define his masculinity in opposition to homosexuality, and this from a boy who, in all likelihood, has not even experienced puberty and may not understand that the term "poof" defines a sexual preference.

The irony of the Elliot household is that at the same time the older men are insisting upon Billy's socialization as a rugged working class male who abhors perceived weakness in men and the more refined aspects of culture, their actions ensure that he will become a much more sensitive male. In the absence of a mother, he is obliged to be the family caregiver, looking after his elderly grandmother and keeping the house. In addition, he is constantly brutalized by his much older brother for minor offenses; and, as brothers do, he insults Billy's masculinity because the boy is smaller and weaker. The father cares about his son but is too preoccupied with his troubles at work to keep track of Billy's activities. His masculine honor is so overblown that his principal motivation in interfering with Billy's dance lessons is clearly the humiliation of having raised a soft and effeminate son.

Billy's insistence that he is not a "poof" and, by extension, that ballet is not necessarily the exclusive province of homosexual men would be homophobic were it not for the inclusion of Billy's close friend Michael, who occupies the opposite end of the masculine spectrum from that inhabited by Billy's father and brother. Michael likes to wear his sister's clothes and is preoccupied with the opportunities to wear a tutu in dance practice, and while he is too young for lascivious interests, he, nevertheless, likes to kiss boys and does startle Billy by kissing him on the cheek. Billy is sensitive and understanding of his friend at the same time that he insists he is not a "poof." Nevertheless, he obliges his friend by taking him to the gym and fitting him with a tutu. Billy's supportiveness toward his friend's unmasculine traits does not necessarily extend to others. Following his disappointing audition at the Royal Ballet School, he assaults a more effeminate boy when the latter tries to console him; Billy reacts by calling the boy a "bent bastard." Billy's response exposes a fear that he cannot fit into either the effete world of ballet or the more masculine world of the coal miners; thus, in his disappointment he returns to his hardy working class socialization, distancing himself from effeminacy with violence. When Billy is admitted to the school, his anger is replaced by compunction, and he confirms his love for his friend and his acceptance of sexual and gender diversity by returning Michael's kiss.

Billy's art signifies a synthesis of the high and the low. He is a working class boy who excels in an aristocratic art form. He signifies the productive infusion of proletarian energy into the decayed aesthetic conventions of the upper classes. The performance that he prepares for the academy audition is a fusion of ballet and contemporary dance. While he performs to a classical composition, he choreographs the dance, listening to contemporary music. His movements for the review committee are erratic, sometimes awkward, and shockingly unconventional; however, his energy, expressiveness, and enthusiasm win him a place in the school. Even in the final shot of the film, the synthesis of high and low art is emphasized. Billy, much older, prepares to dance the lead in an all male version of *Swan Lake*, yet as he leaps onto the stage with a highly disciplined form, the musical score changes to a popular composition, such as those he listened to at the beginning of the film. While he literally dances to the traditional composition, he hears, in his imagination, the more strident rhythms of his origins.

The negotiation between contending cultural impulses is extended into gender politics of the film. Billy embodies androgyny, a compromise between conflicting perceptions of masculinity. While he is heterosexual, he no longer needs to affirm this masculinity through the repudiation of homosexuality or through over-determined public displays of bravado. He can pursue a profession that is traditionally stigmatized among the lower classes, the effete pursuit of queer aristocratic men. The inclusion of Billy's father and brother, as well as the fully grown and openly gay friend Michael, in the audience of Billy's *Swan Lake* performance signifies the settlement between contending masculinities. Appropriately, the miners capitulate to the owners at the same time that Billy is admitted to the dance program, suggesting a general compromise of rigid masculinist values, a negotiation that is continued into the end of the film when Billy's father and brother arrive at the very last minute for Billy's performance, only to find Michael and his boyfriend already settled. The final erasure of traditional binary distinctions—masculine/feminine, heterosexual/homosexual, aristocratic/proletariat, high art/low art—is captured in Billy's dance. He dances the female's part, the dying swan, a performance that illustrates the destructiveness of rigid, compulsory gender roles.

The reparation of relations between gay and straight men via the film industry does not come without significant compromise. The successful depiction of these traditionally antithetical gender categories necessitates the suppression of erotic interests among men, and not just between gay and straight men, but also between gay men. Only the verbal declaration of homosexual orientation is permissible, no overt demonstrations of desire. The same negotiation necessitates the sacrifice of diversity within gender roles. Gay male effeminacy is often erased within the context of gay friendly discourse in order to win the good will of straight men, and since effeminacy is the initial pretext for exclusion, originating within the social and gender formation of young boys, its omission may be too great a concession, capitulating entirely to the stigmatization that socializes young boys as homophobes. Such a scenario does little to validate gender difference, offering a visibility within an invisibility and relying entirely upon the goodwill of heterosexual men. Gay men can be seen only so long as they act straight; they can proclaim their sexuality so long as they do not act it out. Despite the unsatisfactory nature of such portraits, they do constitute a strategy of inclusion, obtaining a straight male audience for the dramatization of improved relations between antithetical groups.

Conclusion

Queer (Un)Friendly Film and Television examines the legion of new cinematic and television representations of gay man. In classic cinema the representations of alternative lifestyles were, even in their most explicit moments, faint and ambiguous. However, the success of films such as *Philadelphia, The Birdcage, To Wong Fu, The Talented Mr. Ripley,* and *In & Out* have signaled the increasing popular appeal of cinema with explicit gay subject matter; when this is coupled with the increasing prominence of Independent Film, which is more courageous in its cultural politics than mainstream Hollywood has been, it is clear that the conditions have never been more friendly toward the cinematic depiction of alternative lifestyles. The same process has been underway in the significantly more conservative television industry, where programs such as *Will & Grace* have enjoyed considerable success and where virtually every popular program has either a gay character or an episode that attempts to reshape popular opinion on the subject. What we are witnessing is a collective effort to construct a positive new public image for gays and lesbians, one that minimizes the negative stereotypes of the past, paving the way for increased social tolerance and for full participation of gays and lesbians in American society. For me, the fact that three new television programs with gay themes have been produced since I began composing this manuscript is the most compelling evidence of the proliferation and effectiveness of gay friendly discourse and imagery. The fact that two of those programs have already been canceled suggests that there is much more progress to be made.

This study examines the negotiation between contending social forces in the aesthetics of recent film and television, observing the subtle interplay between the progressive and the regressive, between encouragement and caution, and between subversion and containment. For instance, the recurring images of monogamous gay couples in cinema attempt to combat the common accusation that alternative lifestyles are characterized by irresponsible promiscuity. While such portraits are certainly advantageous to a much maligned minority, they are also capitulationist, stipulating conditions under which gays and lesbians should be allowed to co-exist safely within heterosexist society — only through the emulation of the bourgeois couple.

These essays address social issues pertinent to the struggle of gays and lesbians for openness and equality, attempting to obviate the apparatus of oppression and exclusion. The subjects include gay partnerships/marriages, gay romantic fantasies, child-rearing, violence, invisibility, cross-dressing, conversion, art, and genetics. With each subject I expose the mechanisms of social and gender construction that serve to fashion the new gay subject, one less threatening to the dominant culture. At the same time, I reveal the ways in which the subversive potential of such portrayals can be appropriated and rehabilitated to the advantage of the white male hetero-sexist power structure.

The study employs the ideas of several contemporary theoretical schools, including queer theory, cultural materialism, social constructionism, post-structuralism, men's studies, feminism, psychoanalysis, and film theory. Of course, most prominent among these are contemporary men's studies and the cultural materialism of the 1980s, popularized in part by scholars such as Jonathan Dollimore and Alan Sinfield, two individuals who later became important authors in queer theory. The central enterprise of each chapter is to demonstrate the containment of the socially subversive potential unleashed by the affirmative representation of those formerly demonized and marginalized. The praxis is directly related to the economics of art and film: how does one sell to a mainstream audience a film or program with a formerly forbidden and unspoken subject? This is achieved by mitigating the revolutionary potential of such portraits with judicious casting of the lead roles and through the equation of the values of the gay community to those of mainstream society. The study is also preoccupied by the dialectical quality of queer art. Gay film is an argument, a rebuttal to decades of misrepresentation, but at the same time that it repudiates the abuses and mischaracterizations of the past, it reaffirms a portion of the same through its choice of subjects and its special pleading. The enemy is always present at queer art's efforts to articulate its own legitimacy; their voice is a part of our own voice. One cannot denounce prejudice without re-stating the biases that motivate bigotry, thus subtly reinforcing abuse by judging it worthy of rejoinder.

Hollywood's effort to forge good relations between gay and straight men by removing the stigma and mystery resulting from the compulsory silence surrounding alternative sexualities is the recurring subject of these chapters, and, while productive, provocative, and well-intended, this effort only achieves an incremental step toward conciliation, a compromise which, one hopes, can be renegotiated in the future to forge a more egalitarian settlement, one that allows queer identities to be performed without apology, one that allows such portraits without the antithetical bias associated with the semiotics of representation that compares gay and straight men frequently to the disadvantage of the former, one that no longer sympathizes with heterosexual men's fear and loathing of gay men before it declares the same unfounded, one that no longer needs to portray gay men as sufficiently safe and middle class before it urges their appropriation into the mainstream, and, finally, one that does not necessitate the erasure of alternative masculine gender performances.

Film and Television Listing

The Adventures of Priscilla, Queen of the Desert. Dir. Stephen Elliot. Polygram, 1994.

Beautiful Thing. Dir. Hettie Macdonald. Channel Four, 1995.

Billy Elliot. Dir. Stephen Daldry. Tiger Aspect, 2000.

Billy's Hollywood Screen Kiss. Dir. Tommy O'Haver. Trimark, 1998.

The Birdcage. Dir. Mike Nichols. MGM/UA, 1996.

Boys Don't Cry. Dir. Kimberly Pierce. Fox Searchlight, 1999.

Braveheart. Dir. Mel Gibson. Paramount, 1995.

Chuck & Buck. Dir. Miguel Arteta. Artisan, 2000.

Ed. Prod. Andrea Newman. Dir. James Frawley. NBC, 2000.

Flawless. Dir. Joel Schumacher. MGM/UA, 1999.

From Here to Eternity. Dir. Fred Zinnemann. Columbia, 1953.

Gattaca. Dir. Andrew Niccol. Columbia, 1997.

Get Real. Dir. Simon Shore. Paramount, 1999.

Gladiator. Dir. Ridley Scott. Dream Works, 2000.

Gods and Monsters. Dir. Bill Condon. Universal, 1998.

I Think I Do. Dir. Brian Sloan. Danger Filmworks, 1997.

Kiss Me, Guido. Dir. Tony Vitale. Paramount, 1997.

Love and Death on Long Island. Dir. Richard Kwietniowski. Universal, 1997.

Macbeth. Dir. Roman Polanski. Columbia, 1997.

The Next Best Thing. Dir. John Schlesinger. Paramount, 2000.

The Object of My Affection. Dir. Nicholas Hytner. 20th Century–Fox, 1998.

Oh Grow Up. Prod. Kirk Rudell. ABC, 1999.

Queer as Folk. Prod. Shiela Hockin. Dir. Alex Chappel. Showtime, 2000.

Rambo: First Blood Part II. Dir. George Cosnatos. Tristar, 1985.

Rob Roy. Dir. Michael Caton Jones. MGM, 1995.

Sling Blade. Dir. Billy Bob Thornton. Miramax, 1996.

Spin City. Prod. Walter Barnett. Writ. Mark Barker and Hadley Davis. Dir. Andy Cadiff and Lee Shallot Chemel. ABC, 1996.

The Talented Mr. Ripley. Dir. Anthony Minghella. Miramax, 1999.

To Wong Fu, Thanks for Everything! Julie Newmar. Dir. Beeban Kidron. Universal, 1995.

Tootsie. Dir. Sydney Pollack. Columbia, 1982.

The Twilight of the Golds. Dir. Ross Kagen Marks. Showtime, 1997.

Urbania. Dir. John Shears. Trimark, 2000.

The Usual Suspects. Dir. Bryan Singer. Polygram, 1995.

Vertigo. Dir. Alfred Hitchcock. Paramount, 1958.

Will & Grace. Dir. James Burrows. Prod. David Kohan and Max Mutchnick. NBC Series.

Bibliography

Abelove, Henry. "Freud, Male Homosexuality, and the Americans." *The Lesbian and Gay Studies Reader*. Ed. Henry Abelove, Michele Aina Barale, David Halperin. London: Routledge, 1993, 381–396.

Allen, Garland E. "The Double-Edged Sword of Genetic Determinism: Social and Political Agendas in Genetic Studies of Homosexuality, 1940–1994." *Science and Homosexualities*. Ed. Vernon A. Rosario. New York: Routledge, 1997, 242–270.

Baldwin, James. *Notes of a Native Son*. Boston: Beacon, 1955.

Bakhtin, M. M. *The Dialogic Imagination*. Ed. Michael Holquist. Trans. Caryl Emerson and Michael Holquist. Austin, TX: U of Texas P, 1981.

Babuscio, Jack. "Camp and the Gay Sensibility." *Camp Grounds:Style and Homosexuality*. Ed. David Bergman. Amherst, MA: U of Massachusetts P, 1993, 19–38.

Bayer, Ronald. *Homosexuality and American Psychiatry: The Politics of Diagnosis*. Princeton, NJ: Princeton UP, 1981.

Beneke, Timothy. *Proving Manhood: Reflections on Men and Sexism*. Berkeley: U of California P, 1997.

Benshoff, Harry M. *Monsters in the Closet: Homosexuality in the Horror Film*. New York: Manchester UP, 1997.

Bergman, David. "Introduction." *Camp Grounds: Style and Homosexuality*. Ed. David Berman. Amherst, MA: U of Massachusetts P, 1993, 3–18.

Bozett, Fredrick W. "Children of Gay Fathers." *Gay and Lesbian Parents*. Ed. Fredrick W. Bozett. New York: Praeger, 1987, 39–57.

_____. "Gay Fathers." *Gay and Lesbian Parents*. Ed. Fredrick W. Bozett. New York: Praeger, 1987, 3–22.

Bram, Christopher. *Father of Frankenstein*. New York: Plume, 1995.

Burston, Paul. *What Are You Looking At? Queer Sex, Style, and Cinema*. London: Cassell, 1995.

Butler, Judith. *Gender Trouble: Feminism and the Subversion of Identity*. New York: Routledge, 1990.

Campbell, Lily B. *Shakespeare's Tragic Heroes: Slaves of Passion*. New York: Barnes & Nobles, 1966.

Connell, R.W. *Gender & Power*. Stanford, CA: Stanford UP, 1987.

_____. *Masculinities*. Berkeley: U of California P, 1995.

Dollimore, Jonathan. *Sexual Dissidence: Augustine to Wilde, Freud to Foucault*. Oxford: Clarendon, 1991.

Dowling, William C. *Jameson, Althusser, Marx: An Introduction to The Political Unconscious.* London: Methuen, 1984.

Duberman, Martin. *Cures.* New York: Plume, 1992.

Dyer, Richard. *Now You See It: Studies on Lesbian and Gay Film.* New York: Routledge, 1990.

Foucault, Michel. *The History of Sexuality: An Introduction.* Trans. Robert Hurley. New York: Vintage, 1978.

Freud, Sigmund. *Three Essays on the Theory of Sexuality.* Trans. James Strachey. New York: Harper Collins, 1962.

Gever, Martha, Pratibha Parmar, and John Greyson, eds. *Queer Looks: Perspectives on Lesbian and Gay Film and Video.* New York: Routledge, 1993.

Greenberg, David F. *The Construction of Homosexuality.* Chicago: U of Chicago P, 1988.

Hall, Lee. *Billy Elliot.* London: Faber and Faber, 2000.

Hansen, Ellis, ed. *Out Takes: Essays on Queer Theory and Film.* Durham, NC: Duke UP, 1999.

Highsmith, Patricia. *The Talented Mr. Ripley.* New York: Vintage, 1955.

Horrocks, Roger. *Masculinity in Crisis.* New York: St. Martin's, 1994.

Jackson, Earl. *Strategies of Deviance: Studies in Gay Male Culture.* Bloomington, IN: Indiana UP, 1995.

Jameson, Fredric. *The Political Unconscious: Narrative as Socially Symbolic Act.* Ithaca, NY: Cornell UP, 1981.

Keller, James R. "Masculinity and Marginality in *Rob Roy* and *Braveheart.*" *Journal of Popular Film and Television,* 24 (1997): 146–151.

Kimmel, Michael. *Manhood in America: A Cultural History.* New York: Free P, 1997.

Kincaid, James R. *Child-Loving: The Erotic Child and Victorian Culture.* New York: Routledge, 1992.

Klein, Alan M. *Little Big Men: Body Building Subculture and Gender Construction.* New York: State Univ. of New York P, 1993.

Kristeva, Julia. *The Powers of Horror: An Essay on Abjection.* New York: Columbia UP, 1982.

Lacan, Jacques. *Ecrits: A Selection.* Trans. Alan Sheridan. New York: Norton, 1977.

Lehr, Valerie. *Queer Family Values: Debunking the Myth of the Nuclear Family.* Philadelphia: Temple UP, 1999.

Levin, Harry. *The Overreacher: A Study of Christopher Marlowe.* Boston: Beacon, 1952.

McCauley, Stephen. *The Object of My Affection.* New York: Washington Square P, 1987.

Meyer, Moe. "Introduction: Reclaiming the Discourse of Camp." *The Politics and Poetics of Camp.* Ed. Moe Meyers. London: Routledge, 1994, 1–22.

Miller, William Ian. *Humiliation: and Other Essays on Honor, Social Discomfort, and Violence.* Ithaca, NY: Cornell UP, 1993.

Mulvey, Laura. "Visual Pleasure and Narrative Cinema." *Screen,* 16 (1975): 6–18.

Neitzsche, Friedrich. *Twilight of the Idols.* Trans. R.J. Hollingdale. New York: Penguin, 1968.

Norton, Rictor. *The Myth of the Modern Homosexual: Queer History and the Search for Cultural Unity.* London: Cassell, 1997.

Park-Fuller, Linda. "Voices: Bakhtin's Heteroglossia and Polyphany, and the Performance of Narrative Literature." *Literature in Performance,* 7 (1986): 1–12.

Plummer, David. *One of the Boys: Masculinity, Homophobia, and Modern Manhood.* New York: Harrington Park P, 1999.

Pronger, Brian. *The Arena of Masculinity: Sports, Homosexuality, and the Meaning of Sex.* New York: St. Martin's, 1990.

Ragland-Sullivan, Ellie. *Jacques Lacan and the Philosophy of Psychoanalysis.* Chicago: U of Illinois P, 1987.

Raymond, Diane. "In the Best Interests of the Child: Thoughts on Homophobia and Parenting." *Homophobia: How We All Pay the Price.* Ed. Warren J. Blumenfeld. Boston: Beacon, 1992, 114–130.

Ringer, Jeffrey, ed. *Queer Words, Queer Images: Communication and the Construction of Homosexuality.* New York: New York UP, 1994.

Rivera, Rhonda R. "Legal Issues in Gay and Lesbian Parenting." *Gay and Lesbian Parents.* Ed. Fredrich W. Bozett. New York: Praeger, 1987, 199–230.

Rohy, Valerie. "Displacing Desire: Passing, Nostalgia, and *Giovanni's Room.*" *Passing and the Fictions of Identity.* Ed. Elaine K. Ginsberg. Durham, NC: Duke UP, 1996, 218–233.

Russo, Vito. *The Celluloid Closet: Homosexuality in the Movies.* New York: Harper & Row, 1981.

Sarup, Madan. *Jacques Lacan.* Toronto: U of Toronto P, 1992.

Sedgwick, Eve Kosofsky. *Between Men: English Literature and Male Homosocial Desire.* New York: Columbia UP, 1985.

_____. *Epistemology of the Closet.* Berkeley: U of California P, 1990.

Segal, Lynn. *Slow Motion: Changing Masculinities, Changing Men.* New Brunswick, NJ: Rutgers UP, 1990.

Shakespeare, William. *Hamlet. The Complete Works of Shakespeare.* Ed. David Bevington. 3rd ed. Dallas: Scott, Foresman, 1980, 1069–1120.

_____. *Macbeth. The Complete Works of Shakespeare.* Ed. David Bevington. 3rd ed. Dallas: Scott, Foresman, 1980, 1216–1249.

_____. *Richard II. The Complete Works of Shakespeare.* Ed. David Bevington. 3rd ed. Dallas: Scott, Foresman, 1980, 754–792.

Simpson, Mark. *Male Impersonators: Men Performing Masculinity.* New York: Routledge, 1994.

Sinfield, Alan. *The Wilde Century: Effeminacy, Oscar Wilde, and the Queer Moment.* New York: Columbia UP, 1994.

Straayer, Chris. *Deviant Eyes, Deviant Bodies: Sexual Re-Orientations in Film and Video.* New York: Columbis UP, 1996.

Taylor, Affrica. "A Queer Geography." *Lesbian and Gay Studies: An Introduction.* Ed. Andy Medhurst and Sally R. Munt. London: Cassell, 1997, 3–19.

Terry, Jennifer. "The Seductive Power of Science in the Making of Deviant Subjectivity." *Science and Homosexuality.* Ed. Vernon Rosario. New York: Routledge, 1997, 271–295.

Vaid, Urvashi. *Virtual Equality: The Mainstreaming of Gay & Lesbian Liberation.* New York: Anchor, 1995.

Waith, Eugene M. "Manhood and Valor in *Macbeth.*" *ELH,* 17 (1950): 265–268.

Watson, James D. "The Human Genome Project: A Personal View." *The Code of Codes: Scientific and Social Issues in the Human Genome Project.* Ed. Daniel Davies and Leroy Hood. Cambridge, MA: Harvard UP, 1992.

Weinberg, G. *Society and the Healthy Homosexual.* Boston: Alyson P, 1972.

White, Edmund. *A Boy's Own Story.* New York: Vintage, 1992.

Wright, Robert. "Achilles Helix." *New Republic,* 9 July 1990.

Index

abjection 175, 177, 178, 182, 183, 184, 186, 187, 188
ACTUP/AIDS Coalition to Unleash Power 6
The Adventures of Priscilla, Queen of the Desert 146, 150
AIDS/HIV 98, 99–100, 107
Alien 56, 95
Amedure, Scott 176
American Beauty 180–183
American Psychiatric Association (APA) 66
An American Tragedy 79–80
Aniston, Jennifer 161, 162
Astaire, Fred 39

Babuscio, Jack 124, 145
Bakhtin, Mikhail 5
Baldwin, James 80
Baldwin, Stephen 110
Ball, Alan 180
Barrile, Anthony 188, 189
Beautiful Thing 10, 19–29, 44
Benshoff, Harry 61
Billy Elliot 194–197
Billy's Hollywood Screen Kiss 10, 34–41
The Birdcage 146–147, 150, 151, 154, 155–161, 171, 173, 199
Black Rain 95
Blade Runner 95
Blanchet, Kate 72
Boogie Nights 149
Boys Don't Cry 44
Bram, Christopher 58
Bratt, Benjamin 168
Brave New World 107
Braveheart 84
Bride of Frankenstein 62, 66
Burston, Paul 7, 8

Butler, Judith 139
Byrne, Stephen 110

La Cage aux Folles 155
camp 27–28, 37, 38, 39, 66, 124–125, 126, 136, 145, 159, 160
The Celluloid Closet 69
Chuck & Buck 192–194
Connell, R.W. 13, 44, 55, 82, 109, 177
Cooper, Chris 181
cultural materialism 200

Dahmer, Jeffery 68
Damon, Matt 69, 77, 78
deconstruction 12, 13, 35, 60, 63, 119, 175, 177, 183
Del Toro, Benicio 110
DeNiro, Robert 139, 141, 148, 149, 189, 192
diologism/diologic 5, 83
Dirty Dancing 9
Dole, Bob 151
Dollimore, Jonathan 4, 44, 150, 177, 200
Dreiser, Theodore 79–80
Duberman, Martin 98, 127

Ed 179
Ellen 122–123, 131
essentialism 12, 106
eugenics 97, 100, 101, 103, 104
Everett, Rupert 168
Everybody Loves Raymond 124

Father of Frankenstein 58
feminism 83, 121, 167, 200
Flawless 137
Forster, E.M. 51
Foucault, Michel 98, 178

Fox, Michael J. 179
Frankenstein 62, 63
Fraser, Brendan 59
Frazier 122, 124
Freud, Sigmund/Freudian 25, 28, 38, 45, 53, 79, 98, 177
Friends 124
From Here to Eternity 35, 37, 38, 39, 40
Futterman, Dan 155, 183

Gattaca 107
Get Real 10–19, 20, 28, 29
Gibson, Mel 84
Gladiator 82–96
Gods and Monsters 50, 58–67
Greg and Dharma 124

Hackman, Gene 155
Hall, Lee 194
Hamer, Dr. Dean 99
Hamlet 74–75, 113–114
Hayes, Sean P. 35, 123, 124, 134
heteroglossia 5
heterosexism ix, 29, 34, 44, 45, 50, 60, 65, 106
Heywood, Carter 179
Highsmith, Patricia 70, 71, 72, 77, 81
The History of Sexuality 98
Hitchcock, Alfred 39
Hoffman, Philip Seymour 69, 141, 149
homophobia/homophobe ix, 1, 2, 4–6, 7, 13, 14, 23, 29, 59, 60, 61, 63–65, 78, 79, 81, 83–85, 88, 89, 94, 99, 101, 106, 108–113, 117, 119, 122–125, 130, 137, 141, 142,145, 146, 150, 151, 161, 166, 170, 172, 175–178, 181–184, 189, 196, 197
homosexual panic 175–176
homosocial bonding 13, 20, 30, 31, 52, 53, 55, 58, 87, 110, 112, 120, 181, 183, 188
Horrocks, Roger 27, 138–139, 142, 143
Human Genome Project 97, 100, 101, 103, 106, 107
Hurt, John 50, 55–56

I Think I Do 10, 29–34, 35
In & Out 199
invisibility viii, 16, 64, 80, 151, 197, 200

Jameson, Fredrick 121
Jannie, Allison 163, 181
Jenny Jones Show 176

Karloff, Boris 62

Kerr, Deborah 40
Kiss Me, Guido 188–192
Klein, Alan 108
Kramer, Larry 6
Kristeva, Julia 175

Lacan, Jacques 27, 45
Lancaster, Burt 40
Lane, Nathan 155, 157
Law, Jude 69, 78
Leguizamo, John 146
LeVay, Dr. Simon 99
Love and Death on Long Island 50–58, 63–67

Macbeth 69–81
Madonna 168
male autism 27, 137, 138, 139, 142, 143, 152
male masochism 85
masculine protest 59, 62, 108, 109–110, 111, 113, 117, 118, 119, 120, 186
masculinity/masculinities ix, 4, 5, 12–14, 15, 42, 44, 50, 55, 56, 59, 60–63, 77, 83–86, 91, 95, 108–111, 113, 116, 117, 119, 120, 124, 125, 130, 137–139, 141, 143, 144, 145, 147, 149, 150–151, 152, 173, 186, 191, 192, 195, 197
McCauley, Stephen 161, 162, 164
McCormack, Eric 123, 124, 134
McKellen, Ian 58–59
Meloni, Chris 186
Melville, Herman 104
men's studies ix, 5, 139, 143, 200
Messing, Debra 123, 125
Michelangelo 104
Minghella, Anthony 69, 72, 75, 77, 78, 80, 81
misogyny 111, 112, 113, 117, 151–152
Mullally, Megan 123, 125
Mulvey, Laura 32

Native Son 80
Neeson, Liam 84
The Next Best Thing 154, 155, 167–174
Nichols, Mike 146, 154, 155, 156
Nietzsche, Friedrich 103, 104
Notes on a Native Son 80

The Object of My Affection 154, 155, 161–168, 172, 173
O'Donnell, Rosie 102
Oedipal Complex 25, 53
Oh Grow Up 180
Oz 185–188

Pacino, Al 189, 192
paedophilia/pederasty 52, 92
Palminteri, Chazz 112
Paltrow, Gwyneth 69
parenting 153–174
passing 160–161
Pesci, Joe 148
Philadelphia 199
Plummer, David 175, 177–178, 180
Polanski, Roman 77
political unconscious 121
Pollack, Kevin 110
polyphony/polyphonic 5
post-structuralism 200
Priestly, Jason 51, 56–57

Queer as Folk 1–4
queer theory 179, 200

Ragland-Sullivan, Ellie 27, 45
recruitment 44, 129, 153
Rice, Anne vii, 56
Richard II 74
Ring Cycle/Der Ring des Niebelungen 97, 104
Rob Roy 84
Romeo and Juliet 9, 16
Rosanne 130
Rudd, Paul 161, 162
Russo, Vito 69

Saturday Night Live 148
Schlesinger, John 167, 170
Schmitz, Jonathan 176
Schumacher, Joel 139
Scott, Ridley 95
Scotti, Nick 188, 189
Sedgwick, Eve 25, 53, 80, 87, 179
Segal, Lynn 108, 142, 145
Seinfeld 122, 132
semiotics 4, 32, 40, 50, 201
Shakespeare, William 52, 54, 68–81, 85, 116, 148

Shepherd, Matthew 175–176
Sinatra, Frank 39
Sinfield, Alan 50, 61, 194, 200
social construction 4, 5, 106, 109, 119, 129, 200
Sontag, Susan 126
Spacey, Kevin 111, 181
spectatorship 26
Spin City 179
Survivor 137

The Talented Mr. Ripley 68–81, 199
Tennyson, Alfred 51
To Wong Fu 146, 150, 151, 199
Tootsie 172
transvestism/transvestite 145–146, 150, 151, 152
Twilight of the Gods 97, 103, 104–105
Twilight of the Golds 97–107

Urbania 183–185
The Usual Suspects 108–120

Vaid, Urvashi 43, 98, 107
Veronica's Closet 179
Vertigo 39
voyeurism 32, 182

Wagner, Richard 97, 104–105
Wasserstein, Wendy 161, 163
Weinberg, George 176
Whale, James 58–67
White, Edmund 127
Whitman, Walt 52, 55, 56, 57
Wilde, Oscar 194–195
Will & Grace 121–136, 199
Williams, Robin 155, 157
Williams, Tennessee 104
Wright, Richard 80

You've Got Mail 9